'An inspirational work that allows us to understand lesbian lives in a different historical and cultural setting. *Lesbiōt* gives voice to Israeli lesbians who are trying to make sense of a sexual, religious and geographical frontier.'
Joan Nestle, author of *The Persistent Desire*

'Far from constituting a single identity for Israeli lesbians, this powerful collection helps us to understand the complexity of their lives across lines of difference. This book will change our understanding of what it can mean to be a Jew, a lesbian and an Israeli. It is essential reading for Jewish Studies, Lesbian Studies and Women's Studies courses.'
Professor Evelyn Torton Beck, University of Maryland–College Park, editor of *Nice Jewish Girls*

'These oral histories provide an absolutely fascinating insight into the lives and loves of a previously silenced and invisible group. The tragedies and triumphs of these brave women are moving and inspiring. This is a must read.'
Rabbi Sharon Kleinbaum

'Though much has changed in the official response to homosexuality in Israel during the past decade, the gay community is still at the very beginnings of its struggle for popular recognition and civil rights. These women's stories are poignant, inspiring and revealing of the constraints and the joys of being a lesbian woman in Israel.'
Marcia Freedman, former member of the Knesset and author of *Exile in the Promised Land*

'A ground-breaking book that pulls together the parallel strands of lesbian history and the history of Israel by gathering the disparate voices of lesbians from Tel Aviv to New York. An eye-opening achievement.'
Victoria Stagg Elliott, *New Moon*

'I look forward to this book with great interest. It's time the voice and experience of unknown Israel was heard.'
Rabbi Lionel Blue

'There is no world without politics and with the intimacy of their words, these women invite us to re-examine what it really means to be a lesbian in the larger world. The stories of their lives suggest hope for change and for peace.'
Jewelle Gomez, activist and author of *The Gilda Stories*

A new series of books from Cassell's Sexual Politics list,
Women on Women *provides a forum for lesbian, bisexual and heterosexual women to explore and debate contemporary issues and to develop strategies for the advancement of feminist culture and politics into the next century.*

COMMISSIONING:
Roz Hopkins
Liz Gibbs
Christina Ruse

Lesbiōt

לסביות

*Israeli Lesbians Talk about
Sexuality, Feminism, Judaism
and Their Lives*

Edited by Tracy Moore

CASSELL

Cassell
Wellington House
125 Strand
London
WC2R 0BB

387 Park Avenue South
New York
NY 10016–8810

© Tracy Moore 1995

First published 1995

British Library Cataloguing-in-Publication Data
A catalogue record for this book is available from the British Library.

ISBN: 0-304-33156-2 (hardback)
     0-304-33158-9 (paperback)

Typeset by Fakenham Photosetting Limited, Fakenham, Norfolk
Printed and bound in Great Britain by Mackays of Chatham plc

Contents

Foreword

I CAME to political activism through my lesbianism and to activism around Jewish issues through the US lesbian/feminist movement, whose primary Jewish preoccupation was Zionism and Israel. Raised in a secular Yiddishist environment, I was indifferent to Israel throughout my growing-up years. After a three-month stay in Israel in 1963 when I was twenty-one, my indifference changed to alienation and anger. I found Israelis (all of whom, I assumed, were Jewish) were 'not my kind of Jews', too hostile to and rejecting of the destroyed Eastern European culture which was the bedrock of my Jewish socialist identity, too ashamed of alleged Jewish passivity during the Holocaust. Back home, even in the privacy of our apartment, I could only whisper the unspeakable to my mother: 'They're anti-Semites.' I carried these feelings around with me for years.

In 1963–64, I was neither a feminist nor a lesbian and my concept of Jewish identity was limited to Yiddish cultural secularism. It took almost fifteen years for my views of Jewishness and Israel to broaden. Then, like so many other US Jewish lesbians coming out in the early 1970s and 1980s, I found myself trapped: on the one hand, I was alienated from Israel; on the other hand, I was angry about anti-Semitism in the women's and lesbian movements, much of it disguised as criticism of Israel; on the third hand, I was quite ignorant – about Israel, Zionism, Israelis, Palestinians. But I did know this: during that period, the women's movement and the lesbian and feminist presses in the USA (and also in England) were so hostile to Israel that Jewish lesbians, whether or not they affirmed their Jewish identity and remained loyal to the Jewish community of their origins, were often isolated and scapegoated for Israeli policies. Israel's 1982 invasion of Lebanon accelerated my education and ongoing contacts over the next decade with Israeli lesbians, who eventually became friends, drastically reshaped my views, my politics and the focus of my activism.

My history is not unique. Greater familiarity between US and Israeli Jewish lesbians has resulted in strong personal and political ties and more visibility and understanding by the broader movement about Israeli lesbians and peace activists. Thus, *Lesbiōt* is ground-breaking, not only because of its content, but because it represents a collaboration between two communities which would have been almost impossible a decade ago. In 1988, Tracy Moore, neither an Israeli nor at the time a Jew, had the vision and commitment to record the histories of Israeli lesbians; but she also needed and got support in preparing these histories for print from more than fifty-eight lesbians – almost all from the USA – who served as volunteer transcribers and editors.

Undoubtedly *Lesbiōt* will be met with hostility by many Jews inside and outside Israel. For decades, the Israeli government has tried to export a monolithic image of Israelis – politically and otherwise. Despite Tel Aviv's Museum of the Diaspora, which documents Jewish diversity, the government has been slow in acknowledging non-Ashkenazi Israelis and even slower in recognizing non-Jews, especially Palestinian Israelis. Differences in lifestyles and sexual orientation have been denied or condemned, at least until very recently. But as *Lesbiōt* demonstrates, lesbians are now committed to being recognized as a distinct group within Israeli society. The answer to 'Who is an Israeli?' is increasingly varied.

Though lesbians in the international community have much in common, our individual culture, class, political, ethnic and racial histories create enormous differences in how we live and how we perceive the society in which we live. To non-Israeli lesbian readers of *Lesbiōt*, the daily economic struggle and the specific process of coming out to a family, of using forbidden labels and gaining acceptance or rejection will be familiar. To non-Israeli Jews, the internal dialogue about the nature of Jewishness will also resonate. Yet even these take on a different aura in the framework of Israeli society where the Jewish norm, military duty, Israel's occupation of the West Bank and Gaza Strip, on-going conflicts with Arab countries and the authority of the Rabbinate inform Israeli lesbian life and the lesbian movement and make them unique.

That movement's current visibility and strength are the result not only of 1960s and 1970s activists, some of whose work is remembered (albeit not extensively recorded), but of 'ordinary' lesbians who risked coming out to their families, friends, employers and fellow workers. It is these private individuals who, without organized support, have spread the word, raised awareness, nurtured a generation of children with different norms and values. By itself, the family birthday party to which a lesbian insists on bringing her lover cannot achieve civil rights for gays and lesbians or break institutional homophobia. But without it and thousands of events like it, no movement can ever emerge, for it is in such private gatherings and discussions that consciousness is altered, that need for overt political action is defined, that preparations for organized political activities are made.

Lesbiōt is a record of such history beneath the surface of public scrutiny. By allowing Israeli lesbians to speak directly about how they have negotiated their lives in the past and how they envision the future, the present collection brings to the forefront that mysterious, unacknowledged partnership between the private and public. Some of these lesbians do not see themselves as political activists, but nevertheless affirm the need to record their lives if only to break the debilitating isolation which so many Israeli lesbians still experience. Conversely, self-defined activists provide not only the history of their organizing, but also intimate views of the relationships between their political work, jobs and ordinary life crises and between their lovers, allies and families. They recreate their inner dialogues about setting priorities (personal and political) and about the connections between their own oppression and the oppressions of others, linking sexism and homophobia with militarism and racism. Reading these interviews, I am amazed at how complex and overburdened life is for those who want to challenge the status quo, and yet despite that, how much they manage to achieve in actively hostile contexts. The stories in *Lesbiōt* will inspire not only Israeli lesbians, but anyone who is working for or just dreaming about change.

The interviews had to be conducted in English, a limitation which makes me hope that the book will quickly find a Hebrew translator and become available to all Israelis. Tracy herself acknowledges that *Lesbiōt* is a product of her personal network and resources and the time of the interviews (1988–89). These did not include, for example, lesbians from Haifa, nor Israeli Palestinians. The former are known, organized and active. The latter remain hidden to Jews not only because of homophobia, but because of the vulnerable, second-class status held by Palestinian citizens in Israel. *Lesbiōt*, like any 'first' collection, should be read as part of a larger work-in-progress which simultaneously lays the groundwork and energizes us to expand the historical record of lesbian life.

Also, since 1989 much has changed in Israel: the Women in Black movement, the increasing number of lesbians willing to come out publicly, the initial steps towards ending the occupation of the West Bank and Gaza, the establishment in Tel Aviv of national headquarters for the Israeli lesbian/gay/bisexual rights movement, heterosexual support in the Knesset and the passing of an anti-discrimination bill, the opening of a new women's centre in Jerusalem and a gay and lesbian synagogue in Tel Aviv – are all welcome developments. But we know that most progress is accompanied by backlash, that the struggles for peace, for the rights of the 'other' are never completed by one organization, one law or one individual. Things change, but the work to transform institutions and people's attitudes remains the same.

Lesbiōt is an important historical document which will not be outdated. It will remain a critical resource for those who want to understand Jewish diversity and to know how Israeli lesbians live and view Israeli society; for activists and historians eager to understand how change occurs, how history is made and unmade, and ultimately how it alters our sense of self and purpose. It must be translated into many languages so that the ties between lesbians are strengthened and Israelis can fully participate in the expanding international lesbian community.

Irena Klepfisz
Brooklyn, New York
July 1994

Preface

THE chapters in this book are narratives drawn from the word-for-word transcripts of oral histories of Israeli lesbians that I recorded between July 1988 and May 1989. Although I conducted the interviews alone, the project that resulted in this book reflects a vast communal effort by scores of lesbians and allies. How it came to be exemplifies the personal responsibility so many lesbians take for contributing to and preserving lesbian culture and history, as well as the commitment connecting many American Jews to Israeli Jews.

I am not a historian, nor is this an academic project. My preparation for this work was twenty years of activism in grass-roots lesbian projects. For the previous seven years I had worked on the collective of *Common Lives/Lesbian Lives*, a journal to 'document the lives of common lesbians' that Cindy Cleary, Anne Lee and I had founded in 1981. Cindy brought her perspective as a trained oral historian to the passion for first-source documentation that informed the journal. I became fascinated by oral history's immediacy and personal quality.

In 1988 I accompanied my partner, Lisa Edwards, to Jerusalem, for her first year of rabbinic school. There I found myself without political or community work. When I asked about written work by or about Israeli lesbians and learned that almost none existed, I immediately thought of beginning an oral history. I wanted to contribute to the vital lesbian community which had so warmly welcomed us, and I felt that documenting the voices of Israeli lesbians in their own words would be the least invasive method I could offer.

The project began when new acquaintances in the Jerusalem

lesbian community responded with interest to the idea. Dina Waik sensitized me to important cultural elements of lesbian experience in Israel and Miriam Zeevi helped me to practise interviewing. Terry Greenblatt, herself conducting an oral history among Black Hebrews, schooled me in technical, organizational and ethical considerations. Though I designed the project to include a broad spectrum of Israeli lesbians, the activists I met were unable to introduce me to Israeli Arab lesbians. Indeed, they were not acquainted with any Arab lesbians then living in Israel. Thus, the interviews all took place in Israeli Jewish communities. (See the Introduction for more on diversity and representation in the collection.)

Though the excitement of my close friends about the project encouraged me, I realized my qualifications for it were limited. I was not raised a Jew and becoming a Jew was to take me another three years. I spoke no Hebrew and was on my first visit to Israel. Thus it felt a bit *chutzpadick** to ask Israeli lesbians intimate questions about their lives. To my surprise, women readily agreed to be interviewed, referred me to other lesbians – 'You really must record So-and-So's history' – and actually sought me out to tell their stories. As I came to understand, several factors contributed to their open response. They told me that my status as an outsider actually helped them to talk to me: I had no personal stake, no axe to grind, and was not part of a gossip network. Also, at that time (1988–89), the lesbian community was experiencing a 'lull', a result of burn-out among lesbian activists, disagreement about feminist priorities, and the intensified focus on national politics brought on by the year-old *intifada*; perhaps the lesbian focus of this project felt revitalizing.

Most importantly, I believe, virtually nowhere could Israeli lesbians find an accurate reflection of their life experiences in Hebrew, and there were few in English. Marcia Freedman's memoir, *Exile in the Promised Land* (1990), wasn't yet published, although her essay 'A Lesbian in the Promised Land', which contains specific accounts of lesbian history and lives in Israel, had appeared in 1982 in *Nice Jewish Girls: A Lesbian Anthology* (an expanded edition was published in 1989 by Beacon). Also pub-

* Presumptuous.

lished in that volume was 'Letters from My Aunt', which told Helen (now Ilana) Weinstock's story of moving to Israel. *The Tribe of Dina: A Jewish Women's Anthology*, the 1986 special edition of the US journal *Sinister Wisdom* (Melanie Kaye/Kantrowitz and Irena Klepfisz, eds., reprinted by Beacon in 1989), contained a section on Israeli women, but only two identified themselves as lesbians, Chaya Shalom and 'S. Tall'. (The late Lil Moed decided not to be out as a lesbian in *Dina* for fear that it would damage her peace activity. Ilana, Chaya, Lil and S. Tall, who here calls herself Ora Yarden, are included in *Lesbiōt*.) In any case, English-language material is not necessarily accessible to Israelis.

In spite of a rich lesbian history in Israel, as of 1988 no one had publicly recorded her own – not in newsletters, not in underground journals, certainly not in books. Why? One assumes the base causes to be lesbophobia and sexism, institutional and cultural as well as internalized – the same kind of biases that have kept any non-mainstream experience hidden, except when exploited by the mainstream to serve its own markets. In addition, in Israeli culture, the social group is valued above the individual, so, for example, even the hypothetical Israeli lesbian who considered herself safe enough to survive public identification would have been less likely to write her autobiography than to lend her energy to a group project, whether social or political. Until recently, Israeli lesbians as a group have felt themselves better off outside the limelight, developing their own culture, building feminist institutions or simply living their lives.

The factors that led the lesbians in *Lesbiōt* to record the personal details and secrets of their lives include an amazing courage and willingness to take on whatever consequences result from this publication. Because there has never been a book like this one in Israel, nobody knew what would happen – within families or friendships, at work or in the media – when *Lesbiōt* appeared. Recognizing this uncertainty, about half the lesbians in the book chose to use pseudonyms. The participants who have chosen to use their own names are Avital, Barbara Becker, Chaya Shalom, Elena, Gaby F, Gila Svirsky, Ilana Weinstock, Lil Moed, Millie Ben David, Na'ama Shapira, Nurit D, and Saron. Within their accounts, some names may have been changed. I honour all of them for their proud, trail-blazing spirits and their contribution to lesbian history in Israel, and am grateful for the immense pleasure it has been to know each of them.

Although publication was always a stated goal of the project and everyone who participated had agreed in principle to allow some version of her story to be published, even after I returned to the United States in 1989, the eventuality of a book was a vague notion. To make the oral histories more accessible, the first task was to transcribe the 73 hours of tape. I placed ads for volunteer transcribers in lesbian, feminist and Jewish publications and sent flyers to women's centres, bookshops, and lesbian/gay synagogues. Although a few friends transcribed, nearly all the volunteers were strangers who responded to an ad. Most transcribed one tape, and one stalwart in Kentucky did nine! The project could never have been completed without these forty people, and I want to thank them here: Alaina Zipp, Aliza Orent, Amanda Joseph, Amy Boyd, Amy Ollendorf, Audrey Miller, Aviva Tirosh, Barbara Donelan, Bernice Schneiderman, Beth Rose, Betty Bershak, Carol Waymire, Chana Pollack, Deborah Margolis, Erica Moore, Jenney Milner, Jerry Hanson, Jessa Goodwin, Jessica Needle, Julie Saxe, Karen Endor, Kati Newman, Katia Frischer, Lia Lynn Rosen, Marcia Cohen, Marjorie Winkelman, Nadine Dolby, Pam Carter, Pam Wax, Patricia Bailey, Riqi Kosovske, Robin Berkovitz, Sally Koplin, Sandra (the stalwart) Barr, Shifra Teitelbaum, Susan Kane, Thais Carr, Tracy Riordan, Wendy Goldman, and my lesbian sister, Wendy Miller.

Transcription took 3½ years. I proofed each transcript against the original tape, then mailed a copy to each participant to correct and approve. The editors of the chapters were volunteers I reached through lesbian writer and editor friends. Working full time, I couldn't edit all the chapters myself. More importantly, I felt that bringing fresh eyes and ears to each lesbian's story would be a benefit. Shaping an average of three hours of tape/fifty pages of transcript, retaining the speaker's voice on paper, and deciding which themes to organize around are difficult challenges, with multiple solutions. Having twenty different chapter editors enriched the project immeasurably and made completion possible; I thank the editors for their caring work.

Other acknowledgements

Necessary to every aspect of this project has been Lisa Edwards, dear heart-partner, lover, companion, inspiration, teacher, editor, comfort, challenge and laff-riot. Along the way many friends and strangers provided valuable assistance, and I wish to thank some of them here: Amy Beth, meta-librarian; Chaya Shalom, lesbian visionary; Doctor Jo-Jo, of slash and burn renown; Elana Dykewomon; Elise Asch; Ellie Kellman; Galia Golan; Hadas Tagari, law maven; Harriet Perl; Herman Edwards, gloss maven; Ilana Brody, fax central; Irena Klepfisz, true believer; Irene Zahava, fount of good advice; Jenn Milner, my almost-co-publisher; Judith Pendleton, illimitable source of (cold) comfort; Karla Jay; Katz (a.k.a. Spike), who found us Cassell; Liora Morial; the Lesbian Herstory Archives; Mary-Ellen Carew; Maxine Wolfe, for her network; Nancy Bereano; Nina Warnke; NYU Law School; Ron Dayan; Sarah Schulman; Tal; Tali; the UAHC; Yaffa Weisman. There are others who do not want their names included, and doubtless those I have, unfortunately, forgotten to list.

The disks and transcripts of the Israeli Lesbian Oral History Project are housed at the Lesbian Herstory Archives in New York (LHA, PO Box 1258, New York, NY 10116), until a suitable archive opens in Israel. Only when *Lesbiōt* is translated into Hebrew will I feel there has been appropriate repayment to the pioneering Israeli lesbians who contributed so much of their lives to this book.

Tracy Moore
Los Angeles
October 1994

Biographical statements by editors

Amy Beth

I wish to thank Tracy Moore for initiating this important lesbian oral history project and collection of Israeli lesbian voices. I would also like to thank all the women for agreeing to keep the project documents at my favorite home away from home, the Lesbian Herstory Archives. I am a co-ordinator of LHA, and I am thrilled to be living as its neighbour in Park Slope (aka Dyke Slope), in Brooklyn. I am an academic librarian and an activist working for lesbian visibility; a peaceful resolution to the Israeli occupation of Palestinians and a free Palestine alongside the state of Israel; an end to the AIDS crisis and improved overall health care in women's lives; and more time to adore my lover and friends, without whose care and cleverness I would have long since expired.

Melanie Braverman

I am a nice Jewish girl with tap-roots in the Midwest. My work in poetry has appeared in various journals, among them *Calix*, *HOW(ever)*, and *Thirteenth Moon*. Fiction is forthcoming from *Five Fingers Review*. I am co-founder, with my partner Sarah Randolph, of Cosmos Press, and have recently completed a first novel called *East Justice*. I live year-round in Provincetown, Massachusetts, where I practise therapeutic massage.

Marla Brettschneider

'With a little help from my friends', I am learning to opt for concrete daily *naches*, rather than succumbing to the fears of potential *tsuris*. In addition to my activism, I am an assistant professor of political philosophy doing Jewish, feminist, and multiculturalist theory. I am currently editing an anthology on Jewish perspectives on multiculturalism and preparing a book on the role of the American Jewish left in communal pro-Israel politics.

Mary Ellen Carew

I was born at the end of the Great Depression in Omaha, Nebraska; raised in Fargo, North Dakota; spent five years in a convent in St Paul, Minnesota; married a man from Elcho, Wisconsin; lived with my dyke lover and my four kids in Mt Vernon, Iowa. I'm a writer, a grandmother, blonder than blonde, and deaf as a post. Right now I live on the queerest street in Washington, DC, and work for Gallaudet University Press.

Kate Chandler

I'm a former law slave, and an ongoing lesbian, Jew, screenwriter, film student, friend, cat mama, and recently, to my surprise and delight, once more a lover.

Alexis Danzig

When I left the lesbian feminist community in Anchorage, Alaska, in 1982 to return to New York I reduced the lesbian Jewish population there by 20 per cent. I fondly remember baking some of my best *challahs* there. *Pesach* is my favourite holiday, even if there's no challah. I've been the co-convener of the Annual Queer Seder with Gregg Bordowitz for the past four years, bringing together queer Jews and our friends and lovers working in ACT UP, the direct-action AIDS organization.

Currently I teach HIV/AIDS prevention education to adult learners in basic education programmes throughout New York City, and am a co-ordinator at the Lesbian Herstory Archives. I hope more lesbian Jews will consider the Archives as a place for keeping and showing their film and video work. Write to the Archives at P.O. Box 1258, New York, NY 10116.

The daughter of an English Jewish feminist mother and a gay Jewish father from Brooklyn, I know that there are all sorts of ways and places to be both a Jew and queer, and that the struggle to realize one's identity is fierce, lifelong and a continuous source of conversation.

Lisa Edwards

I am the rabbi of Beth Chayim Chadashim, the world's oldest gay and lesbian synagogue. In 1984 I received a PhD in English Literature from the University of Iowa, where I wrote a dissertation on post-Holocaust Jewish American fiction. I am also Tracy Moore's lover and partner, and it was because of my rabbinic studies that we went to Israel.

My teacher, Lawrence Hoffman, distinguishes between pilgrims and tourists: tourists go places to see 'sights', pilgrims go to see 'sites'. Tourists bring home souvenirs; pilgrims bring back objects sacred to them. Tracy's sojourn in Israel offers a perfect example of Hoffman's distinction. Had it not been for her oral herstory project we might very well have been simply tourists passing through, taking in the sights. Instead we carried home with us something most precious, most sacred: herstories of our people, a *torah* of lesbian lives, sacred stories heretofore unrecorded and mostly unknown. I know this is supposed to be my bio, but who else can tell you about the care with which Tracy duplicated and packed up those audio-cassettes and computer disks, carrying the shoe-boxes filled with them on the plane home the way other 'pilgrims' might carry the shard they found at an archaeological dig? Who else can tell you of the care she took with each woman's story and each woman's ownership of her story? Who else can tell you of the dollars spent and the hours of painstaking transcription and editing, of project management, of encouraging other lesbians and allies to contribute their energies and hours in order to bring this project to fruition as a community effort? Who else can tell you of the passion with which she did all this, or of the undying appreciation and admiration she has for each woman who told her story, and each who helped bring those stories to these pages?

Like Jews, lesbians have come to understand the value and

joy of recording the lives and the culture that might otherwise go unnoticed or unrecorded, being of little interest to majority peoples who see us only as 'Other', if they see us at all. Tracy has given us a record in the tradition of all Jewish sacred texts: texts that tell the stories of the journeys of our people[s], thus allowing us to join our lives to that long history of struggle and survival, trauma and triumph, and to see in their stories the reflections of our own.

Jyl Lynn Felman

I am a Jewish lesbian writer and performance artist. I am also an attorney and lecture widely on racism, anti-Semitism and homophobia. As I edited Avital's story, I was struck by the similarities in our childhoods. That is, I felt most uncomfortable in the traditional female roles and expectations. I too, could be close to boys/men as long as it wasn't sexual. My identity as a Jew has always been strong. I grew up in Dayton, Ohio, surrounded by restaurants, businesses and country clubs that excluded Jews. My father parked cars for a living and my mother was a teacher. We were observant Jews and my mother's kitchen was kosher. I went to Israel as an ardent Zionist when I was seventeen. We had been taught nothing about the Arabs or Palestinians. My own feminism, lesbianism and rejection of the policies of the government of Israel developed simultaneously, beginning twenty years ago.

Israel is a part of my life and my imagination. In my work, I try to write about the Israeli occupation of the West Bank and Gaza Strip – not only that it is wrong but also that it is destroying the daily lives of Israelis and Palestinians. My stories appear in over twenty-five different journals, anthologies and newspapers; some lesbian/gay and others mainstream or Jewish. My writing is often controversial in both the lesbian and Jewish communities. I struggle to keep my censors down and liberate my voice. I am in search of Jewish identity in the *galut*/Diaspora and want to write more about the contradictory realities of assimilation, visibility and passing that reflect Jewish life outside of Israel; and about the relationships between African American and Jewish American women. For me, art is activism as well as sacred text. I am a cultural worker in the tradition of Audre Lorde. My collection of short fiction, *Hot Chicken Wings*, was a 1993 Lambda Literary Finalist.

Amy Bragdon Gilley

A first-generation Estonian-Irish-American, I hold a PhD in Dramatic Art from the University of California, Santa Barbara. After two years of trying to crash the academy, this radical feminist lesbian tries to retain her sense of irony. I am looking forward to claiming a place within the up-and-coming field of gay and lesbian studies. In addition to a projected work called 'Lesbian Kitsch, or the Post-Modern Lesbian in Sarah Schulman's Work', I am working on studies on Jane Bowles and Cherrie Moraga for *Gay and Lesbian Literary Heritage*. Currently working on *The Diaries of E. Soomann*, the irreverent life of the first Estonian-American Lesbian private eye, I am encouraged by my publications of poetry and fiction in various lesbian periodicals.

Pamela Gray

I am a Jewish lesbian poet, screenwriter and playwright, born in Brooklyn in 1956 and now living in Santa Monica, California. My work appears in many anthologies and journals including *Love's Shadow, Naming the Waves, Dykescapes, Bubbe Meisehs by Shayneh Maidelehs, Cats and Their Dykes, Common Lives/ Lesbian Lives* and *Sinister Wisdom*. I co-wrote the play *Healin' Dirt Diner*, which has been produced in Los Angeles and San Francisco, and I wrote the 'Violations' episode of *Star Trek: The Next Generation*. I won the 1992 Samuel Goldwyn screenwriting award and the 1993 Woman in the Moon poetry prize. I'm the author of a poetry chapbook, *the lesbian breakup manual*. I'm a co-parent to Andrew, an eleven-year-old boy, and cat-parent to Coyote and Artemis.

Sarah Jacobus

I am a forty-one-year-old Jewish lesbian feminist. I have lived in Los Angeles since 1983, where I am an independent producer for community and public radio, a teacher of English as a Second Language in a public adult school and activist in the movement for a just peace between Israel and the Palestinians. My work for peace in the Middle East has informed my life for over ten years. I have spent time in Israel, the West Bank and Gaza almost yearly since 1983, interviewing Israel and Palestinian peace activists and establishing important friendships and alliances. Much of my radio work has focused on the women's peace movement and dialogue between Israeli and Palestinian women. Along with a Palestinian woman in the Los Angeles area, I founded a dialogue and political action group of Jewish and Palestinian women. I have also organized vigils of Women in Black against the Israeli occupation. I do public speaking on Middle East issues to a variety of community groups, on college campuses and in the Jewish community, often speaking in tandem with a Palestinian woman. My essays and short stories have appeared in *Sojourner* and *Common Lives/Lesbian Lives*. Another short story will be published in the anthology, *Indivisible II*, new short fiction by West Coast lesbian and gay writers. I am currently at work on a collection of personal essays focusing on my experiences in the Middle East.

Lil Moed was a friend, ally and someone with whom I had the opportunity to work politically during her annual sojourns in the United States. She was a consistent source of inspiration and optimism for me around Middle East peace work; I learned a great deal from her clear thinking and gifts as an organizer. Her death has been a major loss in my life. Thus it has been especially enriching to have spent this time with her words and thoughts. The experience has enhanced my understanding of Lil's sense of her lesbian identity and affirmed for me the importance of shaping a life in which the integration of all parts of one's self is possible, and the psychic necessity of coming out.

Irena Klepfisz

I am a poet, essayist, and, for the past twenty years, a lesbian/feminist activist in the women's, lesbian and Jewish communities. I was a co-founder and editor of *Conditions* magazine, a co-founder of the Jewish Women's Coalitions to End the Occupation of the West Bank and Gaza, and, for almost two years, Executive Director of New Jewish Agenda. I've taught Yiddish, Jewish/ Women's Studies, English and creative writing and am the author of *A Few Words in the Mother Tongue: Poems Selected and New* and *Dreams of an Insomniac: Jewish Feminist Essays, Speeches and Diatribes*, and co-editor of *The Tribe of Dina: A Jewish Women's Anthology* and *Jewish Women's Call for Peace: A Handbook for Jewish Women on the Israeli/Palestinian Conflict*. A committed Yiddishist, I serve as editorial consultant for Yiddish language and culture on the Jewish feminist magazine *Bridges* and am currently researching and translating the Yiddish writing of eastern European Jewish women writers, intellectuals and activists.

As Ora Yarden's oral history indicates, there are phases in which we emphasize one part of our lives above another, but the visible and public political work and personal crises never take place in a vacuum; all our lives go on simultaneously – connected or not. Political ideas, political action, money and work issues, family, friends, lovers, inner psychological pain and turmoil are sometimes interconnected, but, more often and more typically, evolve parallel to each other. One of my aims in editing was to retain that sense of parallel lives – parallel in time and importance, outwardly contradictory criss-cross of issues, the 'impurity' of phases. It was important to me to listen directly to an Israeli lesbian *sabra* speak insistently about her life in the historical context of Israeli society. I was moved by Ora's view of herself as an emerging and then fully mature and older activist.

Finally, editing this interview can be for me only a partial acknowledgement and expression of gratitude to Israeli lesbians, who first educated me in the mid-1980s about general political Israeli issues and, specifically, about the Israeli–Palestinian conflict. Their perspectives and work gave me strength, information and inspiration to do my own.

Jenifer Levin

I've been writing all my life and publishing professionally for more than a decade. My most recently published novel is *The Sea of Light* (Dutton, 1993). Previous novels are *Water Dancer* (Poseidon

Press/Simon & Schuster, 1982), *Snow* (Poseidon, 1984), and *Shimoni's Lover* (Harcourt Brace Jovanovich, 1987). I've written for *The New York Times*, *Rolling Stone*, *Ms.*, *Mademoiselle*, *The Advocate*, *Lambda Literary Review*, and other publications. Also taught fiction writing for two and a half years at the University of Michigan.

Travel's been an important part of my life, over the years, and I've pretty much done it whenever I could afford to. In addition to living in North America and spending quite a bit of time in Israel, I've been around Europe, Britain, the Mediterranean, South America, Thailand, Cambodia.

I was born in New York in 1955, and grew up along the rural East Coast in a secular, hard-working, lower-middle-class Jewish family (father's side mostly Russian and Polish Ashkenazim, mother's side some Turkish and Romanian Sepharadim) that had no sense of religion but a strong sense of modern history. For whatever reason, though, I've had a lifelong fascination with religions and, from an early age, took it upon myself to learn what I could about Judaism and Zionism. I went on an extended visit to Israel in my teens, and as a young adult (1977 and 1978) lived there, intending to immigrate, working on a kibbutz and in a steel factory, studying Hebrew intensively, studying kibbutz management, travelling around the country. Later, I spent a few months doing (non-citizen) volunteer service in the IDF. My political outlook gradually changed from a rather severe form of militant Jabotinsky-ist Zionism to a more moderate one. While I eventually decided not to live in Israel, my relationship with the country – and with my people, both here and there –continues in its volatile way, see-sawing back and forth on the emotional spectrum. Thrown into this emotional stew is my lesbianism, of course, and everything I am as an American and a woman, as well as my artistic commitment to making a living from my work.

Stew and all, I spent some time in Israel again in the mid-1980s, and will no doubt return. My lover Julie DeLaurier and I currently live in New York City with our adopted son, Nakara.

Alexis Lieberman

I am a twenty-eight-year-old, upper-middle-class, sometimes bisexual/sometimes lesbian Ashkenazic Jew, the third generation in the US. I love being Jewish and find that I am happiest when my level of observance is at a high point, and when I am involved with the wonderful, progressive Jewish community in the Mount Airy section of Philadelphia, where I live.

My work is learning to use my intuition, my sense of caring, my touch, and the sophisticated drugs and therapeutic methods developed by 'western' medical research and experience to help prevent and heal illness in children and adults. I am learning through a resident training programme in Pediatrics and Internal Medicine at Albert Einstein Medical College in Philadelphia. As I develop skill in this work, I find that I love it and am excited by its many possibilities.

I've been a volunteer editor on and off for the past ten years, beginning with my college weekly magazine – the one that meant the most to me – and then including the *Lambda Valley Monthly* in Allentown, now defunct, and *Vital Signs*, the monthly at the medical school I attended. I also co-authored a book, *Positive Living and Health* (1989, Rodale Press). This is the first oral history I have edited – a welcome challenge.

Jenney Milner

I am an Ashkenazi Jewish lesbian. I lived in Israel for a year in 1988–89; if I had found lesbians sooner, I would have stayed longer! Instead I ended up on Mount Desert Island in Maine, where I work at the local YMCA. I also serve as book section co-editor of *Sojourner: The Woman's Forum.*

Tracy Moore

Born in 1943, I'm Anglo and a new Jew. I live with my heart-partner, Lisa Edwards. I'm a co-founder, with Cindy Cleary and Anne Lee (of blessed memory), of *Common Lives/Lesbian Lives*, and worked with that collective from 1980–1987. I started doing lesbian things in 1963 and came out in 1970 in the Iowa City lesbian community, a fierce and wonderful place. I've been an English teacher, a house-painter, an editor, a non-profit administrator, and a fund-raiser.

Joan Nestle

I am a fifty-three-year-old Jewish fem from the Bronx who lived through the queer fifties, the lesbian sixties, the feminist seventies, and since then have tried to integrate all the wisdoms these experiences have given me. I am co-founder of the Lesbian Herstory Archives, author of *A Restricted Country* (Firebrand), and co-editor of *Women on Women I and II: Anthologies of Lesbian Short Fiction* (New American Library) and *The Persistent Desire: A Femme-Butch Reader* (Alison). I believe oral histories are at the centre both of how we survived in the past and how we will pass on the passionate and brave ways we fought to change the world.

Spike Pittsberg

I grew up in the States, spent fourteen years as a martial arts instructor in Israel, and am now working at a 'normal' job in London. I spent much of the last quarter-century writing and have published articles and stories in the feminist and lesbian press in all of those countries. I still contribute the occasional journalistic piece to the gay page of an Israeli daily, but haven't been writing much the last couple of years because of my new obsession: ballroom and Latin American dancing. I am an activist in the Pink Dancers, London's dazzling lesbian and gay dance club.

I am, by inclination, a perpetually (some say chronically) single woman, an old-gay butch who feels like an anachronism in the trendy London scene. This is particularly ironic because when I just didn't feel I could lug the necessary closet around Israel any longer, I decided to leave my 'home' in order to come 'home' to a lesbian culture. 'Home', however, is where the heart is, so I feel quite thoroughly internationalist.

Gila Svirsky edited her own oral history.

Yaffa Weisman

Born in Israel in 1951, I spent the first thirty years of my life there being a closeted lesbian. The little energy that was left in me after developing it into an art form went into reading, writing and completing my BA in Theatre Studies at Tel Aviv University. Before coming to Los Angeles in 1980 to come out and to write my doctoral dissertation, I managed to be, amongst other things, an au pair, an archivist, a freelance writer, and a theatre critic.

Nowadays I am living happily ever after with my spouse, Tina, dividing my time between teaching, writing, translating, and earning a living as the Judaica Librarian at the Hebrew Union College in Los Angeles.

Introduction

I collected these oral histories not to 'study', but simply to document as much Israeli lesbian experience as I could; thus it was never my intention to draw any 'conclusions', and I hope readers will be similarly hesitant to do so. I want to note that these narratives are *edited* versions of lengthy oral history interviews. Including all twenty-one stories necessitated shortening each interview drastically, thereby making choices about which episodes to include, which thoughts to leave out. This process reduced the inevitable overlap among the stories and resulted in a lessening of the echoes and similarities of experience that exist in the collection. For instance, every participant discussed Israel's occupation of the West Bank and Gaza Strip and took a position against it in some way; the fact that only several of those opinions are included in *Lesbiōt* not only obscures this political similarity but suggests a lower level of political concern/involvement than is the case. Another reminder I wish to make is that *every one* of these lesbians speaks 'accented' English, whether English is her first language or not. Not being able to hear the shapes given to English by the rhythms, phonemes and idioms of Hebrew or French or Spanish or deafness or Scots – not to mention the tonal expressiveness of each woman – homogenizes these voices in a false way. Nevertheless, these stories grant us the remarkable opportunity to become acquainted with twenty-one individuals on a deeply personal level.

From August 1988 to May 1989 I interviewed twenty-seven Israeli lesbians. Each oral history covered five interwoven subjects: family history; personal biography; lesbian sensibility and experience; Jewishness, Judaism and Israel; and feminism/political issues. The interviews were loosely scripted and open-ended.

Although diversity was always a goal, my identity, experience, skills and resources shaped the group of interviewees in basic ways: I was limited to English-speakers; only ten participants lived outside Jerusalem (I travelled to them by bus); and people I met led me to people they knew, so certain similarities persist. For instance, in spite of political differences, nearly all fall somewhere to the left of centre, and all are social progressives. Also, the networks I was interviewing did not lead me to any Israeli Arab[1] lesbians. With few exceptions, Arabs and Jews in Israel live in separate districts and towns, attending different elementary and secondary schools. In and around Haifa, however, Jews and Arabs interact more frequently, and had I networked in the Haifa feminist community, the result might have been different. Although two participants live in the north, I interviewed no one in Haifa, an important city with a unique feminist and lesbian history that is only indirectly included in this oral history. And although the activists included in *Lesbiōt* were involved in the feminist, lesbian culture, and peace movements, I interviewed no one in the Israeli gay and lesbian rights movement.

I attempted to reach a divergent and inclusive group. Participants' ages range from twenty-one to seventy; ethnically, eight are Sepharadi/Mizrachi Jews, seventeen are Ashkenazi Jews, one is a Puerto Rican–American convert to Judaism and one is a European-American of Christian heritage; fourteen are *sabra*[2] and thirteen are immigrants (ten from English-speaking countries). Ten were single lesbians; eight lived with female partners (of these eight, two self-identified as bisexual[3]); five had non-live-in lesbian lovers; one sometimes identified as bisexual and at that time had a male lover; and three were married to men while identifying as lesbians and having woman lovers. Eleven had been aware of their lesbianism since childhood or early adolescence. Ten were mothers: two with grown children, five with teenagers, and three with youngsters. Divided 13:12 along working-class/middle-class lines,[4] their jobs included student, driving instructor, substance abuse counsellor, estate agent, agency administrator, ecologist, dental student, draftsperson, music therapist, journalist, police administrator, childcare worker, foundation director, translator, retired professor, office worker, nurse, woodworker, TV producer, travel agent, retired hospital orderly, kibbutz director, and community development social worker.

Of the twenty-seven participants, twenty-one eventually agreed to publication; three withdrew for personal reasons and three lost touch with me during the approval process.

Clearly, neither the oral histories I collected nor this book are definitive. This is just one step, and those who see the gaps will, I hope, be stimulated to continue documenting lesbian life in Israel.

*

Those who have some familiarity with Israeli society and history will have little trouble placing these narratives in their social-historical context. For others less familiar with Israel, I have attempted to gather some facts pertinent to the lives of Israeli lesbians in 1988–89, the period when these histories were recorded. Other than some of the books cited in the bibliography, my sources have been Israelis, mostly lesbians, and I have tried to present a perspective relevant to Israeli Jewish lesbians.

Israel was established as an independent state in 1948. In 1947, the UN proposed dividing the area called Palestine, which was under British rule, into two states, one Jewish and one Arab. However, Arabs living in Palestine and the governments of the surrounding Arab countries rejected the proposal, and war ensued. By 1949, the Jews had won the war and established the modern state of Israel. Many Palestinian Arabs either fled or were driven out during the war, but those who remained became Israeli citizens. The decades of Zionist settlement and the complex local and international manoeuvres that preceded statehood are the subject matter of many books; some study of Middle Eastern history will give the reader a richer appreciation of the oral histories in *Lesbiōt*.

About the size of Wales or El Salvador, Israel had a population of 4.2 million people in 1988, of which 81 per cent were Jewish, 14 per cent Muslim, 3 per cent Christian, and 2 per cent Druze and others. As is still the case, Hebrew and Arabic were the official languages and English was a required subject in schools.[5] A US dollar bought 1.7 shekels and the per capita annual income was just over $5000.

Israel's 1950 Law of Return grants automatic citizenship to almost any Jew. Immigration is known as *aliyah* ('going up'), reflecting the goal of many dispersed Jews to return to the land of their tradition. For more than a century, religious beliefs and Zionist ideology have motivated Jews to migrate to Palestine/Israel, and Jews in countries such as Iraq, Romania, Yemen, Ethiopia and Russia have been flown there in Israeli-sponsored rescue missions. To many Diaspora and Israeli Jews, Israel represents and offers a safe haven from millennia of anti-Semitic persecution.

In the late 1980s, about 53 per cent of Israeli Jews were *sabra*, the rest having immigrated from all over the world. Ethnically and culturally diverse, with no single ethnic group constituting even 20 per cent of the Jewish population, Israel's two main Jewish groupings are Sepharadi (also known as Eastern/Mizrachi or Oriental), who come from Africa, the Middle East and Asia, and Ashkenazi, from Europe and North America. At the time of statehood, Ashkenazi Jews comprised over 80 per cent of Israel's Jewish population; by 1988, as a result of immigration in the 1950s, over half were Sepharadim.

Whether part of a mass immigration or following individual impulse, Jews who emigrate to Israel undergo a process fraught with culture shock. Usually housed in absorption centres or development towns, they learn Hebrew at an *ulpan* (language school), while trying to find employment and establish independent living. Because massive Jewish immigration to Israel isn't controlled or carefully planned, over the years there have often been shortages of goods, services, housing and employment, resulting in dramatic downward changes in lifestyle and profession for many. Although the drop-out rate for immigrants approaches 50 per cent, immigration nevertheless accounts for most of Israel's population growth.

Because of government housing policies, most Israeli Jews live in cities and towns, in apartments which they purchase, not rent. In contrast, about 3.5 per cent live on kibbutzim, Jewish collective agricultural settlements subsidized by the government, where members share the work and take their meals and educate their children communally. (Five of the 21 lesbians in *Lesbiōt* were raised on kibbutzim, though only one has remained a member of her kibbutz.) The kibbutz movement began in 1909 as part of Zionist pioneer doctrine. Although the kibbutzim were theoretically based on socialist notions of equality, women never have been equal to men in kibbutz jobs or decisions, and early practices of communal child-rearing (which was always carried out by women anyway) have given way to traditional organization by (heterosexual) nuclear family. The *moshav*, a co-operative agricultural settlement where people own their houses, accounts for another 4 per cent of Israeli Jews. In 1988–89, while the vast majority of Jews lived in towns and cities, most Israeli Arabs lived in rural areas.

★

Israel has no constitution, but its government is democratically elected. A multiplicity of parties vie for seats in the Knesset, the parliament modelled on that of Britain. When citizens vote (more than 80 per cent do), they elect parties, not individuals. Each party offers a list of candidates, and whatever proportion of the votes the party wins determines the number of its candidates to be seated in the Knesset. Whichever party secures the greatest number of seats then forms a government. In previous years, either the left-wing Labor party or, from 1977 to 1984, the rightist Likud party had been able to form a majority coalition with parties generally aligned with their positions. However, in 1988, neither could amass a majority, so Labor and Likud were forced to form an unprecedented 'national unity' government, along with two small religious parties. The national tensions over policies of occupation and peace, as well as the disproportionate power of the religious parties, were reflected in this government, with Yitzhak Shamir (of Likud) as Prime Minister.

★

Despite the democratic process, in many ways Israel is a theocracy. Although Orthodox Jews number only 20 per cent of the population, Orthodox rabbis and tiny religious political parties have effectively controlled family law, especially marriage and divorce, and greatly influence health, education and welfare policies. In the Knesset, religious parties often hold the balance in voting on national issues, which gives them inordinate leverage to pass or defeat social legislation.

The thirteen-month Hebrew calendar and Jewish religious holidays shape the official Israeli calendar, yet only about half of Israeli Jews could be termed 'observant'. These range from the Ultra-Orthodox, who number only about 4 per cent, through Orthodox and so-called 'modern Orthodox', to those who may keep a kosher home but seldom attend religious services (or vice versa). The other half are those who call themselves 'secular Jews' and progressive Jews, and includes the Conservative, Reform, and Reconstructionist movements of Judaism.

As a matter of theocratic state policy, Israel recognizes only Orthodox Judaism, and thus only Orthodox rabbis are sanctioned by the state-approved rabbinate establishment. As a result, in 1988–89, Conservative, Reform and Reconstructionist rabbis could not perform marriages or hear divorce cases, and their synagogues were not supported by the state as are Orthodox synagogues. The issue of religious pluralism is especially important to Jewish women because of the stranglehold the Orthodox have on all laws pertaining to marriage, divorce and burial.

In the areas of marriage and divorce, the Israeli legal system grants exclusive jurisdiction to religious courts.[6] Unless a (heterosexual) Jewish couple travels outside the country for their wedding, they must be married by an Orthodox rabbi. And no matter where they were married, in order to divorce they must obtain a *get*[7] from an Orthodox rabbinical court. In Jewish law, the man must grant the *get* to the woman. If a husband disappears or refuses to grant the divorce, a wife has no recourse and is considered still married. Child custody is always determined in religious court; there is no obligation to pay alimony. With older, socially conservative men as judges, double standards often influence the judgment (such as if the wife has had an affair), and with Judaism's patriarchal model of the nuclear family, the bias is towards keeping a family 'intact'. One can imagine how frightening and discouraging the prospect of divorce proceedings would be to lesbians married to men. Homosexual marriage or the extension of heterosexual privileges to same-sex partners, if and when they do arrive, will have to be achieved through civil law and policy reform.

As for abortion, religious tenets and the value placed on having children have kept some restrictions on abortion in place, although in practice abortion is generally available.

*

One of the factors most influential in Israeli Jewish culture is the military; indeed, the centrality of the military to the minds and plans of Jewish citizens is a recurring theme in these oral histories. A history dependent on military security and a policy of universal Jewish conscription have woven the structure and experience of the military into the daily lives of Israelis to a very great extent. The military's paramount importance is in part an outgrowth of Israel's status as a small, young nation surrounded by countries hostile to its establishment, with a history of several major wars.

The war most critical to Israeli domestic and international politics was the Six Day War of 1967, as a result of which Israel occupied the Golan Heights, West Bank and Gaza Strip, as well as East Jerusalem, which was immediately annexed,[8] and the Sinai (returned to Egypt in 1982). In December 1987, after twenty years of worsening conditions with no political resolution in sight, Palestinians in the Occupied Territories launched their *intifada*, or uprising, against Israel's occupying forces. During 1988–89, the daily events of the *intifada* pushed to new levels of intensity the national dialogue/argument between peace advocates and those wanting to expand Israel's borders by annexing the Territories.

The army in Israel is known as the IDF, the Israel Defense Forces, on the theory that its duties are security and self-protection, not aggression. Yet in 1988–89, Israeli feminists cited militarism and ultra-nationalism as bulwarks of sexism in Israel, because they encourage violence and machismo in Israeli men. Feminists pointed to a culture of macho expectation pervading all aspects of Israeli society, including social relationships and political analysis. They argued that the occupation led to increasing violations of human rights in the Occupied Territories which, in turn, threatened democracy in Israel itself. Because security is accepted as the primary duty of government, the military agenda had been allowed to monopolize resources while subordinating or sweeping aside issues such as women's rights, civil rights and economic development.

Even a casual observer will notice the ways the military permeates Israeli daily life. Especially in Jerusalem and in areas along the 'green line', Israel's pre-1967 border, one sees young men in army khaki with machine guns tucked casually under their arms walking in the street or riding a bus. Even on leave, soldiers carry weapons, and anyone still eligible for reserve duty may choose to carry a sidearm. Young women soldiers seldom carry arms because women are permitted so few combat roles; most women inducted to the army handle firearms only during their three weeks of basic training.

In theory, all Jews are required to perform military service after high school.[9] All men (except the ultra-Orthodox) serve three years, from age eighteen to twenty-one, and then are reservists serving a yearly stint until the age of fifty-five; women serve two years, and are technically on reserve until twenty-four, though they are seldom called on. The role the military plays in socializing Israeli Jews cannot be understated, especially because it is a shared experience of most young people. Being drafted means leaving home for the first time, a rite of passage to adulthood. Even when Israeli Jews criticize the actions or policies of the military, they generally view army service as a positive contribution to what it means to be Israeli.

Army service is important for more than its socialization. Success in the army and connections made there provide much of the basis for entry or promotion in the work world. Military training and performance can be as important as a university education, and in some cases are acceptable substitutes. But whereas nearly all men serve in the army,[10] only about 50 per cent of women actually serve. Many women seek exemption on the basis of religion or marital status, or other reasons of 'unfitness'. Moreover, those women whose basic skills are low miss the remedial education that poorly prepared men receive from the army. Since women serve only two years as opposed to men's three, less is invested in their skills, and because women do not serve in combat roles but are usually relegated to support positions, they have less opportunity to lead and develop responsibility. Thus their status both within the army and in the culture at large is reduced and marginalized.

True, army training and army careers can be seen as an

equalizing force for some Israeli women, who are at least exposed to physical training and firearms, and often hold important technical and intelligence jobs. Nevertheless, the majority of women serve in traditional clerical functions. Those women who choose a military career are mostly limited to the command of other women or to non-combat staff positions. With army service a jumping-off point for high positions in government and business, an 'old boys network' is firmly in place in the country's leadership.[11]

Even though male experience and values define the military in Israeli society, there has been no organized resistance to military service by women. Male protest groups like Yesh Gevul ('There is a limit') refuse service in the Occupied Territories, not in the army itself. And for gay men and lesbians, the IDF has not been the enforcer of homophobic attitudes as has, for instance, the US military. Even though intelligence positions were routinely denied to gays because the army believed gays were at risk of extortion, homosexuality as such was seldom a disqualification for service or, of itself, grounds for dismissal. As was the case generally in Israeli civilian life, gays and lesbians negotiated their army experiences depending on the climate of acceptance in their units. Among lesbians and gay men, basic training and army life often figure importantly in coming-out lore.

Any discussion of the Israeli military and its history must include the importance of national dissent and opposition movements. Indeed, some degree of opposition to the occupation of the Territories characterized the politics of all of the lesbians who participated in the oral history project.[12]

Israel's continued occupation of the West Bank and Gaza Strip after 1967 eventually aroused outrage and opposition among Israelis on the left.[13] At least since the early 1970s, leftist women, including lesbians, have been active in a variety of movements favouring peace with Palestinians and other Arab neighbours. The breakthrough agreement with Egypt in 1977 gave hope that Arab–Israeli relations were mutable and might improve, and Israel's unpopular war with Lebanon in 1982 increased the number of Israelis critical of the military and inclined towards peace. Although the previous twenty years had been characterized by a near-consensus governmental hard line against negotiations, by 1989 fully 50 per cent of Israelis favoured entering a peace process with the Palestinian Liberation Organization (PLO).

By the late 1980s over forty peace groups existed in Israel, expressing various opinions but all aimed at pushing towards peace with Arab states and especially with the Palestinians. The *intifada* made a peace agenda more focused and urgent. A disproportionate number of lesbians (a common estimate is 30 per cent) were among the founders and activists in several peace groups, notably SHANI: Israeli Women Against the Occupation and Women In Black, as well as among the organizers of women's peace conferences.

Women in Black, a weekly vigil held on Fridays from 1 to 2 pm, was organized in January 1988 to protest against the Israeli government's 'iron fist' response to the *intifada* and to call for an end to the occupation. The women dressed in black, a symbol of mourning for both Israelis and Palestinians, and held hand-shaped signs proclaiming 'Stop the Occupation' in three languages.[14] Initiated in Jerusalem, Tel Aviv and Haifa, by 1989 Women in Black vigils were springing up throughout Israel, both in smaller cities and along roads near kibbutzim. The organizing principle united women who held varying opinions as to how and when the occupation should end, but were in agreement on ending it.

As in other pluralist and democratic countries, Israeli society is often threatened by dissent and suspicious of the individualism that dissent reveals. When dissent is voiced by women, whose opinions are devalued in a society that marginalizes them, the outrage can be intense. Women in Black endured insults, slurs, hurled objects and counter-demonstrators who sometimes had to be controlled by reluctant police. A few male supporters were also in evidence, however, offering water, snacks and flowers.

Women's peace groups, Women in Black, and women's leadership and visibility in more mainstream peace organizations like Peace Now presented Israelis with a strong female presence urging peace. Straight and lesbian women peace activists also organized international dialogues and conferences with Arab and Palestinian women.

By 1988–89, the urgency of the political situation led many lesbians to divert some or all of their energies from lesbian- or women-focused projects to organizing for peace. Most lesbian-feminists saw no contradiction in a peace priority for their activism, holding their politics to be inclusive of national issues, most notably peace, as feminist and fundamental. Although rueful about the diversion in some cases, most activist lesbians agreed that opposing the occupation, and the militarism and violence of Israeli society, demanded priority. These oral histories reveal the anguish, outrage, and determination to work for peace that I saw so often then.

★

As in all cultures, in Israel sex discrimination of all kinds exists throughout the economy, even though it is increasingly prohibited by ever more liberal laws. What, then, characterizes the economic situation for Israeli women and lesbians?[15]

In general, Israel is a working society, in which most people work a six-day week. Though wealth and poverty may not be as extreme as in the USA, Israel battles problems of un- and underemployment and in 1988 the Israeli economy went into recession, after a decade of unparalleled economic growth. Its economy is part state-managed, part free enterprise. Immigrants and young people are subsidized in education. Housing subsidies are available to everyone, with more benefits if one has children, is married or of a certain age. Women are heavily idealized as mother, worker and even freedom fighter/army recruit. Women have to do everything, but especially they are expected to do motherhood. For many lesbians, one result of this pressure is that they feel compelled to marry; however, unmarried lesbians with children are finding a degree of acceptance accorded them because of their motherhood. And because most lesbians are closeted and thus invisible as lesbians to government and social institutions, lesbians usually receive treatment equivalent to straight women.

In spite of the 1964 Equal Pay for Men and Women Act, in 1989 the average salary for women was 60 per cent that of men; the hourly wage, 80 per cent. The 1988 Equal Employment Opportunities Act prohibits discrimination in recruitment, hiring, working conditions, promotion and training and dismissal based on sex, or marital or parental status. It also prohibits sexual harassment. In a victory for the lesbian/gay/bisexual rights movement, sexual orientation was added to the list of protected categories in 1991.

Legislation providing maternity leave or special hours to meet the demands of pregnancy, childbirth, nursing and childcare leads employers to believe that hiring women will be more costly to their operations than hiring men. (However, Israeli men serve in their reserve units one month a year, clearly a heavy economic toll.) Many jobs in industry or in certain workplaces exclude women so as to 'protect' them from health hazards or reproductive risks. However, childcare and health care services are affordable and far more widely available in Israel than in countries such as the USA and UK, making single motherhood comparatively manageable. In general, it is attitudes, not restrictive laws, which disadvantage women in the workplace.

The workplace reflects common sex roles: 75 per cent of employed Israeli women hold 'women's jobs' like secretary, teacher, seamstress, childcare worker, etc., while 78.9 per cent of men are employed in traditionally 'male' jobs like welder, locksmith or electrician, where 13 per cent of women are employed. Motherhood perpetuates this disproportion, as training programmes seldom offer childcare and few aim to reach women returning to work after children are grown. Basically, government policy does not favour changing this imbalance, but encourages it. Even in 'women's' occupations, senior positions are usually occupied by men. Women are also considered 'secondary wage earners' and are usually laid off first. Arab and Druze women are relegated to the lowest-paid jobs, with little or no training. In 1988–89, about 8.5 per cent of Arab and Druze women and 34 per cent of Jewish women worked for pay.

★

Though surely lesbians have lived in Israel since well before the state was established, the lesbians I spoke with locate the origin of today's lesbian movement within the feminist movement of the late 1960s and 1970s.[16]

The political situation in Israel in the early 1970s, as in other countries, created an environment for progressive ideas; the best-known in Israel was the social grass-roots movement called 'Black

Panthers', which demanded equality between Sepharadi and Ashkenazi Jews. During this period, the Israeli New Left began demanding peace with Arab neighbours and Palestinians and withdrawal from the Occupied Territories. Not surprisingly, women too started to demand their rights.

The three major cities – Jerusalem, Tel Aviv and Haifa – saw the birth of grass-roots feminist movements evidenced by consciousness-raising (CR) groups and political organizations. By the late 1960s, Tel Aviv and Haifa feminists had formed separate organizations, each called The Feminist Movement, while Jerusalem feminists had established an organization called the Women's Liberation Movement (WLM). Although varying somewhat on Israeli politics and their own priorities, the groups were similar in their fervour about feminism and in their determination to bring about change in the lives of women in Israel.

Although hundreds of women organized around feminism, the effect of Marcia Freedman, a Haifa heterosexual feminist who later came out as a lesbian, was especially noteworthy. Freedman ran in the 1973 Knesset elections on a slate led by Shulamit Aloni, who had broken from the Labor Party and needed Marcia's link to feminist organizations to gather signatures to launch the new Citizens Rights Party (CRP). When the CRP garnered three times as many votes as anyone had expected, Freedman became a Member of Knesset (MK) – and, at that time, was the only avowed feminist to serve in a national government anywhere in the world. As MK she spearheaded abortion, domestic violence and peace initiatives. Out of office in 1977, she formed the Women's Party,[17] and went on to co-found the first women's bookstore/centre in Israel, Haifa's Kol HaIsha, as well as a battered women's shelter.[18]

A central feminist issue of the mid-1970s was the social clause in the abortion law, which sought to permit abortion for reasons of choice and not just health. Other issues centred on unequal wages and benefits, domestic violence and childcare. In general, women were realizing the nature and extent of their unequal position in a country which had long promoted a myth of gender equality.

Lesbians were, of course, among the first feminist organizers, but lesbianism was often viewed as a divisive or discrediting influence on the feminist agenda. Although lesbian CR groups eventually did form, issues of lesbian rights as distinct from women's rights were not raised in the public dialogue. In fact, as reflected in these oral histories, several lesbian organizers of feminist groups and projects believed women's rights (and issues of militarism and nationalism) outweighed their oppression as lesbians in terms of priorities for activism.

⋅ In 1975, in Haifa, a group of twelve gay men and one lesbian started the Society for the Protection of Personal Rights (SPPR).[19] Soon moving to Tel Aviv, it organized social activities and advanced an equal-rights agenda. Although SPPR had always advertised in newspapers to try to involve more women, in 1988–89 it was still predominantly male.

The first Israeli feminist conference took place in 1978. A legendary event in Israeli lesbian history occurred there when 'the lesbians stood up'. At a call from the podium by Haifa lesbian Maya Bergman, about 25 of the 100 assembled women rose to their feet, thus identifying themselves as lesbians. They then declared the first lesbian-only organization in Israel, ALEF: the Association of Lesbian Feminists.[20] Though it lasted less than two years, it succeeded in its goal of letting Israeli society know that lesbians existed in Israel. By the time the 1982 feminist conference was held, 500 women attended and lesbians were so visible that the scandalized Israeli media vilified the feminists as 'man-hating perverts'.

Meanwhile, the opening of feminist centres in Haifa, Tel Aviv and Jerusalem in the late 1970s gave lesbians a place to gather and meet each other. Tel Aviv and Jerusalem, an hour apart by car, and Haifa, two hours from Tel Aviv and three from Jerusalem, are close enough geographically for centres to share knowledge of each other's activities and for women to attend events in the other cities. Though the geographical closeness has always helped national mobilization efforts, each city retains a strong sense of its own feminist identity.

Tel Aviv's Feminist Movement operated a centre from 1976 to 1978. In 1979 a group of more radical Tel Aviv feminists (said to have been made up of 'half lesbians, half leftists, and one plain feminist') broke away over the Feminist Movement's perceived homophobia and liberal ideology, opening a centre called Tsena

U'reina,[21] with a goal of developing women's culture through a bookstore, films, lectures and social events. It was modelled on Kol HaIsha[22] in Haifa, which had grown out of a bookstore organized in 1978 and which gave Tsena U'reina half its book inventory to help get it started. Jerusalem's centre, also called Kol HaIsha, was begun in 1979 by two lesbians who moved there for that purpose, inspired by the Haifa centre.[23]

Feminist ideology fuelled these activities-driven women's centres. These centres crystallized the women's communities around a safe, supportive environment available nowhere else. They served women through a broad range of programming and gave their organizers the opportunity to develop leadership and political skills. At least half of the leaders in the centres were lesbians.

The women's centres all closed after three or four years as a result of leadership burn-out, but feminist projects such as battered women's shelters and rape crisis centres continued. Lesbians, whose issues had only marginally been addressed at the centres, were back to organizing social events among themselves or going to women's night at Divine, the gay disco in Tel Aviv. A number of English-speaking immigrants left the country for lesbian meccas like London, Northampton (Massachusetts) and San Francisco, though this was not an option open to most Israeli lesbians. Closing the centres left lesbian hopes and political energy unfocused until 1987, when Chaya Shalom founded CLAF, the Community of Lesbian Feminists, to support the evolution of Israeli lesbian culture.

*

In 1988–89 the environment in Israel was characterized by a somewhat organized and self-aware lesbian community existing in a society that generally ignored them. Though the lesbian community's twenty-year history was generally known among feminist lesbians and social activity among lesbians was thriving in many circles, public information and awareness of lesbians were meagre. Radclyffe Hall's *The Well of Loneliness* (first published in English in 1928) had been available in Hebrew since 1952,[24] and several mainstream Israeli periodicals had carried gay and lesbian personal ads for a decade or more. The gay disco in Tel Aviv provided

Tuesday as 'women's night', SPPR's and CLAF's presences were occasionally felt in the media, a gay (mostly male) magazine was published, a lesbian's fight for child custody was covered in the newspapers, an anonymous interview with a lesbian couple appeared in a national magazine, the lesbian actress Noga Eshed had a six-month run of a performance piece, and two books by the Israeli lesbian poet Gabriella Alicia were in print. Probably the only out Israeli lesbian known to the public by name was Chez, a rock singer.[25]

In spite of their lack of political standing and the ebb in lesbian organizing, in 1988–89 lesbians provided regular social and cultural activities for themselves. In Tel Aviv, an SPPR-affiliated lesbian initiated the 'moving coffee-house' in private homes, including social events and discussions. Later the Feminist Movement, which had reopened its centre, offered its space for these gatherings twice a month. Jerusalem lesbians organized dances and potlucks, and often travelled to Tel Aviv for events there. In Haifa, a new centre called Isha L'Isha/Woman to Woman made public its policy of giving space to Jewish and Arab/Palestinian, straight and lesbian women, providing social and political activities for women in the Israeli north. Because the centre created a safe space for lesbians within its own roster of activities, lesbians didn't need a separate organization, although they held gatherings where specific lesbian issues were discussed.

In 1988–89, when these oral histories were recorded, CLAF in Tel Aviv had managed to provide a national communication link for several hundred lesbians and to organize regular events. It used SPPR's basement club room for parties and the Feminist Movement's meeting room for lectures and discussions. Nevertheless, energy was at a low ebb, as CLAF's collective shrank to two.

To understand the challenges to the feminist/lesbian movement in the late 1980s, it is important to remember the political environment. Most pressing was the *intifada*, which began in December 1987. Activist lesbians were putting most of their political energies into organizing around peace, which they generally agreed to be the most crucial issue.

Another challenge was burnt-out, younger lesbians filling the leadership roles. Meanwhile, in Tel Aviv, a growing SPPR offered a mixed organization, where women who felt comfortable working with men could organize around gay/lesbian issues.

*

The environment for lesbians and gay men in Israel improved dramatically in the early 1990s, soon after these oral histories were recorded.[26] In 1992, a media breakthrough occurred when a lesbian couple, Liora Moriel and Susan Kirshner, were interviewed on a prime-time TV talk show, along with Liora's mother, Ruth, who lent strong parental support. The political and social turning-point came in February 1993, at the Conference in the Knesset. Convened by Member of Knesset Yael Dayan (Labor) in her capacity as chair of the Committee for Lesbian and Gay Affairs and in coalition with SPPR, the Conference brought over 100 lesbians and gay men to the Knesset to testify to the size and legitimacy of the gay/lesbian community in Israel, and to demand rights equal to heterosexuals. Since then, public attitudes towards gays and lesbians, as expressed in the media and as felt by lesbian and gay people themselves, have markedly improved.

Two legal milestones for gay rights preceded this event. In 1988 a statute dating from the British Mandate (1917–48) that outlawed homosexual relations was rescinded, and in 1991 discrimination on the basis of sexual orientation was prohibited in the workplace. More recently, El Al airline was compelled in a civil action to grant flight benefits to the partner of a gay flight attendant, and a gay professor at Tel Aviv University is attempting to gain pension and other spousal rights for his partner. The Israeli military clarified its traditionally laissez-faire stand on gays by forbidding discrimination in recruitment, posting and promotion as well as anti-gay harassment. And as of this writing, Adir Steiner, the long-term lover of a high-ranking, openly gay army medical officer, is suing the IDF to be recognized as an army widower with attendant rights.

In the 1990s, energy and activism are much in evidence in Israeli lesbian communities around feminist and lesbian issues as well as issues of peace and anti-racism. The CLAF collective is large and active, scheduling discussions on such diverse topics as a feminist Haggadah, breast cancer and AIDS, and lesbian families. It now publishes a magazine *Claf Chazak* (*The Strong Card* or *The Successful Card*), a forum where Israeli lesbians at last can record their history, thoughts and politics. As a challenge to the concept of the family, lesbians in growing numbers are having children through alternative insemination.

Although lesbian social and political organization has been growing in smaller cities and towns, lesbian community activism in the large cities is better documented. In Jerusalem and Haifa, lesbians have organized social activities in pubs and coffee-houses, so there are known times and places for lesbians to gather. Potlucks, parties, discussions and cultural evenings are held in women's homes or in the women's centres. Metropolitan Tel Aviv, a more pluralistic and open-minded city, boasts gay bars and discos. In addition, the SPPR has opened a national centre there in a beautifully furnished apartment. However, although the leadership of SPPR was lesbian from 1992 to 1994 and CLAF co-ordinates some activities there, SPPR's hierarchical structure led CLAF to insist on remaining independent from it.

In general, the social environment for lesbians and gay men in Israel has greatly improved in the 1990s. In 1993 the first annual Gay Pride event was held in Tel Aviv, with singers, speakers and festivities, marking the first time Israeli gay people gathered in public to celebrate their identities. Indeed, the presence of so many photographs and actual names in *Lesbiōt*, decisions about which were made in 1994, is a testament to the improved situation; had this book been published in 1989, perhaps only one or two lesbians would have felt able to print their names, and I doubt if any would have risked a photograph.

In 1994 on my first trip to Israel since recording the oral histories, I spoke at length with most of the participants, as well as with many other lesbians. I was struck by the ways Israeli lesbians now so confidently express their awareness that they are the makers of their own culture. They are integrating what is useful from 'outside' while shaping a sabra lesbianism rooted in a distinctive lesbian history that has been growing for decades.

Tracy Moore

Notes

1. In general, Palestinians are those Arab peoples who inhabited, or whose ancestors inhabited, the area called Palestine before 1948. For clarity, I have used 'Israeli Arabs' to refer to those who remained in Israel when it became a state; they are Israeli citizens. 'Palestinians' refers to Arab residents of the West Bank and Gaza Strip and to those in the Palestinian diaspora. The terms are not necessarily mutually exclusive.

2. Native-born Israeli; for explanations of other unfamiliar words and phrases, please consult the Glossary (pp. 321–6).

3. Although everyone came to her interview knowing the project was a lesbian oral history, lesbian sexual identity evidently had varying meanings among the participants. I have chosen not to make judgements about sexual classification, believing that each woman understands that she rightly claims a place in Israeli lesbian history.

4. This statement recognizes that the families of many Israelis arrive in total poverty and the category 'middle class' encompasses many professions that are modestly paid.

5. Hebrew, Arabic and English are taught in all public schools. Arab schools teach in Arabic, Jewish schools in Hebrew. Hebrew and English are compulsory for all students; Arabic is compulsory in Arab schools and an elective subject in Jewish schools. In the 1980s, the Jewish literacy rate was 92 per cent, and the Israeli Arab rate was 70 per cent, partly due to Arab reluctance to educate girls.

6. These religious courts are rabbinical for Jews and Muslim for the majority of Israeli Arabs; the small Druze and Christian communities have their own religious courts. Rabbinical courts, or *Bet Din*, are composed of three rabbis. Judges in religious courts are not trained in civil law.

7. The Jewish document divorcing a married couple.

8. As of 1994, most countries had not recognized Israel's annexation of East Jerusalem.

9. Druze are conscripted; Israeli Arabs are not, but may enlist.

10. Exemptions for ultra-Orthodox, who do not recognize the legitimacy of an Israel before the coming of the Messiah, are routine. Other exemptions include mental illness or physical limitation.

11. For instance, in 1988, only 8 out of 120 Members of Knesset were women.

12. Su Schachter's unpublished manuscript, 'Lesbians in the Israeli Peace Movement', provided much of the information on this topic.

13. Though its origins lie in Socialism, the left in Israel is increasingly defined by issues of security and not economics.

14. 'Who we are,' *Women in Black National Newsletter*, Fall 1992. Since 1989, a number of books have been written about women's

involvement in the Israeli peace movement (see the Bibliography).

15. Material in this section relies heavily on Miriam Benson and Dorit Harverd (eds), *The Status of Women in Israel: The Implementation of the Recommendations of the Israel Government Commission of Investigation* (Israel Women's Network, Jerusalem, 1988).

16. This section draws heavily on Chaya Shalom's 'My History of the Feminist and Lesbian Movements in Israel' (unpublished manuscript) and on *Exile in the Promised Land* (Firebrand, 1990), Marcia Freedman's fascinating memoir of her odyssey in Israel, including her experiences in women's, national and lesbian politics and her personal coming-out story. Thanks also to Emma Gilbert, Liora Moriel and Avital for their input.

17. The Women's Party, whose slate did not include Freedman, garnered 7000 votes, not enough for a seat in the Knesset, but enough to raise consciousness.

18. Although Freedman was the driving force behind these landmark events, other lesbians and straight feminists were involved and critical to their success. The women's centre in Haifa was later renamed Isha l'Isha (Woman to Woman).

19. Now called the Society for the Protection of Personal Rights of Lesbians, Gay Men, and Bisexuals in Israel.

20. Alef is the first letter of the alef-bet, the Hebrew alphabet.

21. Literally 'come out and see' (in the feminine plural), Tsena U'reina is the name given to sixteenth-century books of spiritual writing in Yiddish distributed among women because they weren't permitted to learn Hebrew or study Torah. In *Lesbiōt*, Emma Gilbert's oral history discusses women's centre politics in Tel Aviv.

22. Literally 'woman's voice', with a pun on 'all women' (see the Glossary).

23. The oral histories of Nurit D, Chaya Shalom, and Ora Yarden chronicle different aspects of the history of Jerusalem's Kol HaIsha.

24. Published as *The Depth of Loneliness* in 1952/53, translated by Ytzchak Swerdlik, and as *The Love of Women* in 1975/76, translated by A. Levy.

25. 'Chez' is a Hebrew acronym for 'temporary name'. In the early 1990s she began using her real name, Efrat Yerushalmi, and gained renown for her poems, stories and a play. She returned to public performance as part of the *Hot Night* lesbian cabaret in 1994.

26. Much of the material in this section comes from Chaya Shalom, 'Conference for Homosexuals and Lesbians in Israel', *Off Our Backs*, April 1993, and Ron Dayan, 'Gay Rights in Israel', unpublished manuscript.

אלינה

Elena

Edited by Kate Chandler

● *Elena, born 1961*

Elena, twenty-seven and Sepharadi, is a TV film producer in Jerusalem. Gesturing with her cigarette, her intensity is frequently punctuated with ironic laughter.

ISRAEL is not such a dangerous place to be a lesbian. You see, I come from Uruguay, where it's not a question of lesbianism being difficult or dangerous: you just can't. Although I love my country very much, the society is oppressive. I think it must be something like Spain during Franco's rule – really square! Very closed. Very Catholic. Very restrictive for women. An environment so hostile you consider yourself sick even *thinking* about loving another women! Like many other places in South America, lesbians there can't make anything together; they can't imagine to be lesbian can be something happy or good.

Israeli lesbians compare their country with the occidental world; they say, 'Here is worse, here is more dangerous, here is not like America.' Maybe it is not so easy as in America. Maybe it is difficult and traumatic. But it's *possible*. They don't appreciate that you have the opportunity to choose. That is very important. In Uruguay, we don't have that possibility.

By the time I made my aliyah at twenty, I knew I wasn't happy in Uruguay, pretending to be heterosexual. Although I didn't admit it to myself, I was not only suffocating sexually, longing for an adventure, but I needed to get away from my parents.

My sister was already living in Israel. The Israeli government had secretly liberated her from a jail in Uruguay, where she was imprisoned for her leftist political activity. She told me, 'In Israel, it is different; we are free.' I said, 'Freedom, that is what I want!'

I went to the Jewish Agency and asked to make aliyah; my parents thought I was joking. I left Uruguay, promising them, 'I'm only going for a short visit; I'll come back.' But I didn't.

Prior to leaving Uruguay, I had known for almost six years that I was a lesbian. At fourteen, I fell in love with another girl, older than me – she was fifteen! We met in HaShomer HaTzair, the Jewish Youth Movement.

I felt a lot of excitement when I was close to her. I didn't want to go to bed with her; I just wanted to be near her. It's funny because when other girls talked to me about what it was like being in love with a boy, their feelings were very similar to mine. So I began to think, if they feel like that when they are in love with a boy, then maybe I am in love with her.

I talked about my feelings for this girl with a woman psychiatrist I had been seeing for about a year. I didn't go to her because I was lesbian, but because I was 'difficult', I was all the time closed in my room, doing 'strange things', according to my parents. I had problems with them too. My father was very depressed, so my mother had to work very hard as a clerk for the Ministry of Justice.

Although the therapy probably gave me a certain degree of consciousness, I still dreaded it. I was always sick beforehand, and I remember trembling as I waited for her. I considered going to the psychiatrist as you would consider going to the dentist, because you have something that is wrong, and must be cured. We talked a lot about my attraction to girls, so I was pretty sure it was part of my sickness. Also, she was so happy when I talked about boys. She never said anything directly, but I felt the suggestion.

I also told my sister, who I went to with all my problems, that I was in love with a girl. She was completely shocked and called me 'sick'. She convinced me I was the only girl who felt this way about other girls! It was a terrible feeling.

I was so worried I went to the National Library, and I looked in the card catalogue under 'homosexuals' and 'lesbians'. I found three books all listed under homosexuality. At first, I was too afraid to ask for the books. Finally, I took courage and asked. Nothing happened. Nobody even looked at me!

I read about my sickness with fascination in the very big and dark Uruguayan library. The books made it definite: by definition, to be homosexual was to be sick. But even though I was 'sick', I was happy to learn that there are other 'sick' people like me! Although I couldn't grasp most of it, one book contained some love letters written by a woman to her lover in prison. They described feelings I could understand so well.

I met Alicia when I was seventeen, in preparatory school. It was funny, how do I say it – in the South American schools, if you are very brilliant, they give you the flag to carry in the ceremonies. I had to carry the Uruguayan flag, and she carried the flag of the national hero, Artigas. We met at the ceremony.

She was quite intellectual, and we were able to talk about Thomas Mann, Hermann Hesse, William Faulkner, Graham Greene, Howard Fast and all kinds of writing. We were very big heads! It became an important friendship. Not only did we read together, but we went to the movies together, we smoked marijuana for the first time together, and we dreamed together.

One day she told me she was in love with her Spanish literature teacher: a woman. So I began to think, maybe she feels like me! When I told her I was also sometimes in love with women, she told me she was in love with me! So we had a romance.

We didn't have sex exactly – we just kissed and hugged. Even though we didn't do much, almost nothing, we felt *so* guilty; it was terrible. She was much more afraid of sex than me. I asked her to come home when my parents were not there. But she refused. She repeatedly told me, '*You* are the sick one. *You* are the one who is the lesbian because you try to seduce me.'

So I decided, yes, I am sick. I am lesbian. And that's that! I wanted to have sex with her, but she didn't, and we managed to have a fight, and put an end to our friendship. Afterward, she had a boyfriend.

Soon I made aliyah. When I arrived in Israel, I went to a kibbutz full of South Africans in Matsuba. During my six months there, I missed Uruguay. There was no one who could speak Spanish, and I was speaking all the time bad English. I also went out with men, thinking somehow that would make me heterosexual. I was exhausted by the change in language as well as my inner voice pushing me to change my sexuality.

Soon I began studying at Tel Aviv University. Even though it was all in Hebrew – a language I hardly knew – it was wonderful. I made such a big effort to catch things, to understand people talking to me. I had to go to class with a tape recorder! The other students took notes for me, explained what the lesson was about, and helped me find things in English. People were very good in the university, even though generally the people in Tel Aviv are the most unfriendly people in Israel.

I lived in the dormitories with two Uruguayans and a Mexican girl. I got to speak Spanish, so much Spanish! It was full of South Americans with similar problems. For all of them it was exactly the same – they couldn't understand a word of Hebrew. Hebrew was Chinese! So everybody was all the time with the Spanish–English dictionary, trying to read something in English.

That first year in the university, I met a wonderful guy, a pianist at the Rubin Music Academy, who became a good friend. Our relations were very funny. We slept together, we ate together, we were all the time together, but we didn't have sex. And we didn't talk about it, it was so right for us. People thought we were a couple, but we knew we didn't have sex between us. After a while, I was sure he was homosexual, but we didn't talk about that, because he was Argentinean and I was Uruguayan, and we don't talk about such things.

At the end of the year, when it was Pesach, he told me his friend, Celia, a cellist, was coming to Israel, and she was going to stay at his house. I was very jealous. I thought she was going to take him from me. But I was wrong!

Things went so *fast*. I think it happens sometimes in life that you just feel you have a special kind of communication with a person, and you want to be with the person the whole day, to talk and talk. We talked about my childhood and her childhood in Argentina. She explained music to me.

I remember something very special. One day I went to see her, and she opened the door and said, 'Oh, I am so happy you came. I think I am going to love you very much.' She hugged me tight. I was astonished. She was the first person who was so open and so tender.

Celia cooked things for me, bought wine for me, and took me many places. There is an expression in Hebrew, 'to fall from the lines'. It means I was just crazy! I almost stopped studying. I was running down from class to see her, going to concerts, and not paying any attention to my own life.

One Shabbat, I said to myself, 'I love Celia; I want her.' It was the first time I felt that way in a long time. When I was seventeen I didn't talk to myself that way about Alicia. Now I was twenty-one, and it was completely different. After I admitted this to myself, I went back to the dormitories and I drank the whole day. I was afraid I would tell her I loved her.

Then I went to see Celia. She knew why I had become drunk, so she said it for me: 'I think you are in love with me.' She didn't feel the same, but she understood. She added, 'It happened to me before; it was horrible. I was with an older woman for almost five years, and now I am cured. I am free of that. I have been going out with boys.'

I went back to my room destroyed completely. I didn't see her for almost two weeks. I said to myself, 'It always will happen exactly the same. I will be in love with a woman in that way, and she will say no.' I remember being so down I could do nothing. She came to my house at the end of two weeks and asked, 'Do you want to go to Egypt with me?'

'I am studying at the moment.'

'Take a week and come with me to Egypt.'

We went to Egypt and had a *wonderful* time. We came back and were together a month, and I had sex for the first time in my life. And after that she went back to Argentina!

I remember it with *such* intensity, but I think it's not worth so much intensity. She was my first love, and it's funny because it took me at least two years to forget her. Of course, I didn't actually forget her. I mean: to forget her in a way that I could begin to start loving someone else.

Later I found that like many lesbians I had a hard beginning. You know, things happen because you look for them to happen. I was so weak when she met me – alone, with only this boyfriend. I didn't have money because I could only spare a few hours from my studying to clean houses. She had an impact on me that in different circumstances she wouldn't have. But in that moment I was Elena, twenty-one years old. Sometimes I miss that excitement, that passion, because it was love, that big! But it also is very harmful.

After that, I met another guy, also gay, who helped me. I didn't know how to reach the community, so he said, 'Why don't you come with me to Divine?' – Divine was the place for the gays – 'on women's night'. It was funny because he thought women's night is exactly like boys' night – I'd go there and just pick someone up, and go and fuck on the beach or in the bathroom. And it was very different, because women are different.

I sat alone in a corner and watched people all night. No one came to sit with me, but it was fascinating, because I saw women kissing and dancing. Everybody seemed like a friend of somebody, but nobody knew me. Later I began going almost every week, and I understood it was because I wanted desperately to make contact with other women like me. It's funny because now when I go to Divine I know everybody, and I go there and just talk. But it takes time to know people.

★

Because I was a new immigrant with a scholarship, the Jewish Agency asked me to do service for the Rape Crisis Center. I agreed and ended up liking it very much. There was a workshop about how to be a volunteer. It was wonderful; Esther Elan, who gave the workshop, completely impressed me. She talked about feminism! It was the first time in life I heard about it. There was a library at the Rape Crisis Center; I took books out: *Rubyfruit Jungle*, *Sexual Politics*, *The Second Sex*. That was my feminist year.

One night I met two women from the Rape Crisis Center in Divine! One of them was so embarrassed she didn't want to talk to me, and the other one was friendly. We decided to go together the next time. When we made the arrangements, she told me another woman from the Rape Crisis Center, someone married, wanted to come along. I complained, 'Why are you bringing this heterosexual woman with us? She's going to look at us like strange animals!' I was very angry with her because I wanted to have an affair with her.

So I went, and the married woman was – Rachel. We fell in

love, and I was with her two and a half years. That first night, I found out she was from England, and although she was still married, she was separated. She lived alone in the centre of Tel Aviv in a small room. The second time we met at Divine, she came alone. She asked me lots of questions – she was curious about so many things. After Divine, she was afraid of going home alone, so I went with her. When we got there, I told her I wanted to stay. She was very confused – she didn't understand my intentions. But we slept in the same bed, so I had the opportunity to let her know what I had in mind.

It was her first time with a woman. But although I considered myself a lesbian since I was a teenager, Rachel was the one who didn't have a problem about coming out. She was so happy – she told her mother, her friends, her husband – everybody!

She also told everybody about us. She embarrassed me so much sometimes! We went with my friends from the university for drinks, and she took my hand and told one of them we were lovers. I wanted to kill her! I complained, 'You can't tell everybody; you must respect my feelings.' Oh, but Rachel took it wonderfully. She said, 'There isn't any problem.' The funniest thing is I didn't convert her, she converted me. I became more and more open, until now I feel more or less like her: strong and happy to be a lesbian.

In my last year, when I was sure of my choice as a lesbian, I made two films in university, both about lesbian relationships. The first, a five-minute film in 16-millimetre, is about two friends. I liked it very much because both actresses are lesbians with strong faces and bodies, and one of them is very butch. They walk in the market in Tel Aviv on Saturday – it is closed and empty. There is a sexual tension between them. When they go home, one of them tries to kiss the other, but she's rejected. The girl who rejects the advance leaves the room, tries to calm herself. Here you see all her fears, doubts and hesitations. She returns and kisses the girl she rejected. In the morning she rejects her again, leaving a letter saying she doesn't want to harm the other, but must end the affair completely. The other girl searches for her in the city, goes to her house, and knocks. She opens the door, doesn't say anything, and leads the other girl in. She sits silently beside her boyfriend, who is sleeping. They have a dramatic exchange of looks and then part.

My second film, which is seventeen minutes long, is not well done. It's about the same kind of experience as in the first film. Two women fall in love, get close physically, and in the end one woman goes off with her boyfriend.

Where I work at the studio everyone has seen these films. Although I don't think they have a healthy reaction to seeing my films, they don't have a hostile reaction either. My friend tells me I am crazy to show the films, but I said to her, 'If they want to know, it's all right.' Later, she told me everybody was talking about them. I don't mind about people saying behind my back that I am lesbian. I don't hide, but I don't talk about it. People at work don't respect me less because there is talk that I am lesbian. I think men don't have hostility against lesbians. They have a curiosity about it – I don't think they feel it's something menacing. They are much more menaced by gay men.

I think we need more positive films about lesbians. My films are based on my first experience that lesbian love is something difficult and frustrating. It took me a long time and being with Rachel to convince me that lesbians can have a satisfactory sexual relationship.

I also discovered with Rachel that lesbian relationships which last a long time have problems similar to any relationship. We made a lot of silly mistakes. If we had a chance to do our relationship over, this time it would be much better. It's a pity, but it was my first couple, and it was her first woman couple.

Ever since Rachel and I separated in 1986, I didn't find a person I liked so much to live with. I have been with many women, and I think it's not so good, for me at least. You see, after we split I got into the lesbian community and got disappointed. When I didn't know lesbians, I supposed they must be wonderful women, very intelligent, very intellectual and very sensitive and very – I don't know what, many kinds of idealistic ideas. Now I understand lesbians are normal people: intellectual, not intelligent; people who screw people and people who respect people in the community; impressed by the same things that impress heterosexual people: looks, money, clothes. So I was quite disappointed by the lesbian community – it's just a group of people that the main thing connecting them is they are lesbians.

Still, I think considering the lesbian community is so small, it is wonderful, and in a way it is wonderful because it is so small. It is important to have a lesbian community: to have places to go when you feel you want to act lesbian, to be what you are more easily. It's much more important to me to have a lecture or films or to talk than to have a disco.

Along with my lesbian friends, I have South American friends who are heterosexual. I don't have problems, being lesbian with them in Israel. However, in 1987, I returned to Uruguay for a short visit and I didn't tell even my closest friends that I am lesbian.

I have been out with my family since I went to the psychiatrist. I sent them photos of Rachel when I was with Rachel, and I sent them photos of all my girlfriends. My father says if I am happy like this, okay. My mother, no. She does not dislike my homosexuality because it is morally wrong. It's just that if my sister doesn't marry, and I don't marry, and we both don't have children, it is her fault: she did something wrong.

*

I think we Jews have a problem because it's not very clear, at least for Jews like me who are not religious at all, why am I Jewish. My parents brought me up as a Socialist-atheist, but I feel Jewish. I can't just say, 'I'm not Jewish anymore.' It's good I have accepted myself as Jewish, as it is good I have accepted myself as lesbian.

For me to be Jewish, it was always to be different. I looked different from Uruguayans. My face is not very Uruguayan, and people said, 'Ah, you are Jewish,' almost to the point of saying, 'Ah, you are not Uruguayan.' Though I was accepted at HaShomer HaTzair, they didn't understand I could be Jewish and not be Yiddish or Ashkenazi. As Sepharadi, we were really strange! In Uruguay, I wanted to be Communist and Uruguayan like everybody – to be part of the people. But Communists don't like the Jews very much! Still, I suffered more from my lesbianism than I suffered from my Judaism.

Israel is getting more and more occidental. For gay life, it's good. But I look at Israel not only from a lesbian point of view, but from a Jewish and Zionist point of view, and things here are getting exactly like in other countries. It is a disappointment. People here are so indifferent to other people, and they are running all the time after money and worrying about the same materialistic, ugly things that everybody worries about. It's a pity for Israel to lose its ideals.

My political hope is that the Palestinians will get the territories. I want them to live peacefully with us, to have their own country – but not because of the Palestinians, but for us Jewish people. We need to have our country alone – without Arabs. We shouldn't live together. Why?

Well, it's difficult because there are problems of culture and economic development, and if we continue to live together, they will continue being our workers, our servants. They won't have the opportunity to develop. We are not today in a normal situation, morally. Jews work in special things – artistic things, or intelligence things, or business. They do the physical work; we don't. If Jews think from childhood that Arabs do only certain things, that's the most terrible thing that can happen to a people. To think that for them there is a special future because they have this Arab people to dominate, that's very sad. We must finish with that, and I think the only way to finish is to separate completely, and to have our country for us, and be ourselves again, afresh.

I think the social development of Israel is a catastrophe. I don't know how you can correct when things have gone so much wrong. We need to teach children not to be militaristic, not to be aggressive. This country is teaching children to be proud of horrible things. We are becoming a little Sparta, proud of our Raphael and Lavie, military projects. Ask a child, 'What is Raphael? What is Lavie?' They know exactly! They know everything about the army.

In the last year I have sometimes felt I don't want to get older here in Israel. I am getting tired of the Israeli mentality, I am tired of the intifada, worrying, having to be afraid of stones or petrol bombs. But I don't see myself back in Uruguay, and I don't see myself anywhere else.

I know Israel is making terrible mistakes. But I *like* Israel inside me. If I leave Israel, I will worry about it. I get angry because

33: Elena

I expect my people, victims of the Holocaust, to be better. It's disgusting to see that we are not better. We are the same as the Germans, the Americans – countries that do horrible things.

Either I can live in Israel or I can't, but I will always be concerned about Israel; I will always consider myself a Jew and an Israeli. It doesn't matter what Israel does; I will be concerned about it.

נעמה

Na'ama Shapira

Edited by Tracy Moore

Na'ama with her daughter Yael

• Na'ama Shapira, born 1942

Na'ama was born on a kibbutz founded in 1936. Her father, an idealistic, bookish man, emigrated from Russia to Palestine in 1926. Her mother and grandparents fled from Germany to Palestine in 1934. At the time of this history, she was forty-seven. An emphatic humour invigorates Na'ama's voice, and even when talking at length, she is seldom still, gesturing and hopping up to walk around.

Shortly before this interview, Na'ama's daughter, Yael, had her bat mitzva *party, for turning twelve. Like most* bat mitzva *parties in Israel, this one was completely secular, involving days of cooking and attended by scores of adults, who showered the* bat mitzva *child with gifts, money and attention. Among the guests were Na'ama's current lover as well as at least seven former 'friends', both male and female.*

I WANT to give my history because I remember when I was young – maybe eighteen or twenty – I realized I live a life different than other people, and I wanted to know about it. So I looked all over, but I found nothing! I think it's very important that people who feel they want to live as a lesbian – or they must – will not feel they are alone in the world. Reading about me, they will know some other people live like that and it's a life. It is a normal life.

I have tried to look for books in Hebrew about lesbians. I found very few. There was only one book I read about a relationship between two women. I don't know the name in English – it's something about deep loneliness. Yes, *The Well of Loneliness*. It has been in Hebrew for a long time. I think it is the only book we have that deals with the attraction between two women. But in the book, it was forbidden and they felt guilty. I don't remember the end, but I remember it was not a full relationship. It was not like a family, they couldn't live together.

Myself, I never felt guilty about it, not then when I was fourteen and not now.

*

My first relationship was when I was fourteen years old, living on a kibbutz, but I didn't understand that people thought it was bad. My teacher tried to tell me but I think she was embarrassed or afraid to talk about it. She never used the word, and I didn't know what 'lesbian' meant anyway.

We lived in a group of twenty-five children. One of the girls,

Tami, came from the town to live in the kibbutz. One day everyone was picking on her, and she was crying. I said, 'Leave her, you don't hear what she is saying. She never had a father, and she has a cruel mother.'

Tami was born in Poland and her mother hid her in a monastery, and this mother in Israel was a stepmother. Nobody knew Tami was actually seventeen, though she looked fourteen like the rest of us. Only now, when she is forty-seven, like me, she went to Poland and the monastery gave her the date that was written on a piece of paper hidden in a little locket she wore when she arrived. They kept it all these years! They said, 'You weren't one year when you were brought here; you were four years old.' Suddenly she grew up three years! Now I can understand why she was more adult than us and other things were in her head.

I came to be her defender, and we became friends, just like that. She also began to touch me, and I was so ashamed. I never thought abut sex before. I was on the football field, or playing, or working with the cows. From nature, we knew everything, you know? It was going on all the time – dogs, cats, cows – but I *never* applied it to people. When I was twelve, some girl said, 'You know how adults make children?' She told me, and I said, [laughing] 'Nooooo!'

So when Tami started to touch me, I was very shy. But we talked many times, and I got used to it in time. It was not like an adult relationship in bed, let's say. But, it was the beginning. Touching very shyly.

Before that I never even thought about sex with boys, let alone girls. All the life was so full, with studies and work. My mother worked with cows and I followed her. From ten years old, I began to work alone milking the cows. I loved the cows – big animals, *calm, slowly-moving*. When you came back from work, you had homework. And then, one evening was discussion, one evening a movie, another a basketball game, a club. We had no time of our own! I was like a wide-eyed child – I never thought about sex.

But now I had a friend, and I felt good! Our class lived in one room, two boys and two girls. Tami and I began to use only one bed, so we could be together. Nobody said anything, and the teachers didn't know. The children just thought, 'All right, they are friends. Good!' One day we were giving the children's house a monthly cleaning. We took all the beds outside, cleaned all the rooms, and afterwards I said to one of the boys, 'Let's take one bed to some other place because we don't need it.' He said, 'All right, let's go!' But our class's adult leader said, 'Where are you going?' The boys said, 'They don't use this bed, so we want to take it out, to have more space in our room.' She said, 'Go back, quickly!' 'All right, why are you shouting? We will take it back, we don't care. Nobody uses it, but we will jump on it or something', and we took it back.

Afterward, I understood that *then* she realized something was going on, but she didn't talk to me about it. In the end of the year, all the class leaders and my mother had a conference, and they threw my friend out of the kibbutz because of me. Yes! My leader said my mother asked for it, and my mother said the leader asked for it. I laughed at both of them. I said, 'Look: you are the manager of the education here, and we are only children, so what I will say or think will not influence you. You are adult, I know you can do anything, so do it!'

I was angry, first of all. Second, I was shy because I knew they were lying. My mother tried to finish all my relationships: she was afraid of boys, and girls are bad, so what stays? Nothing at all.

★

I didn't feel any different when I was with a boy or girl. It's a *person*. It's a human being, you know.

My relationship with my parents never was good. We are four in the family: a brother and three sisters. I remember one day, the little one asked for something, and my parents told her not the real thing – they didn't lie exactly – and I said to them, 'That is not the way to educate a little person, by lying.' My mother said, 'When you have children you will educate them in your way. She is my child and I shall educate her in my way.' I said to her, 'You can take me *out* of the list of your children.'

I never was at home, I didn't like to be there. My parents lived together many, many years but I didn't like the *way* they were living together. They argued because they are such different persons. Now I can understand it. That is their *way* to live together. Without arguing, they can't live! But when I was ten or nine or eleven, when they began to argue I said, 'Bye bye!' and ran out because I couldn't stand to hear it anymore! Until today I *talk*, I don't argue about *anything*. You will do it in your way, I will do it in my way. But many people can't give one another the freedom to do the things they think. We have some need to influence, to make people go our way, I don't know why.

After they sent Tami away from the kibbutz I got more and more closed inside. In those days I was having relationships with ones that I loved or I liked. Always it has been the same. But I never hid. When I say I closed myself – I was very angry about the adults that destroyed young people's lives. I knew Tami had no place to go and I said, 'Look: I don't understand why you have to destroy her life. Why throw her out, she has no place to go!' That's why I spoke up for her, you see. Not because of me, because I can always manage – it's not a problem. But to her, it was cruel.

Nothing more happened until I was seventeen. That year I was a leader for children in Beit She'an, a little town nearby. I would milk the cows twice a day – at night from ten o'clock till two in the morning, and at ten o'clock in the morning until two o'clock in the afternoon. And between, on the bike, I rode the five kilometres to Beit She'an and came back.

During the holiday a group of teenagers from another kibbutz came on an exchange for two weeks. They were sixteen-year-olds, one year younger than me. I was asked to welcome two girls, so I invited them to my room. One was talking all the time, and the other was silent – calm, watching. At ten o'clock I said, 'I'm going now – the coffee is here, the dessert is here, feel at home, and come whenever you like; the door is always open.' They came the next day also, and on the third night the calm girl – her name was Hagar – came at one o'clock to the cows. 'What are you doing here?'

She said, 'I came to see you.'

'But you have to sleep, you have to get up at seven o'clock in the morning.'

'Aah, it's all right.' She came, night after night. She was following me! She was a beautiful girl, she is a beautiful woman today. She's a very good friend of mine, until now. She has now a daughter, twenty-one years old. But in those days she was following me around. They are always following me! I never understand why! [long laughing] I guess I'm just blessed.

Her mother was a very open woman, until today. She understood about the relationship. She said to us, 'Look: if you decide to live together, you have to know you will have a very hard life, because society doesn't take in these people. It throws them out.' And I said, 'Look: this *is* my life. I don't feel that I want to live another life.' And she said, 'All right, you decided. Now my daughter has to decide.' I said, 'All right. I won't push. Not her, not anybody. Hagar will decide by herself.'

We talked together, the three of us, many times. Her father, for him it was very hard to accept the relationship between us. Many years after – she got married, had a child, and then her husband died from cancer when he was twenty-seven years old – then I came back to her. We had been friends all along! I asked her if she wanted me to stay with her from then on. She said, 'No, I can't.' I loved her very much, all of the years. It doesn't matter what will be, you know? She's a friend of mine. Also Tami – we just celebrated the thirty-year-old relationship between us. She has a married son!

There is not a special word about friendship that tells which kind of friends people are. I never destroy relationships between people. It doesn't matter if we had a sex relationship or not. When I have a love relationship between me and somebody, I can never hate the person. All right, we have a love affair. I don't know why, I don't know how, things happened; it's not destroyed, it's changed. If I felt love for somebody, he or she will stay my friend for all the life we have.

*

After my last year of school, I went to the army. And in the army it was something fun! I asked to be a driver. They asked me to be some other thing, a very clever thing. But I didn't want to. I wanted to get my licence because I *love* to drive. The three things I love are french fries, driving and sex!

So in the army, they wanted me to be a test administrator and counsellor. I said, 'Look: I worked with children for three years in Beit She'an, now I want to rest, because I know that after the army I shall work again with people. I know that in the kibbutz I can't get my licence, and I *must* get my licence.' I was stubborn and I won! I became a driver.

They sent me to the north. But there was no work! All the time I was sitting and reading books. One day a week, they gave me something to drive to Haifa – all of three kilometres. I was so bored! Then somebody told me that in the south, there was work.

When I began the army, they knew I was a lesbian. It was in my file but I didn't discover it until I went to the interview when I asked to go from the north to the south. They sent the commander of all the women to talk with me. For the first time all my clothes were shining! She said to me, 'Why do you want to go to the south?' I said, 'Look: here, I'm bored, I have no work to do. Also, I have a good friend and a second family there.' 'What family?' It was the family of my second one, Hagar. The commander told me she knew about me, and asked if Hagar was a lesbian too, because Hagar was applying to officer training.

I said, 'Look: I am what I am. But if my friend wants to go to the officer course, I don't want what I am to stand in her way.' She said, 'No, it's not any problem.' I said, 'Look: I want your signature that nothing will happen to her. If you want me to cut off the relationship for two years, I will.' She said, 'If she's fit to be an officer, she will be selected.' I said, 'Look: I don't have a tape recorder here, but I will remember this.' Hagar was selected to go to the course, and I was transferred to the south.

No, the commander didn't ask me to break off the relationship. Look: the point is that if a person is afraid you will tell other people he is homosexual or lesbian, they can control you. My commander said, 'Na'ama, I know you and I see how you are in life with friends and with other soldiers. You don't hide it. When you asked to come to the south, I got your case. I took responsibility for you because I said, "Look: she didn't hide it." If somebody comes to me and says, "Tell me what secrets are going on in the army, or we shall tell everybody you are a lesbian," you would say, "Who do you want to tell? Ask him to come here, I shall tell him myself."' She said, 'You are not a danger for the army.'

Then I said to her, 'You know I love my friend very much. I

don't know what will be in the future. Who knows? But I can promise you one thing. I shall not have any relationship with any girls here in the south. I shall not make you any trouble.' I told her, 'If someone starts following me, you are the first one that will know it.' And it happened, and she was the first one I told! I said, 'Look: I have a problem. That girl Sarah is following me, I don't know what to do. Maybe we should change rooms. She is crying, she is asking me to do I don't know what. If you want to throw me out, here I am. I didn't do anything yet, but it's very hard for me, and she's sleeping in the same room.' I didn't want her, I wanted the commander to change the rooms, to take me out of danger. And she said, 'Na'ama, it's not my problem, it's yours.' [laughs] I said, 'What do you want from me? Help me!' She said, 'No! You said you would come first to me. So, you came. But I didn't say I shall help you to guard yourself!'

So I told Sarah to leave me alone until the end of my army service, because I'd promised the commander! [laughs] But she was around me until I finished the army, all the time. After the army, then I could begin. So – I began! Why not?

★

After the army I went back to the kibbutz and then they sent me to lead young people in HaShomer HaTsair in Tel Aviv for two years. Three years after the army, I left the kibbutz.

Now, Hagar had met a boy named Yoash, and he wanted to be her friend. He and I were also very good friends. She said, 'Look: if he says something against you I shall get rid of him.' I said, 'Wait a minute, you've known me for three years, and you got used to me and you love me. He didn't say anything against me yet. You don't know him enough. You like him. Give him a chance to know you, give yourself a chance to know him.' I said to him many times, 'Look: she can't be with me because she can't be with a girl. She doesn't want to have this life. It's too hard for her. But please, don't press the issue.' I told him, 'I shall go out slowly, and you will come in slowly. I know she will have some hard times because she will not understand it, but if we shall explain it to her she will not accept it. So, slowly, please.'

Over two years, we followed this plan. And we succeeded.

Sometimes it was very hard because on Saturdays, she always asked me to come and I said I can't come, I have some work in the army. And he came and she complained to him that I was throwing her away. Because she didn't know we were acting together, one hand, he and me. Sure enough, after five years they got married.

To give her away to him was very, very hard. And something happened after. She was in the end of the two years in the army, and she had another girl following her, and they had a relationship between them. He called me and said, 'Na'ama, please take her to you, because the other girl is destroying her.' I said, 'Yoash, I can't do it. Look: I love her so much until today, and you know it. If I take her back, I couldn't release her again.' And he said, 'Look: if it's good for her to be with a girl, it must be you. You are good for her. Please.' I said, 'Look: it's better for her to be with you and not with me. She loves you, I know it. Don't give up, please. Be sensitive as you are and stay with her. It will get over.' And it went over. Because I couldn't, I couldn't.

If you saw pictures, you'd see: they *all* look like her. All my girlfriends. Many follow me, but I take the girls that are like her – brown skin, lovely. [laughs] She is more beautiful than most of them, but they all look like her.

She had to be with a man, and not with me, because she couldn't accept sex life with a woman. She never talked about it. When we were something like thirty years old, we talked about it for the first time. After Yoash was dead, and we sat together, she said the times I tried to touch her she was something between sleep and awake. She didn't want to be awake. Something ran away with her mind. She couldn't accept it. She said she remembered a very good and very hot feeling in her body. But she never was fully awake, she never wanted to talk about it. I said, 'Today do you want to know what happened? What was between us?' She said, 'No.' Of course, she never touched me.

So, she got married, and of course, I had a new lover – this girl I refused to make love with when she was in the army, Sarah. I made love with her for one or two years. Then she left Israel. She loved me very much. I didn't love her so much as she; it was not balanced between us.

And in the meantime always I have some boyfriend also – to

have fun! But the relationship with boys – or with men – was first of all, sex, and not for my soul, you know?

★

The first time I built a home, it was with Saron (see pages 199–209). I was twenty-eight. At first, we rented a flat together. But the flat was upstairs, and I don't like to climb up steps – my life was in the kibbutz, on the ground. So I looked for a one-storey house. After about a year I found an old house, and we bought it, together with a third friend. We made it larger and into two apartments, the smaller for our friend.

Now we come to why I went to a shrink. When we had troubles with a neighbour, Saron asked me to talk to a lawyer, to take care of the problem. But that made a worse one! Saron was not in town and I don't know what happened – not to me, not to her. The lawyer used to drink wine, and she asked to go for a drink. I never drink – I don't know why I said yes. And I fell in love and she fell in love!

I had been with Saron maybe two years when it happened. The point was that this lawyer, Michal, was married for ten years then. I didn't know *anything* about her life. I knew she was married, and her husband was in England – some professor. We began to talk in the bar and I said to her that I know she is lesbian. I don't know why – but I never fail, I never miss it. I *felt* it.

She said, 'I'm married,' and I said, 'Don't tell me that. I *know* you are lesbian.' I drank something also and for me, one glass of liquor is enough to confuse me. At ten o'clock we came home, and we talked. But when I drink, before I fall asleep, my head is sharp and clear. I made a bed for her in the living-room and I went to go to the bedroom. But she said, 'No, come to me.' I said, 'No, I have Saron, I can't.' And she said, 'Come, come.' So, I came. And we both were very tired and half-drunk – or full drunk, I don't know. But the next morning we didn't go to work. We closed the door and stayed there for one and a half days and we *both* fell in love like two children or I don't know what – two adults, maybe.

It was very hard for Saron. I felt like a broken glass – all the pieces all over the room. And then I asked to go to a shrink. Look: I didn't do it consciously, you see. I felt she is a lesbian, that she is living a wrong life for her. But I felt a big responsibility about Saron, because she did nothing wrong. I don't even know if I had really been in love with Saron. Was I really in love? Look: I always feel in some way that people love me more than I love them. That I really can't love somebody. I don't understand why they love me so much, you see?

Michal was something else, because for the first time, I felt that I *fell* in love, you know? It's like a tank of benzene that you don't realize how it will burn. In a minute, *boom*!

But Saron was with me and I didn't want to leave her. I went to the shrink, and tried to mend it with Saron. But everything was too broken. After a year I went to Beersheva to study in the university. Mostly, I went to be apart from Saron, to try to divorce. She accepted it, but she didn't want it.

*

In Beersheva I tried to be alone, but I had a boyfriend. I got pregnant! Since years before, I knew I wanted to have a baby someday. But with this one I had a miscarriage after three months. I had a lot of blood and I went to a doctor and he gave me some pills. Now I understand it was not strong enough, the pills he gave me, to keep the child. Because when I got pregnant with Yael I had the same problem. But then I went to another doctor and she said, 'I don't believe the baby will stay after losing so much blood, but try. Use this injection.' So for four and a half months I gave myself an injection every week, in my legs. And so, I have Yael!

But in this year I had this boyfriend. When I got pregnant, he was very afraid. I told him I didn't want anything from him, but he didn't believe me. In Israel you can write up any agreement you want to, but the money is not for the mother, it is for the children. So, the mother can sign all she wants, but it doesn't hold in the law, you see? After the miscarriage, he was afraid I shall make another child. He ran away.

So I found another person, Vitorio. He was divorced, with two boys from his first marriage. I said I wanted a child. He said, 'What will be on me?' And I said, 'Look: I have enough money to raise a child alone. I don't need anything from you. If you want to be a father, you will be a father – whichever kind you want to be.'

All right! That's what happened. He's *something*. He and responsibility never meet. Never meet! He's a very good person. If you meet him on the street and ask him for money, for clothes, he will take off his shirt and he will give it to you, and he will stay without. You see? But as we say in Hebrew, his teacher died when he was in third grade. He is not very clever. He is a good person, a very hot person, very funny. But no responsibility – not for himself, and not for anybody else. He has big hands, and the money is flowing with the wind, it turns to mist and disappears.

He came and he went and he loves her. Always it has been this way with him. Thirteen years ago, when I decided he would be the father of the next baby, he wanted to make a home together. Then, when Yael was half a year old, he disappeared for ten months. He came back when she was one and a half. 'Where have you been?' He said, 'Don't ask.' I said, 'I'm asking!' He said, 'Look: I found a woman in Beersheva, and I fell in love. She has three daughters. Now I have nothing! She took everything – my radio, my money.' I said. 'One year you haven't come and I didn't know where you are? Maybe I'd look in the newspaper, at the obituaries, and see your name inside.' And he wanted Yael to welcome him! 'Come to me, I'm your Daddy!' I said, 'Hel-*looo*! I told you: you will be to her whatever father you will be, but if you are not here she will not recognize you. You will have to work on it! Wait a while, she is a baby, don't press her.'

He loved me. He loves me until today. But then he met a Swiss girl, and she sent him a ticket. He moved to Switzerland! Before he left, I took him to the court to register as Yael's father.

In Israel, if you have a baby and you are not married, you can go to the Ministry of the Interior and both have to declare he is the father. So before he left Israel I said to him, 'All right, let's go do it, because otherwise the rabbanut will make troubles for her when she's twenty.'

According to the law, she is a legal child, but not born in a marriage. What is a 'bastard'? 'Bastard' is a big problem in Israel. A bastard is a child who was born to a married woman, but not from her husband. You know the Ten Commandments: Do not be with another man when you are married, or something like this. Because then the child is not from your husband and it's against the marriage and everything else. But if I'm not a married woman, I *can* have a child. It is a 'child born out of wedlock'. It's all right. But it's still easier when you have the father declare, 'I'm the father.'

We went to the judge. The state pressed him to recognize the child as his. They gave us a lawyer. Oh, it was so funny! When a father claims paternity, he must give his name to the child so when he dies the child gets the money. I said, 'No, not his name – *my* name!' And he said, 'No, *my* name!' And I said, 'Go to hell! No way, I'm going home!' The last day, Vitorio said to the lawyer, 'You want to see her happy? I give up about my name!' I said, 'Yay! Happy Birthday to me!' The lawyer laughed. She said, 'I've never seen a couple like you. Are you crazy or something?' I said, 'No, we're only very good friends. We have nothing to argue about.'

*

He was gone, and then I found a beautiful flower running after me. Seventeen years old! I was thirty-six, she was seventeen and nothing helped me. We were together three years. The first year she was in school. After, she went to the army. When she finished the army she wanted to be free. And I gave her to be free.

After she went to have her freedom Saron came one day and said there is a Children's Village in Arad, and maybe it will be good for me and Yael because I will not have to go to work and Yael won't be alone. So, we drove to Arad. Yael was five years old. She loved the place very much. She said, 'I want to be here, I like the grass and trees and the little houses.' So, I said, 'Why not, it's a good idea.'

Children's Villages are also called SOS Villages. After the Second World War, there were many children without homes, without families, and many women without husbands – on the streets. In Austria, the monasteries gathered the children and the women from the streets. Every woman took care of a group of children. Until today, they have seventeen villages all over the world. In Israel it's a problem because in Jewish society, the family is supposed to be a whole. And in Israel there are not many women that are free, never married, and all the women in these villages must be without husbands. So they compromised that some of the women may be divorced and have their own children. They take children from broken families, or when the families are using drugs or throwing the children out. They take children from three years old until eleven, and raise them until they go to the army. Every family has a house and functions like a regular family – nine or ten children with one woman, like a mother.

I was there for one year. But the other children were jealous of Yael because she had her mother and they didn't. One older child told her to put her finger in the electrical socket and another girl – twelve and a half, and Yael was six – tried to drown her in a swimming pool. Luckily, Yael knew how to swim.

So this was one part of why I left. But the other part was Lily. Lily was a trainer for the new women that came to work there. She was getting a divorce, after many years of wanting to but not finding the courage. Her husband tried to take all four kids, but in the end took only one. She was forty and I was forty-one. The point is, she didn't mean to have a girlfriend. She'd never thought about it before.

We were talking many times at work – about the children, about everything. One day, I was in one corner of the kitchen and she was in the other, and she said, 'I want to give you a big hug.' I put my hands in my pockets and stood like this – like NO! But she didn't mean it the way you'd think. She grew up in a Polish family and when they meet, they always give two kisses, and are hugging all the time. I never did it – not with boys, not with friends, never. Because I grew up in a German family – distance one metre *at least* – you know, hard and cold. But she began to follow me, and didn't recognize what was going on in herself.

Slowly it began. It was hard for her because she'd heard the word 'lesbian' but she never thought about herself in this context. After two years of our relationship, I heard her say to someone, 'Look: I'm not a lesbian. I only love Na'ama.' So simple!

So because of Yael and the jealous children, and because of Lily, I left the Children's Village and went back to driving, my favourite job.

For a while, Lily and I tried to live together, but it didn't work. Yael liked Lily very much and two of the children, but the younger boy didn't want it. He fought his brother, and was jealous that the two girls were friends. In the house it was like *Gehanim* –

Hell! In time it became very hard for Yael to be there because of the fighting. Lily and I never argued about anything else, but the problem with children – what is right, what is wrong – and the fighting between the children, brought us to many fights. I had to move from there.

For me moving out was to cut the relationship, you know? But not for her – and she succeeded! Lily and Yael are still distant. But you know, when you are not living together you don't have things to fight about. Lily doesn't disturb Yael and Yael doesn't disturb her.

As for my plans, I think it will be Lily from now on. You know, we had many hard things together these six years and we got over them. Also, Lily had a cancer operation. Through it, we found out how to give freedom to each other. Because I like to be outside, I like to drive. She likes this sentence: you go your way and I will go mine, and if we shall meet, it will be good and nice.

The love with her is not full balanced on the one hand, but on the other hand she gives me what my needs are in many ways. And I think I got used to her. And she got used to me! Because I learned how to take a person as he is and not how I want him to be – her or him, it doesn't matter. We accept as *really* we are.

Look: I don't think I expect a *full* relationship. It's about time I realize the bottle of milk will never be a steak. That is life, you know? But I must say [smiling] I still feel maybe there is something around the corner!

Only yesterday, I was driving my car, with sunglasses on, and some girl walking on the street went like this – her eyes went all over me! Not only her eyes, all her body! [laughing] I was laughing! I said to my heart, 'Move out! Go from here!' [much laughing] I didn't stop, I ran away, but I *laughed*.

Yes, I've had many affairs – it's not really important. The principles, that's what's important. First of all, this book will show young people not to be afraid to live as they are, and not to get married with somebody they do not want to because they think it's the only life. There *is* some other life, just as good, very beautiful, with a lot of life and children if they want them. It's maybe harder for gay men to have kids, but I think they can – they also can be friends with a girl and raise a child together.

Look: in the Bible it's written that it's forbidden, and two thousand years ago people threw stones at the man who was with another man. But we are not two thousand years ago, we are today. In all communities, there are lesbians. I grew up in nature, and I saw many times when one cow wants to get pregnant, she's jumping on all the other cows, and all the cows jumping on her! So what is this? Homosexual, lesbian? I don't know, it's nature!

The community is afraid of homosexuals – I never have understood why. I can't see the difference between heterosexual people and homosexual people. I have friends all over – taxi drivers, driving teachers, psychologists, professors from the university, Hadassah Hospital. Maya came to me in the middle of Yael's bat mitzva party and said to me, 'You know something? Such different people, from all over the world, from the ends! And it's going so well.' And I said, 'Why not? They are my people!' And every one of my friends, and every one of my lovers through life, came to that bat mitzva. I *never* cut a relationship.

אורה

Ora Yarden

Edited by Irena Klepfisz

• Ora Yarden, born 1946

A kibbutz-raised sabra, Ora has been a radical political activist since the late 1960s. Her seven-hour interview, the longest in the project, allowed her to layer into her account many elements of her identity in addition to those chronicled here, such as her journeys to recovery through twelve-step programmes and co-counselling, insights about her spirituality, and relationships of the heart. Forty-two at the time of this narrative, Ora recounts a history entwined with women's and lesbian progress in Israel.

MY parents came separately to Israel in the early 1930s. My father's ancestors left France at the time of the French Revolution and settled in Nuremberg, where my father was born in 1911. My great-grandfather was a Hebrew teacher, but my grandfather was assimilated. He was an activist of the Esperanto movement. My father also knew Esperanto and while he lived in Germany advocated for it. Like all the men in his family, my father became a lawyer. But when he came to Palestine in 1935, at twenty-four, he became a kibbutznik.

My mother's family was originally from Pshemeshel, a small town in Poland. They emigrated to Dortmund, Germany, where she was born in 1918. Her family were very poor. My father has only one brother, but in my mother's family there were seven kids. Her father was a rabbi. The family was very traditional.

My mother's mother died during a flu epidemic a few months after giving birth to my mother, who was placed in an orphanage where she stayed till she was five. Then her father married her mother's sister – as I said, she came from a very traditional family[1] – and brought her home from the orphanage. But when she came back to the family, she was treated like an outsider. She thought this was why she became an incest victim by her two brothers; they never saw her as part of the family.

My mother only completed grammar [elementary] school – there was no money for more. At fourteen she left home and went to work as a maid for a Jewish family. She said she was very exploited and worked eighteen hours a day for two years. Her family had fled to Belgium in 1932 and she was left on her own. She was afraid to flee too, and miss the chance to get a visa to Palestine. And then Recha Freier[2] organized a youth aliyah, trying to save Jewish kids by taking them to Palestine. In 1933, when she was about fifteen or sixteen, my mother came with the first religious youth aliyah. She joined a religious kibbutz where her brother was already a member.

Both my parents lost a lot of their families back there. My father's father had died of a heart attack and my father's brother had come to Palestine before the war, but his mother was captured in Germany and killed in Auschwitz. My mother's three brothers and one sister came to Palestine before the war. Two brothers, a nephew and her parents were all captured in Belgium and killed in Bergen-Belsen. Neither of my parents knew any of this until after the war.

My mother arrived in 1933 and my father in 1935. They went to different kibbutzim. When she was eighteen, my mother left the kibbutz and worked as a maid in Jerusalem. Then she married her first husband, had my sister in 1938, and went to the kibbutz where I was born. My father married maybe twice before he married my mother. When he heard that she'd divorced her first husband – they'd already met – he came to the kibbutz and persuaded her to marry him. This was in 1944, the year my brother was born. I was born in 1946 and my youngest brother in 1950.

*

On the kibbutz, there was a clear separation between parents and children. The children had special houses where the parents would come to see them. Or the parents would take them away for two or three hours in the afternoon. But the meals, medical care – everything was provided by the caretakers. The theory was that if you eliminated the stress, a pure parent–child relationship could develop. Not all parents were considered to be qualified to raise a child. Also there was the question of kibbutz productivity; most adults were needed for work.

The theory was good. But in reality, 100 per cent of the women did the service jobs and were stuck in traditional roles, people aren't freed up so much, and a pure parent–child relationship doesn't develop; the family structure never changed. If there was any incident or if a kid got sick, it was the parents' responsibility, or rather the mother's. Also on the kibbutz there was a clear hierarchy which the kids were born into. The kibbutz treasurer's son had a better position than a labourer's son and could get a university education more easily.

My older brother and sister raised me – practically my sister took care of us all – and I was very attached to them. My mother abused all of us. I would hide from the other kids in the children's house because I had all kinds of bruises. It was hard to shower or undress without showing them. My older brother and sister and I would comfort each other, cry on each other's shoulders. I had nightmares and was afraid of the dark. Growing up I felt trapped.

Very early I developed a strong love of books. My mother claims that by the age of four, I'd taught myself to read. By seven I was going regularly to the library. I read Jack London and Karl May. My passion was reading and I *loved* school. I always had crushes on my teachers. They were all women except for the gym teacher.

I loved sports, especially swimming, and was quite good. I would practise for three hours at a time. In wintertime I was a long-distance runner, and in the summer a swimmer. Education on the kibbutz included hiking and climbing. I was a strong girl – could endure long trips and thirst and carrying heavy weights. I enjoyed being outdoors in the sun and rain. I took pride in my strength.

My mother was proud of my achievements. She thought women should do well. I give her credit, she did support me: she'd watch me race, she wanted me to do well in school. In part I wanted to achieve to find a way to her heart. But I never felt loved by her or emotionally supported. It's still hard for me to talk about.

Even at twelve and older, I was very into sports – the 'rough ones' like running, climbing trees. I was basically a loner, but my group activities always involved girls. I fought with the boys! I got hit a lot and had to have stitches on my chin, my cheek, my thigh. When my cheek was injured my sister said: 'When will you understand that your face is your treasure? You're a woman and have to protect it.' I gave up fighting when the boys got bigger than me.

I was never perceived as a 'nice' girl. They said I had a black woman's face. If I were black, I'd be considered beautiful, but since

I'm white. . . . . It's amazing, growing up in the kibbutz and having all these racial distinctions. Where did we get them? Also, I am tall. I was told I had football player's legs, my shoulders were too broad, my back too muscular. I wasn't feminine. I wasn't! Good for me! I'm still not.

I've read about some masculine women and how they want to be boys and hang around with boys. But that wasn't true of me. All my best friends were girls. My first best friend was Tova. When we were about nine or ten, the entire class decided to boycott me and Tova told me about it. For this she was considered a traitor. Once when Tova and I were in bed under the covers, looking and touching each other's privates, my mother came over to say good night and pulled up the cover. We felt so ashamed!

The only people I really loved were my teachers. They seemed like goddesses – probably because they were in a sphere where I could excel. In school I was appreciated and felt loved. I was definitely the teachers' pet.

Even so, I had hysterical attacks. Once the teacher and the *metapelet** took me by my arms and legs and threw me out of the class because I was such a nuisance. I kept looking in through the windows, but the teachers told the children to ignore me. I had these attacks until I was fourteen. I also sucked my thumb and wet my bed. It all made me feel different and crazy. In fact, they said I *was* crazy.

By the time I was fifteen I'd decided I would never live in a kibbutz. My plan was to go into the army, become an officer and have an army career. I told everyone. Knowing that I would eventually leave made it easier.

At fifteen all the teenagers in the kibbutz got a new schedule – we went to school for four long days and worked for two. Of course I wanted to work outdoors and chose to work with cows. But when the kids made fun of me and said *I* was a cow, I changed to the vineyards. Looking back, I see I wasn't very strong. In school I understood that in order to survive, I had to conform. I discovered the formula for popularity: pretend you don't give a shit. I did it for a year and became very popular. After a year, though, I realized

* Babysitter, childcare worker (female).

that I'd gained everyone's approval and still wasn't happy. Books were important, so was being a good worker and a reliable person. But being popular? All this just strengthened my decision to leave.

*

Let me go back, though, because I've skipped over the incest, which made my childhood so scary . . . the constant fear of being sexually abused by my father. I remember when I was five someone leaving my bed, leaving the room. After that I was always on the run, scared and avoiding my father. Whenever he helped me with my homework, he wanted me to pet the back of his neck. So I didn't want his help, and I'd be cross with my mother whenever she asked him to teach me. There was also a lot of exhibitionism and I would have to lock the bathroom door. I never let him get close to me or kiss me or anything. I was very angry with my mother. She must have seen – there was only one room.

Once when I was about ten and my brother twelve, we were reading in my parents' bed. My father was washing the floor, so we had to stay in bed until it dried. Suddenly my brother grabbed me and pressed against me. I could feel his erection. I kicked him and he fell out of bed. That was a blow because from a very early age, my brother had been my guardian – my saviour, my angel. We'd been so close for so long. Whenever I'd get beat up, he would comfort me, and I'd comfort him when he was hurt. But that day ended all of that. I'm still mourning, I guess.

No one in the family ever talked about the incest, not until my brother's son was going to be bar mitzvah. My parents had divorced and my sister was refusing to come because my father was going to be there. She told my sister-in-law that she was an incest victim by my father – not in so many words, but my sister-in-law understood what she meant and called me. The second I heard that my sister was 'inventing' some stories about my father – I knew. That was about six years ago. Until then, I'd chosen to forget it completely.

*

When I went into the army in 1964 I had no political aware-ness about Israeli wars or about Israel and the Palestinians. I'd been raised very patriotically. I simply viewed the army as a way out of the kibbutz.

I served in the women's camp which trained new recruits. There were a lot of stories about dykes in this camp, but I never saw any! I took officer training courses, but I had no discipline. I was *always* organizing some rebellion. One time I called an officer a son-of-a-bitch and she had me tried in front of everyone. I was a kind of ringleader, troublemaker, pushing everyone to rebel against authority. Although they gave me my rank and I continued with my officer training, when the two years of service were up, I didn't re-enlist. I also left the kibbutz officially. I was twenty.

My sister wanted me to come to Jerusalem, where she lived. When I was a child, she never failed me. Unlike my mother, she thought I was gorgeous and showed me off. She'd knit sweaters for me and embroider my clothes. So when she asked me to come to Jerusalem, I went. This was in 1966. Jerusalem was still a small town, and Israel was in a depression. A lot of people were leaving the country – like today.

It was difficult economically. For two years I worked as a maid. Then I decided to become a secretary and taught myself to type. As it turned out, I was a lousy secretary, but in the process, I discovered that I could organize an office to run efficiently. So after three years, I became an administrator. And that's what I've done ever since.

In 1972, I began working for a state-owned company. I joined the union and became an organizer for the administrative staff. We had three different unions there. We wanted one contract for all employees, with adjustments for levels of employment. I did analyses and showed how the company could be reorganized. My colleagues accepted my plan and we began to fight for it. I was very committed, but the others were more scared. They kept pulling me back. Though I was good at preparing the material, I was not a good representative for them because I was not willing to compromise and retreat. Only later did I realize that the workplace has limitations and that I should have accepted them.

I pushed for a strike. We did go out and then were called into the labour court. We got a lawyer. At one in the morning we reached a certain stage and I *knew* we could go further, that management was trying to wear us down, to scare us. But my colleagues said they had no energy. They said: 'Let's vote.' I said: 'No point in voting. Go ahead. Do what you want.' I knew I'd be out-voted. And oh, did I cry!

I asked the lawyer: 'How could you let them do it? You're supposed to be working with the union! You're working with *them*, not with us.' And I realized that the lawyer, for his own reasons, was willing to go only so far.

All in all I did union work for eight months. And my employers were 'so impressed' that they gave me the personnel manager position. It's hard for me to admit it, but it was a way of buying me out, getting me out of the union, stopping me from making problems for management. It's a common tactic. Eventually I realized this work was against my political beliefs. I decided it was wrong to work in *any* administrative position. I felt I should leave, but it was hard, because this job was very well paid.

*

Wanting to quit was very much connected with my political development, my concept of the world. It took me back to the beginning of my political consciousness – to 1967 when everyone was wrapped in feelings of glory over winning the war. But after 1967 I was in mourning for all my friends who had died. I felt isolated, and began questioning the myths I'd been raised with: that Israel was in danger from the Arabs, that they would wipe us out or push us into the sea. To me the victory was so clear – there were no real dangers. It was at this point that I started to separate from the mainstream.

During these first few years I didn't have a defined political view. I worked with people from the left in Communist splinter groups. It wasn't until 1973 that I had the courage to break with the mainstream. I felt the Yom Kippur War was our fault, that since 1967, we'd never tried to reach a peace agreement, that we were drunk with the conquest of the Territories. I saw young lives wasted and Israel still not giving in. After 1973 I worked against the government. We called for the leadership to take responsibility for what had happened and for Golda Meier to resign.

In those days I mostly concentrated on the Israeli/Palestinian conflict, not on women's issues. The only non-traditional thing about me was that I felt that marriage wouldn't happen naturally to me, I'd have to arrange it. So, I decided to look for someone. My housemate started keeping track on my door of the marriage proposals I'd rejected. After five scratches, he said: 'You'll never marry. There's no chance.'

In 1974 I joined my first CR group. Yaayy!! At the same time, I fell in love with someone special, Gadi. I thought this would be my last try at a conventional lifestyle. Until then I'd never lived with a lover. As soon as we moved in together, we were at war.

Looking back, I think I was pretty rigid. I was afraid of being backed into a corner, forced into a traditional role. When I finally left Gadi, I knew I'd never marry. I'd wanted to be accepted, to be part of the majority, but I found out the hard way I couldn't make it. During this period I also had a tubal pregnancy and, after going through surgery, I realized childbirth, like marriage, did not come naturally to me. Though I mourned not being able to have children, I was also relieved.

*

My consciousness-raising group was part of the Women's Liberation Movement – that was the name of the Jerusalem organization. WLM consisted of CR groups and study groups with a representative organizing committee which developed plans and proposals to be presented at the monthly general meeting, where we decided what actions to take.

There were three branches of the Women's Liberation Movement – Jerusalem, Tel Aviv, Haifa. Each was completely independent. An umbrella organization made up of branch representatives met about once a month to make decisions about national issues, like in 1976 the social clause for the abortion law, or joint actions – usually demonstrations.

In Jerusalem we had a mailing list of about 200, with 75 active members. The Jerusalem branch was formed by women active in left organizations like Shasi, which was Communist, and Matspen, an anti-Zionist, Trotskyite organization. Marxist and socialist theory was very much behind our feminist awareness. This was not as true of the other two branches.

It also was a very *straight* movement. A lot of the issues we focused on were about living with men, on how not to give in to them. But the group wasn't giving me any deeper understanding of why Gadi and I fought so hard. On a conscious level I wanted to live with Gadi, have a happily-ever-after marriage like the rest of the women in the group. On another level I didn't want that. I stopped going to CR, and a year and a half later, I joined a group in which most of the women were single.

One of the things Gadi and I fought about was living in the Old City. I believed we had no right to live across the Green Line, in the Occupied Territory. My feelings about the Old City stemmed from 1967. I viewed the Territories as Palestinian. Just because Jews had lived there before 1948 didn't mean we had rights there. If Israelis were to start claiming Hebron, the Old City, the West Bank, then the Palestinians had the right to settle in *their* old territories – Jaffa, Haifa and Akko. I believe we have no rights in the Occupied Territories, just the power. I see the intifada as the Palestinians' refusal to accept our occupation of the Territories conquered in 1967. But I also see the need to compromise. We cannot move the clock back to the beginning of the twentieth century. The Palestinians may also compromise and let go of the land we conquered in 1948. The rest we should give back.

In the 1970s I identified as anti-Zionist. I believed there should be a bi-national democratic state for Palestinians and Jews. Since then I've come to accept that Palestinians and Jews each want a state of their own. It's a compromise. I believe that a day will come when there will be no nations, no nationalism, no patriotism. But until then – I accept the present reality. I call myself a post-Zionist. I accept what happened up to 1948. But since 1948 – I don't see that there's been a need for Zionism. We have our state and we have to live within our borders and accept the nations around us.

*

In 1976 I consciously fell in love with a woman for the first time. Looking back, I realized I had already been in love with some of my best friends. But with Dina, I was aware of what was happening.

I became very active in the Movement. I helped form a new CR group and participated as a member. I joined the Movement's co-ordinating committee. I organized actions, demonstrations, meetings. And then I decided to go to the States because Dina was leaving. We planned to live happily ever after in California. Eight months in advance, I began to prepare for the trip. I wanted a work permit, so I decided to find a man with an American passport, marry him and get the permit through him.

Israel is very conservative when it comes to marriage and family. It's a Jewish state and in Jewish culture, family is very important. If you're not married by twenty-four, then something must be wrong with you. When I was twenty-eight, my father said, 'It's better to be a divorcée than an old maid of forty no one wants.'

I married this guy and got *so many* benefits. For example, I was entitled to a loan from the Housing Ministry. My father, who his whole life had never been thrilled with me, suddenly insisted I buy an apartment. He wouldn't help me if I were single and getting the loan myself. But now! I got the loan from the Housing Ministry and money from my father. As for the immigration visa, people pay thousands upon thousands. But I was married, so I got the visa free. And because I was married, I got compensation money when I resigned from my position. I can't tell you how much money I made from that stupid marriage! Years later I realized that I had agreed with my father that being divorced is better than being an old maid. As much as he hurt me, as much as I was critical of him, I still accepted my father's values. Getting married served some inner need to be what my father expected.

During this period I spent all my time on three things; my job, the Movement, and dealing with the bureaucracy involved in leaving for the States. I was exhausted, but I learned how the system works.

*

In 1976 in the Movement was the first time I was a full member of anything. My CR group sent me to represent it on the co-ordinating committee, and once I went I wanted to stay. I loved it. I got closer to the Trotskyite women and learned about their perspective in the Israeli/Palestinian conflict. Also, the Rabin government had a committee which was researching the status of women. Eventually it produced a long report – though not much was done about it afterwards. Many of the Movement's actions involved helping this committee. Also, Marcia Freedman and other Knesset members were pushing for a social clause in the abortion law because abortion was only permitted for health reasons. In Jerusalem we pushed for not having any special abortion law, but to automatically include abortion in medical insurance, like therapy. In 1977 the social clause passed. It was a *great* achievement, even though it was abolished later. But I'll get to that.

Another of our issues was violence against women – rape and battering. We were beginning to collect material and to start organizing. We held demonstrations and did street theatre. The first shelter for battered women was founded by the Haifa feminist activists in 1977–78.

Two other activities focused on women's status in the workplace. We supported a strike by women workers in the Elite Chocolate factory. They were demanding the same salary and privileges as men holding the same positions. And we joined with the women at the Leumi Bank who were demanding the signature right for women. What happened? Elite broke the strike and those women lost. But the Leumi women won, and more and more women began having the right of signature.

Simultaneously we were beginning to build a lesbian community. Back in 1974 at a general meeting there had been a big argument over whether WLM should allow the formation of a lesbian CR group. Women were worried about their image and many of us were afraid to acknowledge lesbianism within ourselves. But by 1977, we were having lesbian parties. It was more than culture – a camaraderie had begun to develop, women's friendships, sisterhood.

The Likud party came into power in 1977 and agreed to the religious parties' demand to abolish the social clause in the abortion law. There'd been a wave of radical changes and then it all turned around. As I see it, progress isn't linear: a wave reaches its maximum strength, uses itself up, ebbs and stops. Without strong opposition, the right wing can backlash. Eventually the wave will rise again – in a decade, a few decades. There are also human limitations. I see them in myself, as an older lesbian, an older radical. I can push my vision just so far based on what I know. A new vision can only come from a new generation which has been raised on different facts.

So the social clause in the abortion law was abolished. Oh! we were disillusioned. We protested against the abolishment, and we broke up into service organizations – shelters for battered women, a rape crisis centre, and in 1979, a women's centre. When you can't fight in full force, you move into a lower gear. You maintain the fire. It's not giving up or giving in. We changed tactics.

On the personal level ... I was talking with Dina about having a relationship and being physically close. But I knew it could never happen in Israel. I was too threatened by society, by my family. I couldn't make the leap and see myself as a lesbian here. So my trip to America in 1978 served a crucial function.

I went to California and stayed for a year. It didn't work out with Dina, but I fell in love with another woman, and we became lovers. So I started to live as a lesbian, but it took two more years before I identified as one – in part because she swore me to secrecy, but also because it was hard for *me*. I still had the urge to conform. I even considered being with men in order to maintain the correct front. Still, living in the States allowed me to change.

I originally thought I'd stay in the States – that's why I worked so hard to get the visa. But eventually I realized I'm too Israeli. I felt uprooted. The structure of the society is the same, but the culture is different. The whole time I was there working for various organizations, I never felt I was doing it for myself, for *my* people, for *my* women. It was for *them*. I was homesick as hell. A year later, I came back.

I'd decided I needed to become a labourer and in the States I'd been a trainee in a cardboard factory. After I returned to Israel I held on to this notion that I should be a proletarian. I took a course for electricians and now I'm licensed. But after working as an electrician, I realized that manual labour bored me. I was already forty.

Then I made another decision. Since being downwardly mobile wasn't building a better society, I would try to use my skills in the best way I could and contribute in other ways. Also, I wanted to try to be happy in my work – something I'd never aimed for before. I wanted work which contributed to a weaker group in society and which brought my political beliefs into the least conflict with the system. I took an administrative job with Project Renewal, which was getting money from the States to help poor neighbour-hoods. I worked on one of these projects for three and a half years. Then I became a manager of an investment fund for an under-privileged group. It's a specific job in a specific structure and has for me few internal conflicts and contradictions, the fewest I've been able to manage so far. Maybe some day I'll have a job with even fewer. There's a saying: 'Poor services for the poor.' But I don't believe in that. I provide the best possible services for these people.

★

The Women's Liberation Movement's greatest contribution to me personally was making me re-examine the myth of gender equality in Israel. When I understood that in Israel there has never been equality between men and women, I could stop being a Don Quixote trying to change things by myself and could start working on a broader framework with other people.

In my study group I was asked to present a paper on the myth of equality in the labour movement in Palestine during the early part of this century. On the kibbutz, I had been taught that women had an equal role in building the State of Israel and that today kibbutz women are equal and everything is fine. So when I was growing up and thinking about a profession for myself on the kibbutz and found the possibilities very limited, I thought this was my problem. After working on this paper, I realized there's a general problem that still hasn't been solved.

From the start, women in Palestine were not equal members in the collectives that built the kibbutzim. The collectives were formed by men who then *hired* women to do services – laundry, meals, cleaning, everything. Only after a lot of struggles were women accepted as members; women's equal participation wasn't a given. Women were also not accepted on road-building and construction crews. They had to form their own groups and collect-ives and deal directly with the contractors. They founded farms specifically for women where they were taught skills for farming, construction or whatever.

I stress this because it was very important for me to learn my past and to understand my present. For the first time I saw myself as a member of an oppressed group and could identify 100 per cent with its oppression and with its struggle. A lot of my present understanding is based on the information I accumulated then.

When I was doing this research it never occurred to me that some of the women in the labour movement in the early years were lesbians. I assumed they were all heterosexual. In fact my paper concluded that women were able to achieve a lot more rights in the early days before they became involved with kids and family, that women lost these rights once they started marrying and having families. I'm sure a minority were lesbians – married and unmarried. But at the time I didn't give that issue respect. No real work from a lesbian point of view has been done about this yet, nor have any national heroines been identified who may have been lesbians.

The whole issue of lesbians was very controversial in those years. There were women in the Movement who were known to be lesbians, but were never out. At that general meeting in 1974 which discussed whether there should be lesbian CR, it was straight women, not lesbians, who presented the issue. It was voted down for fear of the image it would create. You know: 'They'll see us as dykes and won't respect us.'

The solution was for the lesbians to create their own subculture which was not dependent on decisions of the general meetings. I respected that. In those years it was mostly parties, gatherings and meetings. They invited straight women who were allies and also a lot of lesbians who were lesbians but didn't know it – like me. But not everyone was invited. Only the chosen and the privileged!

I didn't mind being taken for a lesbian. I come from a lawyer's family, I have a legal mind. Since I 'knew' it wasn't 'true', it wasn't a threat. I had the best of both worlds. It was heaven. I really appreciated lesbians' acceptance of me. They did *not* judge me.

*

Kol HaIsha started with an idea of having a women's centre, a facility for the Movement. So in 1978 we began to fundraise.

When I left that June for the States, we already had a big sum of money. While I was gone, there was a shift in goals, actually a takeover. Not so nice. The group decided to use the money we'd collected to organize a shelter for battered women. I was very disappointed, though a shelter for battered women is a good cause. During this period the Women's Liberation Movement dissolved. It turned into service-giving agencies and stopped being a political force.

When I came back from the States there was a new group working to start a women's centre in Jerusalem. Marcia Freedman, who'd already resigned from the Knesset, and other women had started a centre in Haifa. They were advising women in Tel Aviv and Jerusalem. For a while we thought we might create an umbrella organization, but each branch became fully independent. A couple of women up north in a kibbutz, Terry and Nurit, saw what was happening in Haifa and moved to Jerusalem with the idea of founding a women's centre here (see Nurit's chapter, pages 117–32).

For years, my vision – mine and my old WLM friend Ofra's – was that the centre would be the seed from which the Movement would rise again. In part we achieved it. We organized in June 1979 – and opened Kol HaIsha in June 1980. From the beginning there was great demand. We were open mornings and afternoons, with programmes in the evenings. The collective had ten women, but the first year Terry, Nurit, Ofra and I lived only on our savings and worked there full time. We worked both shifts, facilitated CR groups, gave do-it-yourself courses – a lot of things. The other women came in whenever they could. This created friction because those who gave more felt entitled to have more say. Women who were not as involved felt we were withholding information. It was hard to work in this framework, yet we managed to do it for four and a half years – one year of fundraising and three and a half years of activities.

Kol HaIsha offered a lot of services: legal advice, private therapy, do-it-yourself courses in plumbing and electricity, a basic course in Arabic, morning groups for mothers with kids, evening lectures, events, parties, CR groups. We provided lectures to the public and were invited to speak at community centres, the university, and meetings of left organizations. We had poetry evenings and art exhibits. We issued a monthly newsletter, created a lending library, ran a bookstore, had an archive, and continued fundraising.

We invited women politicians like Shulamit Aloni to speak. We had contact with the special advisor to the Prime Minister, Nitsa Shapira Liba'i. We lobbied on feminist issues, like restoring the social clause to the abortion law. Following our example, establishment women's organizations like Na'amat and WIZO opened legal and individual counselling services. Sometimes we criticized them because, in cases of battered women, they favoured keeping the family intact. But later on they changed, so we began to refer women to them, though we kept our own counselling service.

We also started a project against violence against women. In San Francisco I had been on a 'Take Back the Night' march and was very impressed. On 8 March 1981 International Women's Day was devoted to stopping violence against women, and we decided that Kol HaIsha should participate. We organized a march with torches and candles in the streets of Jerusalem. People threw stones at us. We had a rally with speeches. It was *very* exciting to be out in the streets confronting society.

After a year, I'd gone back to work. By 1982 the friction within the collective became intense. It's hard to describe. The core was made up of dedicated, hard-working women. A lot of the friction stemmed from the concept that we all should be considered equal no matter what. But it doesn't work that way, because if one person is working at the centre 30 to 40 hours a week, and another five hours – it's just not equal, period. There were a lot of accusations and a lot of defensiveness. Then the collective shrank to five members.

A few months later, I started pushing for the core collective to resign. I thought we'd run the place long enough, and if we stayed, other women wouldn't bloom. It was almost the only project in Jerusalem that was general enough for other women to be part of. So in 1982 we had a meeting where a new collective took over. Ofra, Terry, Nurit and I had been the hard core, the ones who thought we could change the world. Some of us had a hard time resigning.

As it turned out, 95 per cent of the activists in Kol HaIsha were lesbians. Yet we were a feminist centre, not a feminist/lesbian centre. At first there was a lot of homophobia: 'What's to be done about lesbianism?' On the one hand, no one wanted to be known as a lesbian, including me; on the other hand, we were almost all lesbians – so who were we kidding? And on the third hand, we lesbians were providing services to straight women – so what about our own needs? For two years whenever we provided services to lesbians, it was always within the lesbian community. Only in the third year of the centre did we start lesbian CR groups. We did have public evenings focused on lesbian issues, but no one was identified. There were also private cultural events for lesbians only – parties, holiday celebrations. Women would go to their parents and then come over to the centre's lesbian *seder*.*

The second collective worked for almost a year and shut down at the end of 1983. Chaya Shalom (see pages 307–16) was one of the leading members. Chaya could never have been a leader with us barracudas, the old-timers, around. We wouldn't have given anyone a chance. When they closed the centre in 1983 it was doing fine financially. But in terms of women's energy – the collective burnt out.

After the closing we had a few years of what we called 'the lesbian community'. There were general meetings with topics for discussion, or presentations, or plans on how we would build the new world. We had a group for lesbians over thirty-five. Those were the years of big parties when we were in touch with the non-feminist dykes of Jerusalem. Every spring we had *huge* picnics and birthday parties with about seventy lesbians. But it wasn't the same.

*

When we closed Kol HaIsha, I stepped back from activism. I realized my work wasn't providing a solution. With all my understanding of politics and knowing that the revolution wasn't around the corner, with all my cynicism, I still had this faith that our actions would bring salvation. I was crushed, disillusioned when Kol HaIsha closed, when I realized there would be no continuity.

In the autumn of 1983, I got very sick with sinusitis and was treated with antibiotics. I didn't respond well, got a lot of pain-

* Passover meal.

killers which caused other problems so that finally the infection affected my middle ear. I lost my balance and peripheral vision. For a long time, I was disabled.

I ended up going to an alternative doctor, an acupuncturist, to try to heal. Chaya insisted that I organize some women to help me with my physical needs. So I organized shifts – women who stayed with me, took me to the doctor, cleaned my house, shopped, did my laundry, took care of my bank account. I couldn't be on my own, even to go to my therapist two blocks away. So there was a *whole* network of women to take care of me. These women got me back into life. This five-month period is part of my personal history, but also a community achievement. In fact, a lot of the Jerusalem lesbian community's activities stemmed partially from the network taking care of me. Somehow that became an example of co-operation.

Kol HaIsha closed in 1983 and CLAF (the Community of Lesbian Feminists) was founded in 1987, about two years ago. It was Chaya's project – I was only involved because of my close association with her. She asked me to give a presentation about lesbianism for the founding national meeting. My talk was called 'The Roots of Denial of Feminism within the Lesbian Movement'. I compared women's oppression with black oppression. I am a woman, I don't have a choice, I can't hide it. I'm oppressed just by being born a woman. This is hard for women to accept. Lesbian oppression I compared to Jewish oppression – it can be hidden.

The political aim of CLAF is to organize lesbians as a sub-culture, to pay respect to our culture and our needs as a subgroup. In some ways I disagree with it. I believe that our main concern as lesbians is to fight homophobia by coming out of the closet. Culture cannot be our goal. What we have to do is create a movement to give us safety, to maintain our rights. Simultaneously, such a movement would develop our culture. Chaya and I debate about this.

*

The political situation here has great hostility towards lesbians. In Israel, we live in a military, very conservative society. Women have a certain role – period. Of course, women are supposed to do what they're supposed to do all over the world – but more so here: raise kids, raise the men for the army, take care of soldiers. A lesbian is a real threat to this structure. She says: 'I'm not taking care of your soldiers or raising new soldiers. I'm not taking part in these war games you play all the time.' In addition, since Israel is a religious country, there are all kinds of religious laws against us.

Still, we're a small enough group so that we're not harassed. In Israel, it's the Palestinian who gets all the shit. As a Jew, even if I'm a lesbian – I'm still privileged. So if I don't make too much noise, they leave me in peace and continue harassing the Palestinians.

★

My mother had a difficult time relating to my lovers. She took to Chaya the minute she saw her, but she knew that Chaya was not my lover. Sometimes I'd get jealous of how beautifully they got along. The same with Lil (see pages 261–74). She and my mother became good friends. My mother didn't know enough English and Lil doesn't know enough Hebrew, so they chatted in Yiddish a mile a minute. But again, Lil was not a lover.

In 1984 I broke up with a lover. I was in a lot of pain. The first weekend I stayed with Chaya. The second weekend I decided to go to the kibbutz to my mother – you know, the old craving: my mother will take care of everything. And she was *so* sweet to me. She hadn't liked my lover, but still, she saw it as a relationship. She said how sorry she was, how hard it is to separate. She saw I was heartbroken and she was compassionate. I want to give her credit. With all the hardships between us, she could stand up for me and help me when the way got rough.

We'd made amends during the time I was sick. We were having a fight on the phone – as usual something about my brother. I said: 'You never listen to me. You don't want to know the truth. You just make up your mind without knowing anything.' And she said: 'You're so secretive. You never tell me anything.' So I went to the kibbutz and I told her my secrets – about incest. I found out she knew my sister and I had been abused by my father, and it was then she told me she'd been molested by her two brothers.

She said something else which helped me: that in Nazi Germany she'd dreamed about founding a Jewish state which would solve all our troubles and about living in a kibbutz which would provide a better life for her kids than she had. She was crying, and said she was disillusioned that it hadn't worked out the way she thought it would. My interpretation was that nationalism or socialism without feminism cannot be the answer. And that's exactly what she said: coming to Israel and founding the kibbutz were not the answers to her daughters' future. I really respect her honesty and her courage to look at the facts and to own them. It was a gift. After that talk we started a new relationship. The last three years of her life we had a very different relationship.

*

When I was growing up, Judaism was explained to us mostly as a religion. I was taught that whatever happened in the past happened to a different nation. In Israel we were building everything new – a new people, the Israeli kind. The emphasis was on being Israeli, not Jewish. It was the denial and guilt about the Holocaust and what happened to all our people. Our parents were separated from their home countries very rudely, very suddenly. They wanted to believe that here everything was whole, they didn't want to acknowledge the loss. Right after the Holocaust it was generally accepted that Jews went to be killed 'like sheep to the slaughter'. Years later, studies showed they didn't go like sheep to the slaughter and that you can't judge them by today's criteria. But the message I got was that I have no connection with the past, I'm an Israeli – period. Or – I'm an Israeli first, and a Jew second.

A lot of what I've done has been in response to this background, checking out what I grew up with, understanding the development of Israel. The way I see it now, I'm a Jewish woman first. I wouldn't be an Israeli if I were not a Jew. In the leftist groups we used to say that we should care only about the people here and have nothing to do with Diaspora Jews, that we should abolish the Law of Return because it is only for Jews and not Palestinians and, therefore, racist. But if there is going to be a Palestinian state with its own Law of Return, then maybe we can equalize the situation. As it is, only my people can come back now and their people can't – it's racist. I have a hard time with it.

Some people see Israel as a safe haven for Jews – that it counteracts the powerlessness of Jews in the world and counteracts anti-Semitism – but that's not true now. Being a racist country, it only increases anti-Semitism in the world. Israel is, in fact, a good example of how a national solution doesn't solve the problem of racism. Since the creation of Israel, racism hasn't faded from the face of the earth. Jews still have to deal with anti-Semitism – all over – all the time. One contribution that Israel gives to Jews is that it is a place where they're not a minority. And maybe this helps them reclaim their pride. It's a tricky question what other contribution Israel makes.

But though Jews choose to live elsewhere, spiritually they are connected to Israel and spiritually I'm connected to them. It's not as if having a connection to other Jewish people means they should all come here, but spiritually they *are* my people. I'm cautious around non-Jews who visit here. I want to know whether they've educated themselves about Judaism and how much anti-Semitic propaganda they've absorbed about Israel. On the one hand, I'm against Israeli policy and against all the fascist deeds against the Palestinians. On the other, this doesn't mean that Jews should have no place to be or that we should erase the state of Israel or that all Jews are fascists. I want other people to respect differences and not to buy into anti-Semitism.

I also have a hard time being accused of internalizing anti-Semitism. There were women in Women in Black who wanted to hold an Israeli flag. God forbid people should think we were against the existence of the State of Israel! But I won't be in a demonstration where my colleagues wave a flag. Dissent is not anti-Israeli or anti-Semitic.

My Judaism doesn't have to do with religion, but with people and with culture. And here again I would have a much easier time if this culture wasn't so chauvinist and male-oriented. So either I try to change it, or become a Jewish woman separatist. Here in Israel we play with that idea sometimes. But it's more like a dream. All my lesbian friends are very much invested in Israel and what's going on in Israel – more so now than twenty years ago. In the past only the Jerusalem branch of the Movement was strong about socialist issues, class issues and discrimination against other minorities. The other branches were more into women's issues. Today, women all over Israel are invested in the fight against the Occupation and about discrimination and abuse of the Palestinian people. This gives each person a broader feminist ideology, one that deals with all problems. I'm still devoted to women's issues, but looking at other issues helps me to understand and to plan.

*

Outside of work, I choose to be mainly with women. One of my dreams is someday to have a women's or lesbian home for the aged. Now we're all mobile and we can drive and meet and see each other, but when we're old, we won't have that mobility. In my dream, I want each of us to have her own separate space or apartment, but also to have common space, rooms for all of us to be together. But I'm trying not to get too carried away, not to live the future. I'm taking one day at a time. Still, I think this is a dream that can be realized.

Notes

1. A variation on the Torah dictum that a man must marry his brother's widow if she has not produced a son.
2. An early organizer of youth aliyah, followed by Henrietta Sold.

יעל

Yael Omer

Edited by Melanie Braverman

• Yael Omer, born 1961

At twenty-seven, Yael lives with her husband in a small city near most of her relatives, Greek and Moroccan Jews. In addition to Hebrew, Ladino and Arabic were spoken in her family. Her father has a small construction business; the few times her mother worked outside the home, she cleaned houses.

Yael's soft voice is warm and melodious, with an undercurrent of mirth even when distressed. She gives the impression of having thought long and carefully about life, concluding there are few easy answers.

I COME from a line of strong women. My mother's grandmother, my grandmother and my mother are all very strong. But strong mentally, not physically. Very ambitious. My mother loves to study and is talented, but when her family came to Israel from Morocco, they didn't have enough money, so she had to quit school and get work when she was fifteen. She worked as a seamstress, and she was very good at it, but what she wanted in life was to do something in medicine. She married my father when she was nineteen. In 1960 this was quite a disgrace, because nineteen was too old an age to be married. I was born one year after, of course. Then came my sister and then a brother, whom I love very much.

I am ambitious too, but maybe in a different way. I want to be a better person. I want to have confidence. I want to be strong physically, and I want to know how to speak in a way to convince people to do what I want them to do. [laughs] Yes, why not! And of course I don't want to worry about money. Not to have a lot of it, just not to worry about what will I have to eat tomorrow. To be able to have my own privacy, my own car. To be more clever, to understand people better. To be able to read situations, and not make mistakes – these kinds of resources.

Education was very important in our family, because my grandfather, on my mother's side, was hysterical about education. He now has a problem with his eyes, but every day he reads from the Zohar, specific Jewish wisdom books from the Kabbalah – the tradition of mysticism in Judaism that only very clever people can understand. He tries to improve himself every day that he lives, even though now he's so old. So education was very important, that's why I am educated.

But my ambitions were not always like this. I thought at first to be a very successful, respectable woman – one of those who goes with the tie and high heels and James Bond bag. But I soon understood that this is absolutely not my style, and I don't have much respect for this kind of career system. For me, a career is to earn money in a way that won't contradict what I believe. I have only *one* life to spend, and I want to spend it creating a better world. Right now I am doing community work, trying to make a few communities more independent, more self-assured, more optimistic – to fight for what they want. I believe in this I am changing the world. It makes a difference if *I* am doing it or if somebody else does it. It makes a difference if I do it in one way or another.

Luckily, I work in a system that gives me a lot of freedom. Of course, I have to report what I am doing and to hear what they have to say. But they don't tie my hands, and they don't tell me to do it only in one way. If things are open, so there are two ways, and people can choose. Yes, this is the most important thing for a person: to be able to choose, to have the *power* to choose, to have the possibility to choose, and the most important – the *wish* to choose. Yes.

As for my life as a woman ... well, before I joined the army I didn't even notice I was a woman! I mean, when I had a paper to fill in – are you male or female? – of course I knew I was a female. But for instance, one day I was walking in the street, and something fell out of my pocket. A passing schoolboy, much younger than I, called, 'Haaay, lady, woman' – he used the Hebrew words *isha* and *gveret* – 'something fell down from your pocket.' For me it was a very confusing situation, because suddenly someone said that I am not just an adult, I also have a sexual identity. Growing up, all the time we were together, boys and girls, and even though I had a boyfriend, I never *felt* like a woman. Never!

When I was twenty-two, I joined the feminist group in Haifa, and of course I knew I belonged there because I was a woman. But I didn't have good women friends, women I trusted, until I went to the university. When I was a teenager or in the army, I had many female friends that I talked to, but if I had a possibility to spend my time with a male friend or a woman friend, I always preferred to spend my time with men. Not in a sexual sense, no. I thought I could talk to them more about things that are interesting to me. And I was more free to set the subject. And actually *because* I was a woman in the relationship, I had the right to be different. But when I spoke to other women my age, I always felt I had to be like them, to be interested in dresses and fashion and gossip. I don't know if this is everything they talked about – I'm sure it was not, that there were many other things – but I had this impression.

I had my first good woman friend in the university. One day, we started to speak about politics. And I told her, 'You know, you are the *first* woman that I am able to speak about politics with.' But she said she had many women friends she could speak about politics with! And I was very surprised.

I got married when I was twenty-one, and I told my future husband that if we were going to be married, there were some things I would insist on. One of them was that I keep my male friends, because they were the only friends I had. I didn't have anything romantic with them, not physical and not emotional. The second thing was, whatever my parents said was very important, and I didn't want him to say something they wouldn't accept. Because then I didn't have a personality of myself, I didn't have any sense of knowing what was right, what was wrong, so I did only what my parents told me to do. And the third thing was that he must never tell me what to do. Never. I didn't want to tell him what to do, and I didn't want him to tell me what to do. Actually, if you want to know the truth, many times I told him what to do, and I made a fuss any time he had a different opinion. But *then* I didn't see it like this, I thought he was threatening me when he had his own version. Now it's better.

So I had my male friends even though my husband was sure there was a danger. I didn't believe him, but slowly, slowly, I realized the physical issue did step in between us, so I had to drop them, one after the other. Now I have only two male friends, one from the army and another one. We studied together since we were twelve. But both of them are married, they have children, and when we meet, we meet the four of us, not just me and them.

But now I have come into a situation, absolutely radical: I

can't find anything interesting or pleasant in being with men. And I *know* it's not good, because some of them are not incapable of communicating or going into deep thought. But I suppose a few years are going to be like this, until I find the exact balance. Men seem to me very disconnected from their emotions. The world is divided into masculine and feminine, and it's not masculine for a male to be connected to himself. And so men all have the same goals, and the same attitudes, and the same impotence to create intimate relationships. I saw a movie where the woman said, 'You see, you need to have sex to get into intimacy, but I, as a woman, need intimacy to get into sex.' I think this is men's problem.

This is their problem also in a cognitive way, not just in love relationships. You know, if a man doesn't listen to himself, he can damage many things. Like making wars, neglecting the family, and thinking that all the happiness is in the outside world, when actually this is not so. Many men die of heart attacks and things women are only starting to suffer from because now we also get into this crazy round circle. Men don't have a connection to their internal voices to tell them what's right, what's wrong. So they have to be all the time exactly the same as other men. They have to have *achievements*, they have to not do things in the house. They never have confidence that they are 'real' men. For women it's maybe enough to look in the mirror and say, 'I am a woman, whether I like it or not.' But men, they can look at the mirror for ages and still not be convinced they are 'real' men.

Much of what men do against women is because they are so lonely, and embarrassed, and out of touch with themselves, and so confused, unhappy, and frustrated; they become aggressive, they hate the world and hate themselves and feel guilty and imperfect all the time. They demand so much from their surroundings, and this is funny, yes? Because who surrounds them are those who fulfil their needs, and they, of course, are women.

*

How I came to be a lesbian is a story I must tell. I didn't know about myself until I was twenty-two, and it was a big surprise! At first, I thought I was just doing something exciting, exotic, trying myself in another field. But suddenly I found myself in love with someone, and it continued for three years, on and off. After this relationship ended, I said to myself, I just have to forget about this chapter in my life. But when I found my second girlfriend, I decided to continue with this lifestyle and started to call myself a lesbian – something I didn't admit before, because I said I was just bisexual.

The second relationship was very close to whatever I wanted from a relationship with another person in my life. From the first month, I knew I had to make up my mind if I was staying with her or staying with my husband.

After half a year together, my girlfriend made me go to a psychologist. What I found out was I wanted to stay with my husband! I didn't like what I heard, so I went to another psychologist. She was very good – a lesbian too, a divorcee with three kids, in a long-term relationship with a women. I thought that since she separated from her husband, maybe I would separate from my husband too.

When I considered it all, to stay with him or to stay with her, I said to myself, the everyday life is very important to me. My relationships with women are very intense. I thought, if my everyday life is going to be that intense, I won't be able to live! I need my *space*. I don't want my relationship to suffocate me, I need a lot of air. And he doesn't take my air. Sometimes I *want* him to take it, and he gives it up, says 'No thank you!' I don't know if it is just because he is a man, or because this is how he is.

So after half a year of counselling, we got to the same point, that I had to stay with my husband! I blamed my psychologist for this result – I thought she didn't want me to make the decision she did. But she told me, 'We have the tapes of all our meetings; you said it all the time, you can't separate from your husband. This is what *you* said, I didn't say it.'

So these doubts continued for two years, until my girlfriend decided to put an end to it and go back to the States. Of course this was very painful for me. It had been very difficult our first year together. I studied in one city, but I returned to my home city for the weekends. I felt distant every first day I was at home, and I felt distant the first day I was back with her.

But after we broke up, after I finished my therapy, I suddenly felt how it was to have only one relationship in my life. It was great! Only one relationship, even if it's not enough, but it's *one*. So much energy suddenly became free for other things! So life looked bright to me.

But it couldn't last forever, even though I like my husband very much. At the beginning, not so much. I got married when I was twenty-one, in the pressure of the family. I didn't choose it. But I thought, OK, I shall pay my debt to the society. I'll be married for a while, I'll try not to have kids, and after four or five years, it's going to be very easy to separate. We fought a lot in the first year. But, you know, after four or five years I became connected to him. It's like anything we get used to. Like our face, we see it every day in the mirror, and, OK, 'This is us,' and if that changes, then suddenly we can't know who we are. He was so obvious to me, he became part of my life. I just couldn't give him up.

And our relationship is a healthy one. There is good communication between us. I can tell him anything I want. He's a very co-operative person. Everything I say I want, he does for me. He's thoughtful and gentle, and I like the way he looks, the way he talks. He's intelligent. He's so easy to be with, so *easy*. He requires so little from me, so I have so much *space*. I love this space! He likes it, too. I can do whatever I want. This is what I want, I want freedom. I want also to be with someone, but I want to be with myself too. And he can give me all this. But the point is, after a while, this space becomes like emptiness. When each of us has his or her own world it suddenly becomes like a separation, as if something is missing.

So I said to myself, 'That's it, I'm going to get pregnant.' I wanted to be a family, to live in my little town, to be *square*, and *happy*, just like everybody else. Yes! I could go back to being what I was before I met my first girlfriend. But only one month passed, and I found myself with a woman again! It's unbelievable.

Last week I talked with one of my colleagues at work. She is thirty-two and is not married, which in Israel means she is not like everyone. I told her, 'I don't know what to do. I look at you and I say I wish I could be a single person too.' And she said, 'Yael, you have never tried it before, it's going to be very difficult. Show me only one married couple you want to be like.' But I don't know any married couples that have a nice relationship. When I visit married couples, it's amazing: they humiliate each other in front of me, a stranger! Very educated, very gentle people – polite, correct, pay their bills on time, have three kids, everything the way it should be – and they make these nasty remarks to one another, in this nasty tone of voice. No respect, it's *amazing*. I go back to my husband and I tell him, 'Look, I've just visited this family, and the way they treated each other, I wonder, why do they stay together?' He says, 'But you know, all the married couples are like this. Only us, we have a different relationship. You don't appreciate it, but we are the only couple I know that has this kind of relationship.' So here is something else I can lose if I don't have him.

And besides, relationships between women often don't last. You know, I want to be with one person only. I don't want to change all the time. Some people can, because they don't take things so seriously, or maybe this is the way they are built, but for me it's impossible. And anyhow, I've spoken with other lesbians. It seems even a lesbian couple might not have a mutual respect for each other.

So that's why I made up my mind I shouldn't leave my husband, and I should be even more serious about kids and family. I don't want to involve any woman in this situation, because it's not fair to have a relationship that has no future, to be with her only because I need to be with a woman from time to time. It's impossible. I'm trapped! Maybe I should find myself a good friend, a very close friend, a very innocent relationship, and hope it will be enough. But I'm not sure. *I don't know what to do.*

I'm twenty-seven. In ten years I'm going to be thirty-seven, in twenty I will be forty-seven. Maybe it's going to be more difficult when I'm older to find someone I really would like to have, in case I want to live with a woman eventually. If I can't have children, maybe it's going to be easier for me and my husband to separate, because maybe he will want to find someone else who can be pregnant. And then I won't have to decide myself! I'll have some kind of excuse. My husband wants kids very much. He's thirty-four, and for him it's urgent. His friends all have their third kid, and he doesn't have any.

Sometimes I ask myself, if I knew this was going to be my situation, would I start getting close to women in the first place?

Sometimes when it's very difficult, I say, yes, maybe it was a mistake. But other times, I say, I got so much, it made me so rich, developed so many sides in me. It made me feel closer to myself.

Both ways are not that good, to be with a man or to be with a woman. They have their own disadvantages. But what I am afraid of is the third option: to be alone.

It's amazing: I really made up my mind to be straight again. It just doesn't work! Maybe I could be like a friend of mine in town: married for sixteen years, raised her kids, then went with a woman after that. For sixteen years be 'normal' – well, not really normal, because my normal situation is to be with a woman. I just want to be complete with myself, to be like everyone, again.

But everyone is unhappy. And yet it seems to me that, if most people are straight, it might be the best way anyway. Yes, I think, sixteen years, and then the children will be more or less adults, and then I can be lesbian again! Because when you are older, the criticism from society is not as great. You've made your duty already, you've had your kids, it's fine if you want to have some fun! I could split my life in two: one half regular, the other half me, myself. It's *not* good that this is the way, but it's going to help me to cope with everything.

There are still unsolved problems, because I don't know how I'm going to manage for these sixteen years. Sixteen years, it's a long time.

I want to say, I have this emptiness only sometimes, not all the time. Most of the time it's OK, but then, for a few weeks, I feel *completely* alone, you can't imagine. It's impossible to communicate with my husband. When I feel down, or think the world is not so good, and I have doubts, I become nervous. He feels it and loses contact with me, instead of being supportive and relaxing me like my girlfriends used to. It's a different approach to the same problem. I don't feel now such big pressures, but when I have a big family, and also have to work, it's going to be very difficult. And if I can't share it with my husband, what do I need him for?

*

Now there is this third woman. We met at a CLAF lecture, it was so innocent. She thought I was interested in her, and I thought she was interested in me. But I didn't do anything, and then suddenly it happened – and we found ourselves together. It's just unbelievable! Her friends warned her, 'What are you doing?' You know, it's a very small community. They said, 'She is married! Remember her ex-girlfriend, she suffered a lot. She was miserable, she was alone in the weekends, what do you need it for?'

I'm trying to let my identity influence me, I'm trying not to cheat myself. I want to give respect to every part of me. This is the only way to be a complete person. When I am in my own city, I can say I am a woman, I can say I'm Jewish – to be close to my identity. In the moshavim I like to say I am Eastern, like they are – this is also an important part of my identity.

That day I came to the lecture, I asked myself why I was going there. I said to myself, 'Look, you are out of it, leave it alone.' And I answered myself, 'This will be completely the last time.' But having a lesbian community means a chance for me to be myself. I felt so *good* suddenly to see everybody. To have one place where I could say out loud, 'Look, I am a lesbian. This is *me*.'

אילנה
Ilana Weinstock
Edited by Amy Beth

• Ilana Weinstock, born 1919

Ilana was born Helen in Brooklyn, New York, graduating from high school during the Depression. Although she dreamed of teaching, her father ruled out college, so she took commercial classes. After working in many jobs from clerk to radio assembler, in the 1950s she studied nursing and became a registered nurse.

Greenwich Village in the late 1930s and 1940s was where Ilana came up in the gay life. Her stories about that time first appeared in 'Letters from My Aunt', her correspondence with her lesbian niece Maida Tilchen, printed in Nice Jewish Girls *(Evelyn Tornton Beck, ed., Persephone Press, 1982; Beacon, 1989).*

Sixty-nine at the time of this history, Ilana was leading a busy life working as a private-duty nurse, teaching beginning Hebrew to new immigrants, and meeting weekly with several women's discussion groups. She is a short, sturdy woman who strides briskly along and comments on life in gravelly bursts of humour, anger, pain and delight.

I WAS close to fifty and Marion was just thirty. She was working as a bookkeeper and I'd been working as a nurse in the States. We had been living together for close to eight years and the plan was for her to arrive in Israel as soon as she finished her college semester. In the States we had taken a couple of lessons of Hebrew – not enough to know anything. We figured I could go to a regular ulpan with the rest of the new immigrants, and Marion would go to a kibbutz where non-Jews studied while working part-time. It was May of 1970 and she was due to arrive before summer's end.

A year earlier I had made a three-week trip to see what was going on in Israel and to feel out the work and living situations. My parents and my sister were already there and my father asked me, 'What is Marion coming for? She's not Jewish.' I said, 'She thinks it's a wonderful country, and she's thinking of converting. She feels Judaism is the most ethical religion.' Finally he uttered, 'You know I'm very understanding, you can tell me anything.' Naturally I thought, 'Great! He knows already and he justs wants me to verbalize it.' So I told him Marion and I lived together as a couple and neither of us wanted to get married to men. I didn't use the word lesbian, but it couldn't have been any more obvious. 'I'm very understanding,' he said. 'I once had a good friend of my own . . .' Delighted, I wrote to the States and told Marion how wonderful the exchange had been, and we finalized our plans.

Marion had a close relationship with her family, and they in turn were openly accepting of me. When my birthday came they made a party for me, and if her mother went any place she'd bring us back presents of the same thing in different colours. The 'subject' never got brought up, but everyone knew what our relationship was. We had a good life together and with my father's recent approval we felt supported and rich with an abundance of family care. However, shortly after Marion arrived we paid my parents a visit. In an agitated manner my father walked out of the room. The next week I got a letter from him quoting Leviticus. Of course Leviticus doesn't make specific references about women, but my father said it was a 'terrible disgrace'. That was all it took for me to cut my relationship with him. (I still visited with my mother, who despite being a shy women knew from the time I was a child of seven that I was a lesbian. She was always good friends with the lovers I had.) This turned out to be the least of the troubles Marion and I were to face.

*

I was at the ulpan and Marion was at Ramat David, a kibbutz in the north. There was no place for us to be together. I finagled a room to myself at the ulpan so she could come over sometimes, but the whole situation was uncomfortable. A lot of people at Ramat David were taking drugs and my ulpan was unsatisfactory; apart from the terrible teaching, there was a woman and her daughter who were both prostitutes, with men coming from all over. Eventually Marion and I joined a kibbutz. The only reason they accepted us was they were desperate for a registered nurse. They said they would help Marion convert and give us lessons in Hebrew. In actuality they couldn't do a damn thing to help her convert because they were a non-religious kibbutz! And as far as the lessons were concerned, they had me working so many hours in the clinic there was virtually no time for learning.

Hardly anyone spoke English except the volunteers, but if you wanted to become a member of the kibbutz it wasn't a good idea to get close to volunteers because they were looked at as outsiders. Eventually it was just too much for us. At that time there was no gay life where women were concerned. Marion had no family here, mine had pushed her out and we had no friends. She went back to the States hoping to convert there. According to her letters she tried to convert, but they kept extending the date over and over again. Marion developed a lot of psychological problems as a result. She tried to commit suicide, and she's been with psychiatric care ever since. She was at a loss without our supportive relationship; our lives had unravelled into a mess. Still, we wrote and I kept dreaming she would come back to Israel, not knowing then how seldom this dream comes true.

I left the kibbutz and went for two months to ulpan Akiva. It's a private expensive ulpan, and I must confess I was broke and my father paid for it. I put my dog, which I had brought from the States, in a kennel. By the time I completed the ulpan I didn't have any money left, but the woman at the kennel said, 'Come and be a guest of your dog now.' I stayed with her for quite a while. She didn't expect me to do any work, but of course I couldn't stay like that. I worked with the dogs and cats, giving them baths and brushing them, and amidst my grief over the separation from Marion I found comfort sitting outside facing the yard, watching television and eating ice-cream. My Hebrew still wasn't very good and I was increasingly unhappy. In the States I had been the nursing director of a hospital and I worked with open-heart surgery. Here I didn't know enough of the language to do nursing. I thought to myself, 'I came to this country to help. I had a good job and a good relationship in the States. What am I here for? I might as well go back to the States and send them $200 a month!'

*

By 1973 I knew Marion wasn't coming back. I had applied to work as a housemother in an American school in Ashkelon. My thinking was that if I couldn't do my work as a nurse, maybe I could inspire these kids to make aliyah. Luck would have it the school wanted me to be their nurse instead, and at long last I was off to a new beginning. At just the same time I saw an ad about the Feminist Movement marching in Tel Aviv for legal abortions. Until now I could find no evidence of any lesbian feminist activity going on in the country, but I quickly concluded if there was a women's movement here, there had to be lesbians in it as well. I went to the march, and I spotted a couple of women who I sensed were lesbians, but my Hebrew was still limited. Whereas in the States I would probably have gone right over, I had become so used to closing up that I didn't know how to approach my own people any more. After all the years of being in the heart of the gay life in New York City, I now didn't know how to approach the topic!

Shortly afterward, I saw an ad in the paper that said, 'If you want to change the laws on homosexuality in this country, contact S.I.R.' I thought, 'Well! That's open enough!' I knew S.I.R.[1] from the States, but I thought, 'Maybe it's a police thing and they're trying to find out about somebody!' You get a little paranoid after a while. So I wrote saying I was interested in finding out what the laws on homosexuality in this country are. That's when Ziva replied.

Ziva was a sabra, a young woman of twenty-one who had completed her army service and was on the brink of making a career out of getting women into bed. We met in a Tel Aviv cafe where she told me she was the only lesbian she knew of in this country. However, there were gay men who were making an organization which I was welcome to become part of. I figured, 'Well, men or women, it'll be a place I could let my hair down a little bit!' Anyway, I didn't believe there were no other lesbians in the country, so I went and was disappointed when Ziva and I turned out to be the only women in the place. Apparently Ziva had no knowledge of confidentiality and had already told the men my age, where I worked, and all the other private items I had shared with her. Although this was only twenty years ago, it was very disturbing. To make matters worse, I was the oldest individual at the gathering, and by default I instantly became the 'mother'. Needless to say, this was not what I had gone there for.

I went to their dances, but you know, if you go with a bunch of boys so many times, while they're flitting around you could die from boredom. On the third time, one of the fellows told me 'the girls' were having a little gathering. How could I say no? It was like an oasis in the desert! They were mostly married women who were playing around. What went on in this country at the time was as follows: Mrs Cohen was married and Mrs Schwartz was married, and their husbands would go to work and they would get together, *bang-bang*, and then Mrs Cohen would go back to her house and Mrs Schwartz would go back to her house. It still goes on today!

Eventually I met one woman who was not married and who

was looking for a relationship with a woman. But Ziva zapped her up quick. Unfortunately this woman got the same rush job Ziva gave all the others. She would court them, buy them flowers and perfume, and tell them all kinds of sweet things; her idea was to 'find 'em, fuck 'em, and forget 'em'. We discovered Ziva used her job as secretary of S.I.R. to meet women who answered the ad. She'd bring them to her bed, but then never brought them to the organization! Most of these women had never been to bed with a woman before. I think I was the only one who didn't fall over myself for her.

We started meeting one evening a week in the boys' place and sure enough we were like the women's auxiliary. I tried to get us out from the boys and to stand on our own. But the women didn't have the confidence. They were all used to depending on the men in their lives, whether it was their fathers or husbands or their gay brothers. I remember one woman saying to me, 'Really what we are doing is sick, sick, sick.' She thought she was crazy in the literal sense. She would repeat, 'This is against all the biblical laws.' There wasn't a woman there who didn't have a guilty conscience about it.

As the 1970s went on some of us joined the Feminist Movement. This was basically a straight feminist group interested in abortion rights and other things straight women needed. We mixed with them, worked on their projects, and didn't really mention our life-style. I wouldn't claim we particularly hid it, but it never occurred to the straight women that we were lesbians until the first all-women's seder. When the seder was over, we played music and started dancing. Naturally we danced with each other! Suddenly the straight women realized they had a bunch of queers in the joint. They looked at each other and walked into another room. When it came time for future newsletters about the meetings, I didn't get the mailings, and as far as I know none of the other 'known queers' did either. 'To hell with them,' I thought, and we quickly made arrangements to use somebody's apartment for our meetings.

The Feminist Movement soon realized the lesbians were the ones who had been doing all the work. It was about 1977 and the Feminist Movement wanted to make the first National Feminist Convention. Marcia Freedman had just concluded being a Knesset member and she said if we could get at least ten women to stand up as a lesbian contingent at this convention, she would join us. Some of the people were afraid, many of us had jobs with the city, or like myself, had a job in a school. I said not only would I stand up, but I would wear a bright red muu-muu dress, so even on black-and-white TV they would see me. And I did. There were approximately one hundred women who came to that convention, and twenty of us stood up!

We were 'ALEF' – Aguda Lesbit Feministit. After we stood up, one of the big shots from the Feminist Movement said to me, 'We don't know why you people aren't in our organization.' We flat out reminded them they didn't want the queers when they had them, but they denied it. We decided to have a meeting and see if there was a possibility of our getting together. They were offering us membership in their organization, an opportunity to pay dues, and the generous offer of the use of their space provided our name would not be on the door, and provided we 'behaved ourselves' when on their premises. So we said 'FUCK YOU. We have a place we're meeting in which doesn't cost us anything and where we can behave as we want.'

Little did anyone know we had our own internal troubles. We used an apartment in Petach Tikvah and the woman who was overseeing it made it impossible to meet her satisfaction and rules. Women got disgusted with this arrangement and started dropping out. This mother superior – who actually was a converted nun – ended up with all the money, and even when she was the last remaining member, ALEF still received donations from advertisements she placed in American women's publications. As time would tell, our work eventually got done through the Feminist Movement. They realized they couldn't proceed without us and we all made adjustments. Nowadays it is normal to go to the Haifa Women's Centre or elsewhere and feel a strong lesbian presence.

Naturally there are other stories of our queer struggles. For the 1981 International Congress of Gay and Lesbian Jews we made arrangements with a Tel Aviv hotel for meeting space. Some ultra-Orthodox American rabbis found out about it and wrote to the Israeli religious communities. The hotel was threatened that they would lose their kosher licence and despite being on our side, no hotel can afford to do business without one. The next two hotels denied us space under pressure from the same threat, but there was one clever place. When the day of the conference came and the help at the desk was asked where the meeting rooms were, they replied, 'It's not here, you go to this and this address,' and they sent us to another place. Secretly they were co-operating with us to the best of their ability and sending everybody where we were. It was a terrible experience and I know a lot of the people who came from the other countries were angry to have to go through this kind of thing. But you know, it was a beginning, and like the next story I'll tell, it is perhaps an indication of our future here.

*

There's a neighbourhood in Netanya close to where I used to live – a religious shtetl where the men wear peyes and the women never go about without long sleeves. There is a post office, and accordingly the woman who runs it wears a sheitel, a wig. Before she worked in this post office she was the maid to an older couple. She was married off to the man after his wife died, and she says the first thirty years of her life were misery: from the Holocaust where she was in a camp and was tattooed with a number, to a meaningless religious life with a man who to me looked like a block of wood and who drank. What saved her mind and sanity was reading. In a surprisingly personal discussion one day, she asked me about my life. She had caught on to the fact that I was a lesbian and we discussed different aspects of it. When you see this woman, you would think a person with her background would never think of lesbianism. But she does. She says she can understand that lesbians could have so much more in common than a woman and a man. I feel sure if I was the type to take advantage of things, I could have. But this would be destructive of her life. Now her whole existence is just her grandchildren. That's the *naches** that she has.

So this is the myth of this country. Many people come from all over the world and think this is nothing but a holy country with everyone attending synagogue and every hotel holding religious services. They can't fathom how truly secular most Israelis are.

---

* Pride, joy.

People here have a lot of the same feelings as other places in the world, and in many ways people in Israel have broader minds than people in the United States. In Israel the lesbian and gay movement is at least twenty years behind the US, but somehow we are comparatively further along than US lesbians and gays were before the Stonewall Revolution of 1969. It is often the American Orthodox rabbinate which puts pressure on Israeli rabbis to protest our existence where they would otherwise turn their heads. In this country we never really went through the bulldyke/ultra-femme thing we went through in the States. When I first came out in the 1940s, if you didn't decide you were a 'this' or a 'that' and dress accordingly, it meant you weren't with it and you didn't know what you were. The acceptance of lesbians and gays in Israel isn't due so much to the absence of butch-femme and the odd stares and treatment those roles attract as it is a basic reflection of Israel being a conservative country that worries more about national security than about butch-femme roles!

*

My lesbian life began in the early 1940s in Greenwich Village. For protection, the gay guys advised me to pretend I came from some place other than New York, so we decided I came from Texas. I had more nicknames and aliases than I can remember. Folks called me Tex and I even developed a Texas drawl. One day I fell for a woman named Katie who was deaf and mute. She had long black hair, great big black eyes, and I was absolutely enticed and attracted to her. She spoke in sign language with her hearing friends, but I unfortunately didn't know how to sign. One night I spotted her walking ahead of me in the Village. I started to run to catch up to her, and then I fast-walked past her in the hopes some contact would be made. She whistled at me and she picked me up! That was the beginning of our romance. She was a no-touch butch and I was dressed very femme, but I did not have a femme identity. One day, she greeted me with her hair partly cut. I asked what happened and she explained she had got paint in it and cut the ends off. Each time she came around it got shorter and shorter, and by the time she looked like a young boy I lost my feeling for her. I wasn't interested in what I called an 'imitation boy', so I just let it cool off.

The next woman I met was also butch, but her hair was longish and I liked her strong ethics. I got all dressed up and went down to Tony Pasteur's to meet her. Tony Pasteur's was one of the places in the Village with a floor show in addition to the bar, and I was really looking forward to the date. I waited and waited, and then I got mad. 'They're just like men! They can tell you when it's a date, and they can do what they want. I'm going to see what it's like to be one of them!' So I went out and bought myself a brown butch suit and tie. I went downtown with my new clothes to Tony Pasteur's, and it turned out this gal and I had a misunderstanding about when the date was actually called for. Our big romance ended right then because there we were, two butches negotiating a date at a time when butches weren't supposed to romance each other. I realized I needed to be the butch since any other garb would leave me only butches to date and I wasn't attracted to them and their 'no touch' ways, not to mention how much more comfortable I was feeling in my new clothes. From here on in it seemed I was destined to love women and to learn about the ways of surviving this kind of love with as much difficulty as one could only imagine.

*

Kay Ryan was an alcoholic who I lived with for three years starting in 1944. Her whole family was alcoholic. I didn't know anything about alcohol then, and consequently I didn't know much about when she was drinking or when she was drunk. If you gave me a glass of whiskey and said, 'This is beer' or gave me a glass of beer and said, 'This is whiskey,' I wouldn't have known the difference. The only thing I'd ever tasted much of was wine at Pesach.

There really wasn't much else you could do in those days except go to the bars. The gay people I knew were apolitical and weren't thinking of women's rights or anything. The next two years with Kay were hell and full of her drinking. I remember one time thinking, if drinking will solve the problem, maybe I should go out and get drunk. On the way I passed a record store where they were playing Tchaikovsky's *Pathetique*. I ended up in the record store instead of the bar, and went home to cry my eyes out. For my two bucks I got the record instead of a hangover, and I left Kay. I dated a bit, but friends would keep trying to get us back together. I ended up going back to the relationship and for the next two years Kay didn't drink. When she came to my parents' house at Pesach she said she was allergic to liquor and she couldn't drink the wine. Things seemed under control until her alcoholic mother came for a visit and got Kay back on a roll. She had brought liquor into the house while I was at work, and that was it. I told her mother off and I took the bottles and threw them out the window. But it was too late for Kay to put the drinking down all over again and I left her.

*

As best I can tell I went to Japan to avoid slipping back into reinvolvement with Kay. I followed an ad for overseas jobs as a clerk and in 1948 I took a job with the Army of Occupation. After I scored big on a typing test I was placed in a department as an army civilian. Somehow I was assigned to SCAP, the Supreme Commander of the Allied Powers, and then finally in Tokyo with FEAF, the Far East Air Force. In Tokyo they had 'takarazuka', which is Japanese women's theatre where women play both male and female parts; there are absolutely no men in these performances. They even have their own fan magazine, and the audience of women drool over the performers and follow them around.

I learned all of this from Mariko, my Japanese lover at the time. She was a medical student who had taken a job as a night guard in the hotel where I was billeted. She would sit there and study, and in case of a fire she was supposed to ring a bell. I was lucky enough to have her be stationed on my floor. We would talk for hours. After we got acquainted, we went away for a weekend. She had never been kissed by anyone in her life before. Well you can't deny romance, and soon after we paid a tin of coffee a month to rent a room out in the suburbs. You see, no Japanese, whether male or female, were allowed to visit us in our billet. One time we had a very embarrassing thing happen. In Japanese houses, the doors slide and you can't really lock them. I guess our landlady got curious about all the noises, the laughing and carrying on we were doing rolling around on the mat. Suddenly she opened the door and saw us with a head at one end and feet a long way down at the other end! She just slid that door closed right away, and had the discretion never to mention it.

Three things happened about this time. First, I wanted to go on my vacation to visit Mariko's family. I had a written invitation which was required for approval. The request went through channels until it got to personnel, where it was rejected. The second thing was a ruling you could take a religious holiday without having to make up the time. I had taken Yom Kippur off only to return and be told that the ruling had been changed and now I would have to make up the time. The third was that I was not promoted into my immediate supervisor's position when she moved on, but I was still expected to train her replacement. This offence is the reason I most often give for why I left Japan. However, I was actually kicked out, and this story is very painful.

One of the civilians, an alcoholic, was also gay. I was glad there was somebody I could talk to since in the beginning I didn't know anyone else. I thought I had a friend, but she was interested in going to bed with me. I am a very monogamous type of person and I also was not interested in her. She got into some trouble one night, and in a drunken stupor she wound up telling someone all the dirt she knew about everyone, including that I was gay and had a local girlfriend. They picked me up separately from Mariko and the questioning and horror began. An agent raped Mariko to teach her the 'beauties' of having sex with a man. He told her he would do it any time he wanted to. They made sure we were kept apart. I went to a top colonel who said if I left quietly he would take care of the rapist and see that Mariko didn't get bothered any more. From this it was clear, I had to leave.

Mariko's father came by ship from the north to bring her home. We wrote to each other and I was hoping to be able to bring her to the United States. That was before the legal peace was signed and without an enormous sum of money it was impossible to bring a person over. Finally I realized it would be years before I could bring her and she would be having a life of waiting like a Madame Butterfly type. I knew there was a man who was very decent and very much in love with her. Mariko herself had told me she loved me, but that she was not a lesbian and would not go with any other woman. I figured there was a possibility for her to make a good life, so I said what was needed to hint it was all right for her to move on, our relationship was over, and she should make a good life with him. I was in love with Mariko, and it was sad, but necessary.

*

Back in the States I landed in San Francisco and decided to stay a while. There I met fabulous Ida. She was a big fat woman, a wonderful cook, and an overall dream. They say, 'A lady in public, a cook in the kitchen' and that was my Ida. Nobody would have suspected us. She lived across the street from a convent and the nuns deeply respected her. Ida had never been with women before and although she had been with men quite a bit and always had these young, good-looking guys available, she was never with anyone else again until she died. Ida was maybe twenty-five years older than I was, and had a zest for life and hostessing inclusive of happiness and dancing. Years into the relationship Ida was having trouble with her lower denture and a dentist told her, 'It's cancer.' I was shocked that he made this statement, but he knew Ida and he was right. Any other approach and Ida wouldn't have done anything about it.

By this time I had graduated and was working as a nurse. Ida underwent radical surgery and our lives changed forever. I worked at my regular job at night from eleven p.m. to seven a.m., and then nursed her during the day, from seven a.m. to three p.m. I would sleep a bit, and then I would work my job again from eleven to seven. Just before she was going into surgery her family was in the hospital with me waiting. I urged them to go out and get coffee, claiming I needed to fix up the surgery bed. When they left I went into the closet, closed the door, and cried from every limb in my body. I washed my face and went about my business. I couldn't cry in front of the family, but I couldn't believe Ida was going to live through this thing. Ida had more life in her than anyone I've ever known. It was all part of the terrific resilient person she was. But the surgery left her disfigured, and she would not allow people to see her much ... not even me. Afterwards she never let me touch her again. She never had one scar on her body, and suddenly, half of her tongue was missing, she couldn't talk well, she couldn't eat properly, and it destroyed her integrity to be seen. Reluctantly and painfully, I respected her wishes. Ida moved out to another area, and afterwards she died.

★

I look back and my life has been many different things. The jobs I've held on three continents have been as varied as the women I've shared my life with, and the social and political climates are ever evolving. As sad a thing as it is to say, I have given up the idea that I will ever be with anybody as a couple again. I am turning seventy and have lived in Israel over twenty years now. I think the only chance I have of having any life with someone is if she comes as a new *olah** and decides to stay. There have been a few romances here, but each one a little less satisfying than the last. I am not interested in making an attachment with a much younger person. They're always making a great discovery of something I've known or lived. The women I know here who are my age aren't lovers of women, and the one potential romance with a woman my own age didn't really stay all sparks and flames. Instead there are fine friendships and an ongoing list of lesbian socials and gatherings I am certain to organize or attend. There is no shortage of creative ways I find to give the strength of my loving women and to be loved back; life here in Israel is never without its fascinations and pleasures. So I fill my life with things I'm interested in other than relationships. It's a little bit less complicated a life, and from time to time I miss the spice, but never the *tsuris*.†

Note

1. Society for Individual Rights, a variation on SPPR (Society for the Protection of Personal Rights), the homophile organization in Israel.

---

* Female immigrant.
† Woe, troubles.

שירה
Shira Markowitz
Edited by Alexis Danzig

• *Shira Markowitz, born 1963*

Shira has curly red hair and an open, expressive face. At the time of this interview, she was demonstrating weekly at the Women in Black vigil against the Occupation and doing graduate work at The Hebrew University. Having since received a degree in clinical psychology, Shira makes her home in Jerusalem.

MY father's family brought him to the States from Russia when he was two years old. My mother's parents are from Germany, and she was born in the States. Their families considered it an intermarriage! After my parents married my father went to rabbinical school at HUC.[1] My mother didn't finish college because she supported them financially and raised the children. My father was ordained when he was twenty-five – my age!

I have two older sisters – Rebecca, thirty-three, and Debbie, thirty-one. We grew up in a very Jewish, middle-class suburb in New Jersey where my father's pulpit was. My family was Jewishly oriented, which can be expected from a rabbi's family. Zionist. I was young and didn't understand these things intellectually, but it was obvious to me: being Jewish and being American go together well. It was a sheltered environment, with a liberal atmosphere that was never tested, really.

When I was seven, my parents came to Israel for their first visit. This was 1970, three years after the Six Day War. They were enchanted, and decided to move. One reason was my father was sick of the rabbinate – it was a good way to leave without copping out. My parents also believed that Israel is where the Jewish people's future is, and that they had something to contribute. I think it attracted my mother because she saw it as a way out of being a housewife. She was aware that in Israel there would be new options – the norm is that Israeli women work. And since being in youth group as children, they had always considered Israel an option.

My parents' decision to come to Israel upset me a lot. I didn't understand why we should move – I thought it was cruel. My older sisters were ambivalent, but they had more positive motivation – already they had gone to camp, they were Zionist, they had read *Exodus*. But my response was distress. The family story goes: my father announced to the congregation that we were going to Israel and I, at seven years old, got up and announced, 'I don't want to go!' Whenever congregants come to visit they always remind me of this story, which I don't even remember.

The first year in Israel was difficult. It took us a whole year to get settled. I went to day camp to get used to hearing Hebrew, but I don't really remember how I learned Hebrew. I remember not knowing Hebrew, and then knowing it. We moved from an eight-room house in US suburbia to a *two*-room apartment in Israel! Afterwards we went to Jerusalem, where my father got a job in fundraising and my mother got a job organizing study missions and seminars for professors dealing with the Middle East conflict. She still works there – by now, she's become a 'big shot'.

It was after my second year in Israel, when I skipped from fourth to sixth grade, that the transition happened, and I didn't feel like an outsider anymore. It was the beginning of pre-puberty. The kids in sixth grade were older, more developed. It was a social thing – boys and girls, parties, who was wearing a bra, who got her period. It was fun, exciting.

That was when I started, pretty sharply, to be alienated from anything American. When my friends came to the house, I didn't want them to hear my parents speaking English. I was embarrassed about the little things at home that were different, like that we ate a big meal in the evening, the way we made the bed, the fact that we had all kinds of appliances. Today everybody has them, but at the time we had things other people didn't have, like a dishwasher.

I wanted to be completely Israeli. I joined the Youth Movement, I wanted to know all the songs, all the places. I didn't want to speak English, though I continued to read in English all along, and I still prefer to read in English. Only after the army did I get in touch again with my American-ness.

In high school, I was very active in the Scouts, which isn't like Girl Scouts in the States. The subculture of youth movements is basic to Israeli culture. It's very ideological. Youth Movement kids are active in social issues, doing volunteer work and discussing things – their entire social lives are organized around the group.

Scouts is one of the groups in the Youth Movement. It has a connection to the World Scouts, but it's very much an Israeli movement, like HaShomer HaTsair, the youth movement of the political party Mapam, which came out of the kibbutz movement. I chose the group whose members seemed the most committed and ideological. There's a whole way of life that has to do with these youth movements – songs, ways people talk to each other, ways they dress. Usually kids in Youth Movements will dress more simply than kids who aren't, and at our parties we didn't usually dance, except Israeli folk dances. We would have a programme or talk. Very serious kids! We would go on a lot of hikes and trips. It was a whole *world*, and I was very much into it.

I had an orientation towards social involvement, and Scouts definitely reinforced my values. My friends and I were interested in all kinds of social and political topics – like the social gap, or an Israeli concept called 'purity of arms', or the melting-pot versus ethnicity. We would discuss an incident that happened in one of our wars, for instance one in which there had been a dilemma between the optimal safety of the Israeli troops on the one hand, and the idea of humanity and war on the other. I wonder if today they even discuss this in the youth groups – it's become much more complicated.

The idea of the Scouts was to be involved, active, critical citizens, but the values of the Scouts were the national values. It influenced me to see myself as a citizen, a member of society who was obliged to go outside of myself; to see that national and social issues are my issues. Feeling that I care and that it's important to care are values I brought with me when I became more feminist and a lesbian.

I'm also critical of the Youth Movement because of what I saw about being within the consensus. We were critical, but only to a point. Certain things, like refusing to serve in the Territories, we didn't consider. Or worse than that – that maybe Zionism isn't an ultimate truth. We discussed these things, but not with real openness.

I went to the army from the Youth Movement. There's an army programme connected to the Youth Movement called Nachal, where members who have been together since they were kids work on a kibbutz together as part of their military service. However, when I was in the Scouts there was a strong ideological orientation that kibbutzim were not as important as development towns, because the social gap existed there. We were expected to become citizens of the development town – whatever we would do, we would do because we lived there, not do *for* them. I joined a group like this, and very much enjoyed it.

I started in 1981 when I was still seventeen. After a year in the development town, I went to an army training base, to be a junior officer and work with young female recruits. It was a camp with men and women, but it was segregated – the men and women did very different things because their basic training is separate.

Once I started working as a junior officer, I felt good there, especially with the staff, and enjoyed the physical challenges. I remember worrying that I was enjoying the company of the women so much, because I wasn't motivated to solve what I saw as my problem with men. But I *felt* good, so even though I thought this, I didn't dwell on it.

Next, I was sent to the Hermon, a mountainous, snow-covered region on the Syrian border. A unit of soldiers was stationed there, and I was to be their 'platoon clerk', a job coveted by army women. There is one woman in a fighting unit of sixty or seventy men, and while she has a technical side to her work – she takes care of the mail, things like that – mostly the role means being a *woman*. She's expected to be motherly – to be affectionate, to bake cookies for the boys, to listen to their problems with their girlfriends. A few of them fall in love with her, she usually falls in love with one of the officers – it's a role a lot of women want. I had a hard time with this role – I felt it wasn't all right that I couldn't be these things. I was trying but it didn't work. Now I don't feel bad about it. In fact, I feel rather proud.

I had made friends with a woman named Limor when she was in basic training and I was her commander. Later we both moved to the smaller unit where I was commander of twenty or thirty women, and we developed an intense friendship that was different from my other friendships. Although we didn't talk much and weren't really open with each other, there was a strong underlying feeling. I was very excited about this friendship, but I was also uncomfortable: why is this so strong for me? Why is this different from my other friendships?

Years later, I met Limor again in the lesbian community. I had thought she might be a lesbian, and when I found out it was true, it was very exciting for me – it was a step in reconstructing my lesbian past. Things made sense: there *had* been something romantic between us, though neither of us had seen it in sexual terms. But in the army, in general, I was totally unaware of lesbians.

I became partially active in the anti-war movement. As a soldier it was illegal for me to go to demonstrations, but I went. There was a big demonstration after the Sabra and Shatila massacres – allegedly 400,000 protesters. Politically I was definitely opposed to the war, yet it didn't occur to me that being a soldier in the army at the same time was supporting it.

At the end of my service I was sent to an all-women's unit, notoriously lesbian, but I didn't see anything! When I thought of 'lesbianism' I thought of it only as sexuality, perversity, not as a way of life. Nor did I think of lesbianism as having a sexual *and* emotional side. The minute an image of lesbian sex would come into my mind, I would think it was disgusting, and push it out of my head. I could recognize my attraction to women, but would never think of it as, 'I'd like to go to bed with her,' or 'I'd like to kiss a woman.' I couldn't make that next leap.

After the army and just before I started university to study psychology and sociology I went to work for NFTY [National Federation of Temple Youth, an organization within Reform Judaism in North America], where I fell in love, head over heels, with a minor, a girl named Jill. This was different from my other experiences with women, because I couldn't deny it – I couldn't sleep, couldn't eat, couldn't think of anything else. I was shaking, blushing. I couldn't help telling people about it either, it was too exciting. I remember friends asking if I felt it was a lesbian experience, and I said yeah, maybe, I guess so. I didn't see *myself* as a lesbian, I was simply telling them about an experience I was having. It's strange it didn't threaten me. Jill left the country and nothing came of it – but I didn't really think it would. I didn't think, 'If only she could stay in the country, we could have an affair, we could make love.' It's hard to describe where I was at then, because it seems so paradoxical.

During my first year of school I became friendly with a gay man my own age – twenty-one – named Yorum. We enjoyed each other, and I thought, 'Finally! *He* can be my boyfriend.' I don't remember being attracted to him, but I could see myself with him. People asked me if he was gay, and I said no, he's not gay. When I asked him directly, he denied it. Eventually, when I approached him sexually and he didn't respond, I understood that in fact he was gay. I felt bad. I thought it wasn't a coincidence that I was interested in a man who wasn't available. I saw this as *my* problem making connections with men. I decided to go to therapy to work on it.

It was during that period that all of a sudden lesbianism burst! The trigger was a conversation with a number of girlfriends from school. We started a joking conversation about lesbians, because one woman had touched another woman, and I said something like maybe one day I would like to try it. One of those women invited me over later and told me, 'I tried it.' She told me about the relationship she had been in, and I felt – all of a sudden – everything connected. I didn't feel, 'Oh, this means I'm a lesbian,' I just knew the story excited me beyond any proportion. I remember saying to myself, 'Something important has happened, I think my life is going to be different.'

I finally contacted lesbians through the 'White Line', a help line you can call for gay information. It was frustrating though, because the lesbian events I went to were far apart in time, and since I wasn't in touch with anybody, in between events there was nothing to build on. There was also my anxiety! I remember the first party I went to as almost surrealistic. The women there seemed scary – very masculine. Now I know these women, and I see them totally differently. Some of them I find very attractive – women who at first turned me off. But although there was a formal welcoming, nobody was my friend yet. I wanted friends – I wanted to belong.

What helped change things was meeting Ellen and Joan –

they were an establishment, an American couple who came to Israel for a year and started having potlucks at their home in Ein Keren. I made friends there, and a few months later, I met Dafna, the woman with whom I had my first affair, an American about to leave the country. We obviously weren't going to have a relationship, just something fun. She was very patient. It was the first time I had made love with someone of either sex. Looking back, what was fun was that we giggled about it together.

I had this affair during my second year of psychology graduate studies, while working as a staff person at a residential home for disturbed adolescents. At the same time I was also volunteering at the Rape Crisis Center. But my first priority was the lesbian community. If something came up, I would change everything to fit around it. It was an intense period, and I began to feel very good. Later when I was involved with a woman named Nava, I was able to tell my supervisor about the relationship and its relevance for me. That was important since I want to be a psychologist, and it's a big question whether or not there is acceptance of lesbianism within the profession.

A few months after my relationship with Dafna, I met Nava, who was married. What seemed like a casual relationship developed into a deep one. I knew she had a husband and a child, but neither of us knew she was pregnant. I don't know what I would have done had I known. Even so, I thought it was going to be something casual and short-lived. I kept saying, 'But this is crazy, she's married, she's pregnant. What am I doing with her?' But I knew I didn't want to end it.

Nava and her husband decided to separate after the baby was a few months old. On the one hand I was happy that finally we were together. But on the other hand I wasn't used to being with two children. I had those 'second parent/blended family' issues. During the few months I lived with Nava I got to know parts of her I hadn't known and appreciated things I hadn't realized. But it was also difficult. I felt a lot of stress.

One day I got a phone call from Jill, the girl I had fallen in love with five years before when I worked for NFTY. She was in Israel for six months. I wasn't sure I wanted to see her, because the last time I had seen her, I'd told her I was a lesbian and she'd been very cold and anxious; but when we met I found out that in the meantime she had come out to herself. From the time I saw her again, *everything* was there. I was in love with her, I felt high and excited and didn't think about anything else.

And then there was a big dilemma about my relationship with Nava, because it was a stable relationship, she loved me, and we had built something. I knew Jill would only be here for a few months no matter what happened. It seemed completely foolish to ruin everything I had with this infatuation. Yet I had the feeling I had never really chosen the relationship with Nava, that it was something I had developed and grown into, while with Jill I had a strong feeling I was missing out on something!

Painfully, Nava and I separated. And the rest of the story? Well, I did have a relationship with Jill, but it was problematic. Still, I'm not at all sorry. Just to have felt it, just to have experienced the things I experienced and the things I saw her experience! I am disappointed, but now I know it'll happen again. For the years I've been a lesbian, that's what I've been waiting for.

I think lesbianism is very *little* of an issue in my life. I mean, it's an interest – I think about it more than my heterosexual friends think about their heterosexual preference. But it's not an issue I worry about or feel is wrong. I feel it's me and that it's resolved. I don't feel there's something unusual about me or that I'm in transition. The secrecy is not a big issue – the question of the closet. Everyone in my immediate surroundings knows, and some in my wider circles, and there haven't been any problems with that.

Part of feeling more resolved about being a lesbian is being willing to look at the future. It doesn't have to start tomorrow, but my dream is to have a steady, long-term relationship with a woman for the rest of my life. It's important for me to have children in my life, to raise them with a partner, and I know women for whom this has come true. I wonder, maybe that's a heterosexist value, that you have to have someone for your whole life. It could be part of my conditioning, a remnant of the idea of getting married and having children with a man. But I do want to have children, and I know – especially after having lived with Nava and her children – it's much better to raise a child with a partner. It's difficult alone – you need another adult to protect you from that little creature! You need someone to give you strength.

I want to be a psychologist – I'm studying psychology at graduate school – and I'm unsure as to how much of an issue being a lesbian is, how secret I have to be at this stage of my career and later. In the helping professions, there is a certain tolerance towards human phenomena – an openness, an air of liberalism. Yet most of the prominent theories still see homosexuality as a problem.

One of the things I like about being a lesbian is that I belong to a community. I feel I belong to it even if I'm not active in it, just knowing it's there and that I have a kinship with other women. We need it for survival, for life. I like the atmosphere in the feminist lesbian community. It's free of some of the heterosexual norms I don't like. The lesbian community is more tolerant of people who are less normatively physically attractive, less educated. There is less ageism, less classism, although certainly these things aren't completely lacking.

I've gotten to know women I would never have gotten to know – women older than I, younger than I, from different places in the world, different classes – although most of the women I know tend to be middle class. And it's exciting that we have this thing in common which is very central to our lives, that makes us connect.

Note

1.   Hebrew Union College-Jewish Institute of Religion, the Reform Movement seminary.

נורית

Nurit D

Edited by Spike Pittsberg

• Nurit D, born 1949

Nurit is the daughter of survivors of the Holocaust who met after the war while preparing to come to Palestine. She spent her early life moving between Scotland and Israel; after living twenty-one years of her adult life in Israel, in 1989 she was about to move to the US with her long-time lover, Terry. A well-known and respected feminist activist in Israel, Nurit's personal history parallels the ups and downs of the women's movement.

I AM a forty-year-old returnee to academia. I'm probably fulfilling my parents' dream, one that I unwittingly ingested. I clean houses and live with my lover of ten years, Terry, and with my two sometimes adorable children, sixteen and a half years old and thirteen years old. That's my unit.

Terry is more like my mother than my father. I used to be married to a man who was, on the surface, like my father – an achiever, very matter-of-fact. No high emotions. In the end, he wasn't like my father. Nobody's like my father. And he wasn't as strong as my father – he certainly wasn't strong enough for me.

Most of the women I've been with have been anything but cool, calm and practical. They've all been very emotional. Terry is cool to an extent, but she's intense. She has this hard cool exterior, but once you get behind it, you get burned by her interior heat. So she's a little bit like both my parents. But primarily our connection is a vital one, a strong one, and that's like my connection to my mother.

My mother came from an extremely wealthy, property-owning, totally assimilated, large Jewish family in eastern Poland. When Hitler made a pact with Stalin, first the Russians took over, so by the time the Germans moved in, her family was already in trouble because the Russians had taken their properties or at least had filled them with their own people. One of the things my mother learned from the war was not to have property. It took my father years to persuade her to buy a house. 'If you have property, you're tied down.' Every bit of her family's money had been wrapped up in property, so they had to leave everything behind.

A few weeks after the Germans arrived, they did a round-up. My mother's mother happened to be on the streets at that moment. They just closed off two streets, took everybody to prison, and after a few days, shot them. Although my grandfather tried to sell everything for bribes, he couldn't get her out.

My mother was twelve at the time. She became a survivor in the finer sense of the word. She says she learned two things from the Holocaust. One is to do whatever you want, no matter what others think. Fuck everybody else. The Jews tried to assimilate, cared what others thought of them, and died for it anyhow. The other is: there's no time in our lives to waste doing things we hate. Which is, in my opinion, a pretty healthy attitude.

So anyway, after my grandmother's murder, my grandfather got my mother forged documents and smuggled her out of the ghetto as a non-Jew. He remained with her younger brother. She travelled on a train as part of a slave-labour group slated to go to Germany, but instead her train went to Austria, for farm labour.

Have you ever seen *Roots*? Once they arrived, it was just like that. They put a bunch of girls and boys up on a stage and the farmers walked around to look at their teeth, feel their muscles, and pick out people from these consignments. My mother was taken by this one woman, who, *davka*,* looked after her, even after she told her she was Jewish. To this day they send each other Christmas cards, and last year she was in England to visit her.

After the war was finished, my mother went to England. She walked from Austria to Belgium, and from there sailed to Newcastle, England, to visit an English soldier she had met. She actually married him, but after he served a stint soldiering in Palestine, he started saying stuff like, 'It's a pity Hitler didn't finish off the Jews,' so she packed her bags for London.

From London, the Jewish Agency sent her to Bedford to train to go to a kibbutz. And there she met my father. He is a pure Sepharadi who can trace his family back to the Spanish expulsion.

---

* Of all things!

His – my – forebears arrived in England about the time of Cromwell. He's an educated Scotsman, an economist and engineer. And he's a very witty man.

So he was in Bedford for the same reason as my mother: to train to go to Israel. He had been a submarine man during the war, and had decided that when it was over, he'd go to Israel. They emigrated together in 1948.

They lived on a kibbutz for five years, where they had me. But my father felt confined there and my mother didn't like the way they brought up the kids. In those days they were rigid about when you could see your kid, when you could touch or feed or change her – everything was done according to the book. It was a very radical new type of politics. The last straw for my mother was the day I came home and announced, 'I'm not going to call Father "Father" anymore because he's not my father. Stalin is my father.' They moved to the city in 1953 when I was four years old.

But in 1955 my grandfather died of a heart attack. We moved to Scotland to live with my grandmother in Glasgow. I didn't know any English. I was put into this first-grade class with a bunch of intolerant Scottish children who, of course, didn't know a word of Hebrew, and certainly didn't know what being Jewish meant. Not that I did either. I just knew it meant being different. So at six years old, I turned wild.

Then, when I was eight, had finally got English and settled into school, my mother had my sister, this gorgeous blonde baby who was everything I wasn't. I hated her. Later my mother told me she had post-partum depression and went to a therapist for a short time who said to her, 'Get your act together and go to Israel, where you want to be.' So she started nudging my father. By the time I was ten she prevailed. So, here we go again. We moved back to Israel, without my father, who wouldn't leave his job. He said she can go for six months and if she likes it then he'll join her.

I was ten and my sister was two. The three of us lived with my mother's only remaining relative in Kiryat Atta, near Haifa, in a two-bedroom house. She had a husband and two kids – and we all lived there. I went to yet another school. And, to this day, do you know what they call me when I go to visit there? The Wild One! I hated every fucking goddamned minute of this country. After four months my mother couldn't stand any more, and we made the traumatizing move back to England.

*

When I was fourteen, my dad, who worked for the UN, got a posting in Africa. My parents left the country and put me into boarding-school. It was my eighth school. And that's when I first fell in love – with a girl, *davka*.

The boarding-school was in Edinburgh, a Grecian building with tennis courts and rolling green hills. It was a private school – the kind where all the girls were tough and the boys were wimps. One of my roommates – a Scottish girl named Rosslyn – was as attracted to me as I was to her. I don't even remember who first got into whose bed, but we slept together. If she had to 'teach' me, it was a very quick teaching. We were close for a year or more – emotionally and physically. When we broke up, I was miserable. I reverted to my holy terrorism and was thrown out of that school.

I went to London and got a job at a publishing company as a secretary. I must have had about five or six boyfriends – totally blocking out the thing with Rosslyn. I considered it a juvenile phase. Didn't know the word 'lesbian'. I didn't actually hear the word 'lesbian' until I was a lesbian, at the age of twenty-eight!

*

When I was nineteen, I read *Exodus*. I thought, 'This is it.' I closed the book and went off to the *sochnut*,* a returning prodigal. They paid my way.

I went to a kibbutz near Haifa for ulpan. From the very first day I loved kibbutz life. Within three days I had a boyfriend and was all set up. It was perfect for me because it was uncomplicated: four hours physical labour, four hours studying Hebrew, the rest of the time my own. I didn't know anybody, I didn't have any history there. I made friends very quickly.

Unawares, again I had fallen in love with a woman – who is now my ex-sister-in-law. She was the younger daughter in the family that 'adopted' me. You know, kibbutz people adopt people from the ulpan. You go to them for afternoon tea, for holidays and

---

* Immigration office.

Shabbat. They take care of you if you have any problems, help you deal with the kibbutz network and that sort of thing.

There wasn't anything consciously sexual between this girl and me, but when she went to the army, I was miserable. I decided to leave this kibbutz for a young kibbutz, just starting out. So I went to Keren Shalom, where her brother Eran lived. Keren Shalom is in the Negev desert. There were maybe thirty-five or forty people there, all the same age, no kids. It was exactly like what Leon Uris was writing about: completely idyllic. The brother was my key to the kibbutz.

After he and I were already together, I went into the branch of the army called Nachal, the Young Pioneers. Keren Shalom had been an army outpost, and this Nachal group I joined was turning it into a kibbutz. They were all kibbutz kids – they only accepted me because I had been born on a kibbutz. After my basic training, Eran and I moved in together, and then got married when I got pregnant. He was attractive; in fact, he looks very like his sister. I probably only wanted to marry him so I could stay within the orbit of her family.

*

Keren Shalom was the first place in my life that the differences I felt between me and the people around me didn't constitute a barrier. They were interesting differences but they didn't stop me belonging.

I had my daughter Leigh in 1972. Looking back, I still don't know if that pregnancy was an accident or not. This was the phase when everybody was having the first children of the kibbutz. It was a cachet to be one of those 'founding mothers'. I loved it. I was totally wrapped up in Leigh. In my pre-mother days I didn't give a fuck about kids. But with this child I had an inordinate, boundless patience and was into the whole mother thing like a duck in water, really. My own mother said it was absolutely nauseating to be near me.

Leigh lived in the children's house, so I could just be an adult in the evenings. There were no restrictions on the number of times we could see the kids during the day. Then at 7.00 p.m. I put her in the children's home and that was it, I knew she was in good hands.

Leigh was nearly two when I got pregnant again. I wasn't sure if I wanted another kid, and when Eran said he'd prefer not to – he was traumatized having one – I stupidly had an abortion. I was totally unprepared for the emotional aftermath. It was the closest I've ever come to a nervous breakdown. Six months later I was pregnant again and I didn't ask him this time. I had Levana. He was ecstatic to have a second chance.

Levana was premature and was very ill for the first six months of her life. I constricted my life to her and totally ignored anything between Eran and me. When Levana was a year old, in 1977, I fell madly in love with a woman visiting the kibbutz.

Carrie was one of the most intense women I had met in a long time. She was a big, Rubenesque woman – sexy, free with her body. She swore like a trooper – a breath of fresh air. She was interesting and new, talkative and uninhibited. Since my arrival almost ten years earlier, she was my first connection to somebody who was larger than Israel. She liked me, but I liked her first. I didn't know I was in love with her. She asked me to visit her in Jerusalem. I was scared shitless and didn't know why until a friend gave me *Our Bodies, Ourselves*, and I read about lesbianism.

So I came up to Jerusalem already knowing about lesbianism but was petrified out of my mind to act on it. She opened the door and gave me a hug – and I was like a board. I was so tense. She said, 'Listen, relax. Go have a shower.' Meanwhile she rolled a joint, which I hadn't had since before I came to this country.

That joint was all I needed. We made love and I was an absolute goner from that moment on. We stayed in bed for three days and then I staggered back to the kibbutz. During those three days I'd persuaded her to come live in the kibbutz.

At first it was fun. I was walking eight inches off the earth. I didn't think anybody knew, and of course they knew immediately. I dropped out of all my kibbutz committees because I couldn't be bothered with anything except her.

In the beginning it was fine – who cares about anybody else, right? And then I realized this was going to be difficult, and not just because I was married and playing two games. That was schizophrenic, for sure. But also because Carrie herself was crazy, unstable – a totally fucked-up person. She'd been married for a little while to this Israeli, which is why she'd been in Israel in the first place, and he was killed in a car crash and it was her fault. She had tried to commit suicide. She needed me because I was this rock for her: married, with children. Safe.

Within six months it had degenerated into this habit I couldn't do without but which wasn't giving me the emotional nourishment I needed. Yet I wasn't prepared to leave Eran. I decided he and I should move back to the kibbutz where his parents lived. It's big – you can work your eight hours without having to be a part of anything. We tried for six or eight months before I knew it wasn't going to work. I met Terry in that kibbutz.

It was entirely different with Terry. I'd seen Terry around because she and her husband had been living in that kibbutz for seven years. Terry was working in the children's zoo because as an English teacher, she was assigned work in different branches during summer. One day I asked her if she wanted to have a cup of coffee after work. I didn't think she would come – she's very offhand although she's a charmer. Right away we became very friendly, as in *friends*.

It was a pleasure to unburden my soul to someone, and her marriage was on the rocks. We talked for about three months before we actually did anything physical. After playing Scrabble late one night, she said, 'Why don't you stay?' I froze. 'No, no, I can't.' So she says, 'OK, Eran's away, I'll come with you.' We went to my room and all I could do was hold her. We kissed and kissed, but I wouldn't do any more. We only really started serious love-making the third or fourth night.

I was feminist by this time – 1978. In my last year in kibbutz in the Negev I had started a women's consciousness-raising group in the kibbutz and had asked Marcia Freedman – who by then was a famous feminist – to come and talk with us. I'd read everything I could get my hands on. In fact, before Terry and I actually started sleeping together, one of the things that brought us close was exploring feminism. For her it opened a whole new world and for me it solidified and expanded something that was already there.

★

In October Terry was sent to Oranim, the kibbutz college affiliated with Haifa University. Marcia taught a course there on women and philosophy and Terry, of course, took it. By wrangling time from the kibbutz for political work, I was also able to enrol. The two of us sat there in the back of the class feeling each other up. Marcia, of course, knew, and thought to herself, 'Who are those two dykes?' We soon became friends with Marcia and her lover Maya. Knowing them was a revelation.

Marcia was in her first years of out-and-out militant lesbianism, and we just lapped it up. We were rabid lesbian feminists – that glorious time most people go through in the process of coming out. And we were going through it together, emotionally and physically. I had slept with and been involved emotionally with Carrie, but my real coming out was with Terry. And with Marcia and Maya. And the whole building of the Women's Center.

I left my husband, officially, about a month after I started sleeping with Terry. I saw the break-up as something peripheral I had to wrap up nicely and get rid of, because feminism was the really essential business of my life – and Marcia and my relationship with Terry. The feminist movement was so glorious, so exciting and fresh and new and creative. So when we decided another branch of the Women's Center had to open in Jerusalem, Terry and I decided to leave the kibbutz and go help found it. I wanted to leave the kibbutz without the kids to set up the whole situation. I'd never lived in the city as an adult, myself. I'd been a child, a daughter, and then gone straight to kibbutz. I didn't even know where to pay the first electricity bill. But Eran was scared shitless, so I took them with me.

I would house-hunt in the afternoon and have meetings in the evenings. Marcia had been a member of the Knesset so she knew women in Jerusalem and gave me their numbers. My first evening here I phoned Ofra to tell her I had arrived. We had never met. I said I was from Haifa and I'd come to set up a Women's Center in Jerusalem. She said, 'You're crazy.' I asked her to get together all the old feminists to meet with me, so I could put a proposition to them.

By my second night, she had gotten together eight or ten women. I said, 'I'm here, I'm looking for a house so I can live in

Jerusalem and set up a Women's Center. We need a place, money, people who know the city, people who know people; we need to get organized.'

These weren't your idealistic types; these were all hard-bitten politicos. They certainly weren't swept off their feet, but this one woman, Nava, sat up and whipped out her cheque-book. She was a working woman; there were some there who were wealthy, but they certainly didn't whip out their cheque-books. And she said to everyone, 'Shame on you. You have to start the ball rolling somewhere.' The rumour about the Center spread very quickly and women descended upon us.

Meanwhile I found a home and Terry and I brought all our stuff and moved in. From that day, things really started moving. It was a twenty-four-hours-a-day thing, meetings at least four times a week. We had bazaars and wrote for grants. We got one from Woman to Woman, a New York-based group, and some money from individual Israeli women, like $500 and $1,000. Our aim was to get one year's rent.

Marcia, who was the moving spirit, and the other Haifa women gave us a stock of books, for free on loan. We paid it back eventually, but we didn't have to put up any money at the beginning – they absorbed that loss. Oh, it was heady stuff, really exciting. We opened ten months after we started.

We had the year's rent, which we had to pay in advance. And I used my kibbutz severance pay instead of working that first year. Ostensibly, it was to get the kids adjusted to city life after separating from my husband and the kibbutz. It actually took us all about three years to acclimate to city life. It was very difficult.

Terry taught English to adults in the evenings so she was free to work on the Center. And that's how we spent our lives: meetings, peripherally with the kids, and trying to make ends meet. The year flew by.

The group changed all the time, but the core was pretty stable: Ora, Ofra, Terry and me. And others, like Nava and Pam and Aurora. There were two women who turned religious eventually.

We had different visions. Ora was organizational and handled the money. Ofra was the 'spirit of Israel', if you like. Her roots are so Jerusalem and she was sophisticated about life –

smooth, adept at manoeuvering. Ofra knows how to use the system. Terry was poetic, the visionary. I was more towards the nuts and bolts in a different way than Ora. I made the thing work.

The whole core group was lesbian and we all knew about each other. The other women were mostly straight. Lesbianism wasn't a primary issue at that point. It wasn't a centre for lesbians, nor was it meant to be run only by lesbians, but in fact, in the end, it primarily was.

And in the end, when it petered out, it was over exactly this issue. Like, it was too lesbian-oriented and therefore alienated everybody else. There's not a big enough lesbian community to support that kind of centre. It wasn't the only factor in its demise, but it was one of the major ones. It became a struggle to keep a balance between the lesbian issue and feminist issues. In this country, at that time, lesbianism was way out and feminism wasn't even in.

You know, choosing priorities, for me it always was feminism, rather than lesbianism *per se*. I had my lesbian crowd, my lesbian partner. And at that point it was enough.

Everyone worked on a purely voluntary basis, as many hours as she could. It was the usual story – some put in more time and had more to say, so friction developed. For me, it was making sure that this creation be the best, that it reach the most people, that nobody feel alienated. It should provide legal and psychological services. Everything. But, although we reached most of those goals, it was doomed from the start, because it was all voluntary.

The meetings were always at my house, because we were the only mothers. Meetings at least once a week, telephones day and night. And by then I had run out of money and was working, commuting a long distance three days a week.

On a personal level it was acutely problematic. My kids were reacting to a lack of attention, trauma from moving, total inability to deal with anything. Because I was in school, studying carpentry, I dumped the kids on Terry. The two of us were permanently exhausted, and it just wore us down. Every month the collective would have a marathon on Saturday, processing ad nauseum without the tools. It was like, 'Why isn't everyone equal here?'

We were following the usual set mistakes of women's

centres everywhere and burned ourselves out. We broke up in 1983 in a state of total exhaustion and got ourselves a facilitator to learn how to break up. But it took each of us three or four years to get over the void that was created.

Terry and I retreated. I would not touch anything feminist for a minimum of three years. I wouldn't even organize a picnic. It was disillusionment, it was grief, it was anger, it was resentment. I had a very, very hard time coming to grips with the loss of this great illusion of my life – that feminism is a golden key for any woman who opens her mind and heart to it, and that lesbian feminism or feminist lesbianism was the ultimate key. The dream was that it transformed a person into Ms Right, absolute perfection.

I had been sold on this dream, so I had refused to acknowledge the fact that not only was the whole community less than this, but I personally was less than this. I realized I had hurt a lot of people. I had left a trail littered with people who felt abused, manipulated, run over – because I can be very steam-rollerish. I realized a lot of it was power, which I abused.

★

When I came to terms with that I began to put the whole period in its proper perspective and lose some of the grief, although I haven't lost all my cynicism.

The cynicism, I think, is the sardonic view that nothing ever changes. And that the only people who can affect anything are the over-experienced, let's say, over-thirties, over-forties. Because it's only when someone gets over a serious disillusionment in their lives that they can really start to make a difference. But by then you're tired and looking more inward rather than outward. It's like, here I am forty, I have the experience, I have the ability, but I'm putting it towards looking after myself, which I think is true of a lot of women. So it's a kind of sad cynicism, y'know?

Feminism has been co-opted by the mainstream and been changed in the process. Like today we were walking the street and heard two religious women saying they have a feminist group studying the Bible under the leadership of some rabbi or other. *That's* co-optation.

What interests me is the lesbian community, and it certainly hasn't changed much. It is still piecemeal, unco-ordinated, fractured. It's all word-of-mouth, a party here, a party there. It's not visible, it's not powerful, it's nothing. With the Center gone, there's no magnet. You need some people to be the moving spirits. It's true the community is too small, but it's also a leadership problem.

I think you need three things to keep a feminist project going. You need stable funding so it is a viable business. You need staff who are responsible for coming up with and testing out programmes. And you need staff who are in touch with the pulse of the community but have some freedom to be creative and responsible without every Jane Doe who drops by telling you what to do.

I don't know what really goes on in Tel Aviv, but in Jerusalem there are ten thousand problems in general society. To be truly 'out', I think you'd have to be very wealthy and impervious to public criticism. And there aren't many lesbians like that around here.

Meanwhile the relationship between Terry and me had been really damaged over the years. We had to make a lot of adjustments, which, amazingly, we succeeded in doing. We had individually put a lot of bad patterns behind us. Now we're in therapy – to celebrate our tenth anniversary.

Like my mother, I'm a survivor. After the Center, I worked as a carpenter with an American woman and man. We were a team and put together three wooden houses out in the wilds. But after seven or eight months, my kids started being like street kids, so I stopped that. Terry and I started a *gan*** at our house, and then I ran it myself. I gave it up in 1987 when I decided to go to college. I did a degree in linguistics and I want to go on to a master's and a PhD. Maybe I'll go into publishing, like my mother wants.

And – I'm back in my first women's group in four years – for lesbian mothers. It's a bit of nostalgia. The group shows me how at ease I am with myself as a lesbian and dealing with lesbianism *vis-à-vis* my kids. It affirms what I think about my relationship with Terry, too. When I sit in this roomful of lesbian mothers and hear stuff like, 'Lesbians don't care about kids' or 'Lovers and kids don't

* Pre-school childcare.

go together', then I realize how hard I've worked and what a special thing I have. The group's a real ego boost.

My guiding principle with my kids from the beginning has been that they – poor kids – didn't choose to have a lesbian mother. They should not have to fight my battles. That certainly doesn't mean they shouldn't know what the battles are about, but that in their world they set the rules. So I don't say anything about it at their schools and with their friends.

When Leigh was about seven or so, I talked to her about how people hate and fear differences and that I'm different. And that she needn't tell anyone if she didn't want to. After all, there are a lot of people I don't tell either. It's not a sin to hide your lesbianism. Even in the first two years, when I was a rabid lesbian and told anybody and everybody, where the kids were concerned I kept my good two feet on the ground.

★

When I think about leaving this country, I try to imagine what will change for my kids. And I often wonder how much my being a second-generation Holocaust child has affected my own kids – their attitude to people, to being Jews, to being Israelis – because I believe my own relationship to being a Jew is heavily influenced by the fact that my mother is a Holocaust survivor. Without that, I'd be one of your most assimilated, passing Jews who knows nothing about Judaism and wouldn't give two shits about it. I'm virulently anti-religious, as it is expressed here in Israel. I'm practically a bigot. I've had a total loss of perspective because I feel thoroughly threatened and negated and despised by the ultra-Orthodox here. I think they're a blight on this country. They and the hawks are leading it on a total path of destruction.

I'm ambivalent towards Judaism. I don't even think God exists. I do think something exists, an energy in this world. So you could say I'm an agnostic. But I would die before I would convert. On the other hand, I wouldn't mix only with Jews. While I would cheerfully strangle anybody that was anti-Semitic, I wouldn't shove my practices down anybody's throat.

I cannot forgive Jews who treat others like anti-Semites treat us. I expect more from Jews; it's like feminists and lesbians. I'm appalled by what we're doing to the Arabs, the collective punishments and fines and blasting houses. It's an appalling *déjà vu*. I believe making comparisons with the Holocaust diminishes the Holocaust, but the first steps towards organized anti-Semitism in the late 1920s and early 1930s were very like what we're doing to Arabs here now.

But of course, it is a vibrant, beautiful country. For a long time it was the realization of the ultimate Zionist dream. Now I've outgrown Zionism, but it still has weight for me. It was an enormous feat of redemption for a whole people. It's just a pity it was at the expense of somebody else. But in and of itself it was a magnificent feat. I don't think any Jew who lives here for enough time to become really acclimated can leave it and be whole, ever again.

But there are things I can gain by leaving Israel. First of all, it'll bring me some kind of calmness, not such an abrasive life. I'll suffer less from the heat. And I'll get away from this feeling that I'm sitting on a time-bomb.

The Holocaust cut me off from a source of life – from roots, history, the past, and wealth, financial and otherwise. I think people who don't have extended families are impoverished in some way. You don't have to grow up with them or live in the same town with them to feel their importance.

I could leave this country and I will. I don't think leaving is a betrayal or a lessening of my Judaism. My attachment to being Jewish is deep-seated. I feel it's a *davka*: the whole world has done its best to get rid of us – *is* doing its best – and I'm still here. Like, up yours.

גבי
Gaby F
Edited by Joan Nestle

● Gaby F, born 1953

Gaby's quiet smile and gentle, slightly lisping voice are accompanied by frequent laughter. Although she speaks Hungarian, Hebrew and English, the language of her family – all of whom are deaf or hard of hearing – is sign language.

At the time of this history, Gaby was living with her then-partner, Avital, in Tel Aviv. Aware of her lesbianism from an early age, she has experienced gay life both before and since the gay and lesbian rights movement began in Israel.

MY name is Gaby, short for Gabrielle. My age is thirty-six; I live in Tel Aviv and I'm a lesbian. I work in a very big office as a draftsperson – for about eleven years. I'm very satisfied with my work and life.

I live with Avital (see pages 149–62). We've been together three and a half years. We have two cats. Our apartment is small but nice. We just bought it. It is located close to many friends and important places. We have many plans about this apartment [laughing], but not enough money right now.

My father Saul is seventy years old. He was born in Hungary in 1919, one of four brothers, all deaf. They were a religious family. His first years were at home. He helped on the farm, a big farm with horses, trees and cows, a lot of work. When he was six or seven years old, he was sent to boarding-school. Here he learned to speak and write. Because it was not a Jewish school, his relationship with Jewish culture is very weak.

There were boarding-schools for deaf children in Hungary even sixty years ago. It's a sign of a very developed country. This school didn't allow sign language, and because my father can hear a little bit, he speaks quite well. He didn't know sign language when he met my mother, Anna. She taught him. When they came to Israel with my sister and me in 1957, he worked in a factory making trousers. In Hungary he had been a tailor like an artist; he created clothes for people.

When the Germans arrived in Hungary in 1945, he was taken with his brothers and parents to Dachau, a forced-labour camp. He suffered a lot. He saw his brothers dying. He was also in Auschwitz for a short time. We have some pictures of him in England, when he became free; he was very weak and thin – nearly dead.

My mother was one of ten brothers and sisters. She is also deaf. Some of her brothers and sisters – I think another two or three – were deaf. My mother's grandfather was an important rabbi in Hungary. She was also sent to a boarding-school, but a Jewish one. She told us she was the best pupil, and always at the end of the year, she spoke in front of the whole school. She was a leader. According to her photographs, she was very beautiful. I know a teacher of hers who lives in England now. She's very old, but she worked there as a psychologist. She said my mother was a very intelligent student.

Luckily for her, her school was in Budapest. The Germans arrived only at the end of the war. She was saved. She lived in a ghetto, but she really did not suffer. She wanted to go to her family's city, but the manager of the school advised her not to because it was dangerous. After the war, she found out all her brothers and sisters and parents were sent to death camps. She says she couldn't sleep at night for years, she cried every night. She felt very lonely. She wanted to build a new family. She wanted her husband to be Jewish, and not many Jewish men were left. A man she knew introduced her to my father.

He was living in a big city called Debrecen. The first time he met my mother he brought many flowers. He fell in love with her that first time, but my mother was not excited about him. I'm told my father was a very handsome man, but he is shy. They met three times and decided to marry – in 1951 in Budapest.

My mother told me that at the beginning she didn't love him, but when she saw how devoted he was – he worked very hard and gave all of himself to the family – she started to admire and love him. I was born in 1953. A year and half after, my sister was born. Her name is Ilsa. My parents wanted to leave Hungary, but all the borders were closed. Finally, after the revolution in Hungary, they succeeded. They got a certificate and we came to Israel in May of 1957.

In the beginning, we lived in Tiberias. I told my mother, 'Let's go back to Hungary, it's too warm.' Also we found a snake in a neighbour's apartment! There was no electricity in many places, no roads. Everything was sand, sand, sand. All the lives seemed very different from Europe – like a thousand years of difference! But some religious relatives here helped us find an apartment in Holon, near Tel Aviv. My parents found work in a clothing factory. They worked very hard.

In Hungary, my mother had worked in a shoe factory. They prepared the deaf to do very simple jobs – carpenter, tailor, shoe-maker, jobs like these. In Israel, their salary was low, but because of my mother's ambition, she saved money to buy a house and give us everything we needed.

My childhood was very happy. Not because of our family relationship, but because I was almost every day outside with other children, playing non-stop games. We didn't have to worry about anything.

When I was born, my parents already knew sign language. Our family life was ordinary. My father left early in the morning, came back late in the evenings and continued to work on our sewing-machine. During the day, my mother worked at home on the machine, so they had two salaries, very, very low, from hard work – sitting all day at the machine. My mother's food was delicious. She was also very clean. She never stopped working. After she washed the clothes, she folded them and put them on the shelf – straight like soldiers.

In the summer we used to go to the beach for half a day and we never wanted to come back. A big truck took us from Holon to Bat Yam. One came every hour. People didn't have cars in those days, and the roads were very bad. It was fun. My father and mother were members of the deaf community in the Helen Keller Center in Tel Aviv. They had social meetings every Tuesday and Saturday. It was a lovely time to meet other deaf people, deaf children.

My mother and father had more friends than many of our hearing neighbours. They usually went to friends or friends came to them on Friday evenings or during the week.

★

My sister and I were not good pupils. Now I know it was probably because of our hearing problems. It was difficult for me to follow what the teacher was saying, so I didn't listen. I would dream. Everyone said I was a dreamer – my sister too. Sometimes neighbours complained that we listened to the radio too noisily. All these signs didn't indicate to *anybody* that we had a serious hearing problem. When my sister was fourteen, the school nurse examined her and found out my sister had a bad hearing problem, and they decided to check me too. I believe they didn't discover my problem early enough to help me in my studies or in my social development.

I tried to avoid being with other people. I felt uncomfortable to ask them again and again, 'What? What? What?' Most people thought I asked 'What?' because I was stupid. I thought I was a bad pupil, but somehow I was always jumped to the next class.

I can say my lesbian life started from my early, early childhood. I can remember, for example, in Hungary, we went on vacation to another city, and there was a swimming pool. I remember after swimming, my mother took me to the shower. I saw many naked women. It didn't affect me sexually, no. But I remember this picture very clearly, that their bodies were so different from my body, were so mysterious and so interesting.

My memory started very early – maybe from two years old. My mother is always amazed when I remind her of things. The woman, the *ganenet** in the kindergarten, I think I was in love with her. If she would look at me, or touch me, or smile at me, I would nearly cry! [Laughing] If I look back on my life I can see that all the dominant persons in my life were women. They attracted my attention, my feelings and all my concentration, you know?

When I was twelve years old, we made once a journey by truck with the deaf club to Naharia in the north. I remember this journey very well. Suddenly my mother called to me from another corner of the truck: 'Look, this is Shira. She is a young deaf girl from Hungary. She's *olah hadashah*.'† I looked at her and fell in love!

She took me on her lap. She spoke with me all day and told me stories. We spoke in Hungarian, I spoke to her with sign lan-

---

* Childcare worker (f.).
† A new immigrant (f.).

guage and we read lips. I couldn't leave her for a minute. When we arrived at Naharia, we went to the swimming-pool, and I followed her everywhere. She was studying to be a tailor in a boarding-school at the Helen Keller Center. Deaf children could learn some professions there. At the end of this day when I went back home, I couldn't stop thinking about her. I always looked for a way to meet her again.

Not long after, I was invited to visit a relative in Tel Aviv. This woman loves children very much – she spoils them with gifts and everything. She asked me what I wanted to do that day. I remembered I had other relatives near the Helen Keller Center, so I told her I wanted to visit the Weiss family. 'Really? You want to see the Weisses?' I said, 'Yes.' She was very surprised!

The moment we arrived there, I apologized that I needed to go into the Helen Keller Center for a few minutes. Shira was in the middle of a lesson, and she was very surprised to see me. But they let me come in, and I sat near to her and I finally could feel her and touch her. I was in heaven! I forgot the Weiss family. I forgot my aunt who took me there. When I finally came back, they asked me, 'Why did you ask to visit the Weiss family? Where did you disappear to?' I didn't explain – I couldn't tell them I was working my plan. But I couldn't meet her again, and in time, I forgot her.

When I was about thirteen years old, we had a new pupil in the class named Rayna; she was from India. When I was a child, it was very usual that new people came to Israel from India, Romania, Poland, Hungary, Russia – many countries. Usually a pupil adopted the ole hadash and tried to help them with homework and everything else. When I first saw her, she didn't pay any attention to me. But after a few months, in a break between lessons, I was standing against the blackboard when Rayna entered. She had just come back from a sports hour, and she was wearing shorts. She was wet and there was a slow wind and her hair moved very gently. I don't know why and how, but I fell in love with her. Suddenly, she seemed like an angel to me. From then on I just thought about her and tried to find ways to be near her.

But you know, at this age when you want to attract someone's attention, you annoy them. Once she wore a short skirt, and I lifted it a little bit. She was very angry, and she said that from then on, we weren't speaking. I was very stubborn. If she didn't want to speak, I didn't want to speak. But I knew where she lived. Another student in the class was her neighbour. I started visiting the neighbour all day, every day, just for the chance to see Rayna. [Laughing] I could see from the corner of my eye that during lessons she looked at me all the time. But I didn't know how to speak to her again!

Then I had an idea. I was nearly fourteen. I decided to have a birthday party and invite the whole class. Maybe she will come too! [Laughing] Everyone came *except* Rayna. I was standing at the window waiting for her.

Another friend, Eliaz, used to come with me to visit Rayna's neighbour, Rachel. When we left, if we met Rayna on the road, Eliaz tried to make peace between us. He would say, 'Rayna, say "Gaby".' She'd say, 'No.' Then he would say, 'Gaby, say "Rayna".' I'd say, 'No.' She was too proud and I was too proud.

Finally she said my name first. Then we became the closest friends in the world! Many times we took walks around where we lived. Once we talked about sex, but mostly we spoke about her life in India, about her mother who had died when she was very young. She only had a father and big brother who lived in England. When we walked we usually held hands. It was a very happy time in my life.

Just before our class journey at the end of the last year of elementary school – suddenly, Rayna's father died. We all went to the funeral. After that, our teacher took Rayna to her home to live until she could go to England. Soon after her father died, we had the school journey to the north.

We had in class an albino girl. Nobody was friends with her. One cold night, our teacher asked us to divide into groups of two or three and sleep together, sharing blankets. The albino girl – her name was Etzyona – stood in the corner. I didn't want to be with her, but I told Rayna, 'Look, Etzyona is alone. Nobody wants to share a blanket with her.' So Rayna left everything and went to the girl and said, 'Where are your blankets?' She didn't ask her to join us, but she arranged a place for her near us. She just showed her attention. When I saw this, I started to cry. I felt how she is an angel and so good, and she had no father, no mother! A head of a child I had. When we slept together, I didn't fall asleep for hours because I felt her leg near my leg. It was so lovely ... I was so happy.

I don't remember any sexual feelings in these years. Just the real need to be physically close. To feel the warmth, and the hands and the body. But not sexually. I didn't call my feelings at this time lesbianism. I don't think I had heard this word. Maybe in the books we were allowed to read they didn't put in the right word.

At the end of the year, Rayna left for England. It was very sad for me, but I didn't think I could change it. We were both dependent on our families and there was no one to care for her, only her older brother. We wrote letters to each other for about one year, then we stopped.

In these years also, since I was twelve or thirteen, I read a lot of books. I love to read books. Some of them influenced me very much – in good and bad ways. Some books create impossible worlds of romance and beauty, and I had too high an expectation of people as a result of the books I read.

I was also mad about movies. Mad, mad, mad! Close to our home was a cinema which showed a different movie every day. In the afternoon it was not expensive. Sometimes I asked my mother for money, sometimes she didn't agree. Then I would take empty bottles and sell them to have enough money to buy a ticket.

Once I was in the kitchen and I asked my father for money to see a film. 'We don't have the money,' he said. 'What is more important to you, to eat or to see the film?' I said, 'To see the film.' Then he slapped me hard. I looked at him coldly. I didn't say a word, and he asked again. I answered the same way and he slapped me again. And again. And again. Then I suddenly jumped on him and we started to fight like in the Wild West films! When it was over, I decided not to speak to my father.

When I was fifteen or sixteen, there was another family event – this time with my mother. She used to follow me everywhere at home. If I wasn't wearing socks, she would give me socks to wear. If I took a shower, she would follow me into the shower to check if the window was closed. If I was watching TV, I suddenly found I was eating a banana or apple – I was so concentrated on watching, she fed me without my knowing it. She was too deep into me!

★

Remember when I mentioned Rachel, the neighbour of Rayna? When Rayna went to England, Rachel and I continued our friendship. She was an invalid – handicapped. She'd had polio and both legs were paralysed. I used to visit her and it was very nice. Once when I was between sixteen and seventeen, I dreamed Rachel and I were kissing and holding each other in the stairway of my home. It was a very erotic dream! Another girl from my class was standing there, watching us. The dream affected me deeply. Once when I visited her – she was very strong from walking on crutches – we were wrestling, in fun. In the middle of the fight I told her, 'You know, I dreamed about you.' She said, 'Yes, I know. Me too.' I said, 'Really? What did you dream?' Months passed until I agreed to tell first. Then she said she had the same dream! Not in every detail, but very similar dreams. Probably on the same day!

Now at this time I felt I'm maybe the only lesbian in the world, and I would never dare to offer any kind of relationship to any friend because she would throw me away. But now I had met a girl – a nice girl! – who had the same thinking about it. Why shouldn't we do it?

I wanted it very much. She said she was afraid that if we start, it will spoil the friendship, and I will not stay faithful to her. But I kept saying, 'There is nothing to worry about,' until it happened. She had a car, and we kissed the first time in that car. My first kiss with a woman! I had before then kissed a boyfriend, but this!

We had no place to do it, so [laughing] we made love in the car. If we were lucky, once in a long time we did it at her parents' apartment if they went out, or at my parents'. I continued in this relationship for two years but then her jealousy made me tired. Also I was not sure I was a lesbian. I thought, maybe because my sexual relations with men are not so good, that's why I'm a lesbian. I wanted to have a chance to check it out. It was also a good excuse to stop this relationship.

I really tried with men afterward. I had two nice men. One was the manager of my draftsperson school – but that was much later. There was also another young man, handsome and gentle, but it didn't work. They never excited me as relationships with women did.

I will talk about school now. In high school, my social problems and my hearing problems were obvious. I didn't pass the first year. I don't know why, but I wanted to try again – then I was in the same class with my sister. That was a little bit after we learned about our hearing problems.

That year I finished successfully, but the psychologist and social worker decided the best thing for us is to leave home immediately because of our mother's influence and go to an agricultural boarding-school in Petach Tikvah. It was the only place that had openings for new students. In this school I had a boyfriend for a year. All of this was before Rachel. In this year, I saw the movie, *The Killing of Sister George*. It spoke to me very deeply. I don't remember well all the feelings, but the older woman tried to touch the breast of the young woman. She removed the hand and then she tried again. The atmosphere was full of tension! I felt very strongly that this is what I really want. Even though I had a boyfriend and it was very nice with him – we had an exciting sexual relationship, but without him coming inside of me. I felt something was missing, something very deep and important. I remember once when we kissed, between breath and breath, I told him I was a lesbian. He said, 'Nonsense', and continued to kiss me.

*

I will jump to the period in my life when I went to drafting school. My high school studies were not successful. I stopped in the middle and worked about two years in a zipper factory. I made a lot of money there because I liked to work, but I decided there was no future in it. I considered learning another profession and decided to go to drawing school.

This was a lovely year. I became a close friend of a student named Lena. She was seven years older than me. We studied together, and at the end of the year, Lena and I and a young man we studied with, Noam, decided we should live together and try to open an office. We rented an apartment in Bar Ilan, and we saw it was not so easy as we thought.

Lena wondered about some things in me. Once I told her I would never marry. When she asked me why, I said, 'I can't tell you, but one day I will.' She asked me again and again. Noam was in love with me – he told me so. So at the end of this year, I told Noam I was a lesbian. He was shocked. I tried telling Lena, but I couldn't say to her, 'I am a lesbian.'

Oh! I forgot a very important story. While in drawing school, I fell in love with a student named Pazit. At the end of the year, I wrote her a long love letter – but I couldn't send it. So when Lena asked me again why I would never marry, instead of telling her I was a lesbian, I decided to show her the letter. She read it and I saw that she was smiling when she read it. She said, 'That's all?' I said, 'Yes, that's all.'

When I saw the office would not succeed as we thought, I got a job as a draftsperson. Noam worked in another place and Lena got a job as a stewardess. Once she came home from a flight and asked me if I wanted to meet Linda, a bisexual woman that she knew who was also a stewardess. At first, I said, 'No.' Then I started to ask myself, 'Who is this Linda? Maybe she'll know another lesbian, maybe I am not alone. I wonder what she looks like!' I asked myself question after question – I couldn't stop thinking about it. Then I came to Lena and said, 'OK,' and she gave Linda my telephone number.

We decided to meet and Lena took me there in her car. I was so frightened! Finally when Linda opened the door, I saw a tall young woman, dark, so full of energy and self-confidence. I was so shy at this time, I didn't speak much – tried to hide behind Lena's back! [Laughs] I am sure I made a very bad impression.

After that we met one afternoon at her home, after I knew how to get to her place in Givatayim. She told me about SPPR, the homosexual rights organization we have here. I don't know how I had not heard of it! This was the early 1970s, very near the time this organization was established. I was full of admiration for those people – the first to stand against society and say, 'We are homosexuals. We are lesbians.' They were so brave and strong!

She told me the next week was going to be a women's meeting, and she asked me to come with her. But she warned me that there are some lesbians like Don Juan, who want to fuck as many women as they can! This was a shock – I never dreamed lesbians were like these women. I thought lesbianism was something perfect, something beautiful. I became very frightened. I decided to go there and not let anybody touch me or speak to me. [laughing] She named some of the dangerous women, and I decided to be especially careful of them.

Soon we had a sexual relationship. It was not so great because I didn't feel comfortable. I didn't know her well and was very confused by all her stories because of my hearing problem. I hadn't gone out much and I didn't have any hearing aids yet, so social and hearing problems were mixed up together.

We went together to the first meeting of the women's group of the Society for the Protection of Personal Rights. It was a meeting between the feminist group and the lesbian group. The point of the meeting was to discuss if there were common aims. This was in 1976 – I was twenty-three. The evening was a very hot atmosphere of arguments, differences in attitudes. I was also surprised to learn that there are some lesbians that are not feminists. I didn't call myself feminist but my view was feminist. One young lady, Chava, stood there and spoke against feminism. I thought she was lovely, but I didn't like what she said. I said to myself, 'She is not my style.' After that night, she didn't come back for a long time.

This date with Linda was our last meeting. She started to flirt with another woman there. I learned Linda was one of those women she had warned me about!

Chava came back after several months. By this time, I already had hearing-aids, and I started to feel my life was changing, slowly, slowly. I had tried hearing-aids before, but the quality of the old hearing-aids was so bad and the voices so loud I couldn't stand to use them. The new hearing-aids were much better.

Chava tried to seduce me, not once, not twice, but many, many times – she didn't stop. Finally I agreed to dance with her. Afterward when I wanted to go home, she asked me if I would walk her to the bus station. It was on a dark Tel Aviv street, very late. She pushed me against a car and tried to kiss me. Then she apologized, 'Forgive me, I haven't been with a woman in a long time.' I said, 'How long?' She said, 'Two weeks.' [laughing] I was shocked!

She asked to see me again. We went to a movie and then another movie. We went to drink coffee – and slowly, slowly we became closer. She was so different from me that somehow she attracted me very much. She was full of life, full of self-confidence.

So brave and so easy, so gay, you know? She knew how to fight for her own rights! I was too shy and always gave up, never wanting problems or trouble. But she was assertive. I learned a lot from her. And she had hardly any education – she stopped school at the third grade. Her life story is very interesting.

It was the start of a long relationship. We rented an apartment for a few months in Tel Aviv, but it was a terrible place. I wouldn't call it living together because we brought things from our parents to eat, we sent our parents our clothes to wash. It was a place we could make love – this is the correct name for such a place like this.

Eventually I knew this relationship would not be for my whole life. We were too different and also I wanted a faithful relationship. We have different versions of how long it really lasted. I say it was four years, she says it was six years. One of the explanations for these two versions is that our relationship didn't stop all at once. It stopped slowly, slowly. Chava always needed new excitement. Many men never had so many women as Chava had.

I am now thirty-six, but I think I had too many women. Relationship after relationship, I tried to believe finally this was the right relationship but always it was not. Now I can truly say that Avital is one of the very few 'normal' lesbians! Over the recent years, more women have become lesbians and maybe that is why women are more positive. My impression has changed for the better. I think it changed also because we stopped going to the bar and the disco.

★

Now for some of my other views about life. I don't believe in God; I don't feel Jewish. I was born to a Jewish mother and live in a Jewish community, but I don't feel Jewish values mean anything to me. For instance, I feel the Jewish self-view of ourselves as a chosen people is not relevant to me – first of all, because I don't believe in God and second of all, I believe if there was a God, He wouldn't choose just one people. If He created all of us in His image, for example, it is obvious if He chooses one people, the result is hate and anger and war. I believe if people belong only to one group, they mostly will separate and not join together. 'We are Jewish, we are Arab, we are Christian, we are better, you are worse.' There is no end to it.

In some places of the world, people might hurt me because my mother and father were Jewish. So Jews must have their own country, a place where they will feel safe. But the big question is where and what size. My opinion is we should give back the West Bank and Gaza and let the Palestinians self-identify. I don't think we should occupy foreign lands with people who do not want us there. I would prefer there were no countries in the world – that all will be one country. I know on the other side of the 'enemy lines' there are people who could be my best friends, and here with me, I live with some people I dislike.

When I had to join the army when I was eighteen, I didn't have any hearing-aid, and my motivation to be with people was low. In those days, hearing problems such as I had were reasons to be released immediately from the army and that's what happened. But also I am a pacifist. An older man there asked me, 'Really, you are a pacifist?' I think he thought I was unrealistic or a dreamer. The Israeli army is called Ts'va Haganah L'Yisrael; in English it means 'Defence Army of Israel'. Not anymore is it a defence army. A long time ago it became an occupying army.

Lesbians are a minority in this society and when you are a minority, you have to find your own identification. Searching for yourself causes you to think. I became a lesbian because I felt it. But after I felt it, I discovered it's complicated – to find a partner, how to stand against the world. You become more aware of suffering. By thinking about it, my self-identification became clearer. My views about Jews, about religion, about countries and about feminism are all part of one concept of equality among people, women and men, in the world. I am not sure this is a result of my lesbianism directly, but my awareness of the right to live your own life.

אביטל
Avital
Edited by Jyl Lynn Felman

Tal, Arel and Avital

• *Avital, born 1960*

Avital was twenty-eight years old when she recorded her history. At that time she was living with her lover, Gaby, in Tel Aviv, and completing dental school. Today she and her partner, Tal, are leaders in the lesbian-feminist movement and are raising two sons.

While her purring cats lay contentedly on her lap, Avital told her story of determined nonconformity in a light, sweet voice.

IN 1951, all the Jews of Iraq decided to come at once to Israel. Before the Israeli War of Independence, the Jews had a lot of power in Iraq. They were related to the king. All the people who had important government positions were Jews. After the war, the Arabs' attitude toward the Jews living in their countries became more hostile. Bit by bit Jews lost their positions. There were even a few violent events against them. Once a bomb badly injured my aunt's husband and other relatives were killed. It was becoming harder for them to live there, although they were very rich. All these things together made my relatives think seriously of coming to Israel. Working with the Zionist underground, Israel arranged the escape of all the Jews from Iraq.[1] My parents – only nineteen and seventeen, and as yet unacquainted – left everything behind in Baghdad.

The Israelis used military transports to take out all the Jews at once on special flights from Baghdad to Tel Aviv. People came suddenly, not knowing exactly what the situation was here. My mother put on her loveliest dress and packed little things she could take with her. When they landed, they were sprayed with DDT. My mother told me it was a big shock for her, being treated like that! She and her brother came alone because their mother had died long ago, and their father wouldn't leave. They were sent for a few weeks to Atlit, near Haifa, to a *mabarah*, a camp for *olim hadashim.** There were so many Jews coming from so many places

___

* New immigrants.

that the Israelis didn't have any place to put them. It was hard for them – coming from a wealthy house to a tent! They didn't have any money, because the Iraqis took it all just before they left. From my mother they took most of her jewellery. She had really nothing left.

After a year in camps, their sister came with her husband and children. When they were all together they managed to buy a modest wooden house in Tel Aviv. My mother was seventeen and without any profession – she hadn't finished school and didn't have the money to continue studying. She went to an ulpan, but she didn't know Hebrew fluently enough to continue school. She had to work, usually in places like cookie or matzah factories.

Around 1955, she met my father. All the Iraqi Jews, even though there were so many in Baghdad, knew about everybody's family. Two ladies arranged their first date, and that led to marriage. Just before the wedding my father, his brothers and mother bought an apartment in Ramat Gan. My mother moved with him to his mother's place. After a few more years they bought my grandmother a little apartment of her own.

My father was over eighteen when he left Iraq so he finished school. Since he came to Israel, he worked in the post office, starting as a postman. When he came he didn't know the language. Today, after almost forty years, he is the manager of a big department.

My mother worked two years after she got married. They had difficulties having babies – it took five years till I was born, then four till my sister. After I was born my mother stopped working, and didn't continue till many years later. My parents gave me a lot of attention because I was the first one. In the sixties people didn't have much money, and many things we wanted my parents worked hard to get for us – bicycles, guitar lessons. It was hard for them to afford it.

As a child I was very shy. Teachers would tell my mother I was too quiet – they were not sure if I was dreaming or listening. But it didn't affect my studies at all. Even when I had friends in class, I hung back. But when I came home from school the neighbourhood boys and I had a lot of fun playing in a big old orange orchard. I had only one girlfriend who also wasn't interested in the regular things girls do – dolls and things. It was a lovely childhood. When I remember myself from that period I was always the only girl with the boys. We had a detective group! There is an Israeli book about a detective group of children. There was a leader and the vice-leader was a girl, and everyone had his own character. We made such a group of our own. Of course, I was the vice-leader!

At that time, I liked many things that my father did. In the evening he studied electronics. He took courses and started fixing electrical things at home, as an extra job. When I was good, he gave me an old radio set to take every piece out and try to put it back, to have a toy of my own. I liked learning about electronics.

Also the boys who lived there were interested. We built a device that can transmit Morse through a cable. What is important is that I was interested in technical things, not feminine things. In school we had handicrafts classes – separate ones for boys and girls. The girls do knitting and many boring things, and the boys do woodwork – very different. They have a machine shop and we have a lousy little classroom. When we finished elementary school every girl had to know how to sew a shirt with embroidery on it – many flowers. You had to make *two*, one for you and one for a boy from your class, who can't do it of course! I was bored. All the knitting – I started it in class and wrote down how to do it, and gave it to my mother to finish.

In Israel, after you finish eighth grade you have to decide what high school to go to. I went to a school where you study for the *bagrut*.* I enjoyed studying more in high school. There were a few subjects I was very good at, like maths, physics and biology. And because of being the best pupil in that subject, I got more self-confidence, and because it was a new school, I could change my reputation away from 'Shy Avital'. Instead of being an average student I began to be a very good one. I studied in a special Tel Aviv University programme for youth who are interested in science. Two afternoons a week I took biochemistry, microbiology, and computers. I began to change away from being a shy child without any self-confidence. Not all at once, but every time I had more challenges, it made me change.

* Matriculation exams, taken before leaving high school.

Meanwhile, I was still interested in electronics. I was fascinated to discover there is a hobby of people who have their own radio transmitters and talk with each other. In Israel in order to get a licence as a ham radio operator, you have to study advanced electronics and pass hard exams. After studying a few years with the radio club, I got my licence. In that club, I made many new friends, mostly boys. We started a group of teenage radio hams. When I was seventeen my parents bought me a radio station, which was very expensive. During that time there were one or two girls in that club. But I was the first girl who actually got a licence and the only girl to have a radio station of her own. On the air it's quite extraordinary to hear a female voice. So whenever you operate, because you are a woman, everyone wants to talk with you! I would just raise my voice, and then somebody would say, 'There's a YL' – in radio language, YL is Young Lady – 'There is a YL voice; go ahead.' So I never had to wait. Even though my signal was not the strongest because of the pitch of my voice, everyone could hear me. On the air, I also met friends from Australia, Germany and India. We would meet at a certain hour at a certain place on the band. At that time I was the only Israeli woman who was active as a radio ham.

Meanwhile, I started to date a boy from that club, David. He was of course my first one, and I was the first for him. Together with a few couples from the radio club we went on trips. Sometimes we would stay all night at the club transmitting. It took time till we started to have a more physical relationship. We were young and didn't know what to do. After a while, he told me he thought he had a problem with sex. He'd had a homosexual experience when he was quite young, and he wanted to try it again. He wasn't sure he'd be able to have a real, full sexual relationship with me. Of course, I tried to help him, to talk to him a lot. We had physical relations, but not full sex.

Then I went to the army. In Israel, the girls first do a few weeks of basic training. After you finish it, according to the test you took just before you were drafted, they decide where they'll send you – to be a professional or just a plain secretary. I chose a course in meteorology. I studied physics, mathematics and geography intensively from early morning to late afternoon for three months.

Every weekend we had tests. One weekend, if you get more than seventy you can have the weekend off and go home, and the second weekend, if you get more than ninety you can go home.

After the course I was sent to a base in the south. After three or four months I was in charge of meteorology for the base. First we made inspections of the weather – every hour writing down how many clouds, what kind, the direction of the wind, the temperature, the humidity level, drawing some maps by hand. We gave the officers the forecasts. At the beginning it was a shock for me – as a new soldier, new in that profession, to go and stand in front of the head of the base and all the very big officers! They ask you questions and you have to know the answers. But after some time I enjoyed it, because I learned a lot more about the profession, and had more self-confidence. Whenever you stand up and you're sure you know much more than the officers, and especially when you laugh inside when you hear their questions, you feel very confident – although you are just a plain soldier.

I still had a relationship with David, although less frequent than before. He was trying to inquire more about his homosexuality. When he finished the army a year after I did, he actually went out of the closet. All that time I didn't think anything about myself. During the army I had another boyfriend, but it was a very short relationship and I never let it become physical. One soldier – she was with me in the meteorology course and later on the same base – we got very close. We were so close that I thought – I *knew* – I was in love with her. But the funny thing was, I didn't think it was so unusual, and I didn't make any connection between this and how it was going for me with boys. It was all subconscious.

The first person I knew that talked about homosexuality was David. He had some gay friends, and I started to go out with them. It was very convenient. It was the only way you can date boys without feeling threatened physically. But still I didn't think about what it might mean about me.

After I finished the army, I applied to study dentistry and pharmacology. I was accepted to pharmacology, but I decided not to study right away. I went to work as a secretary in a bank. My boss – I won't say he was chauvinist, but he expected me to be 'nice' and to do everything according to his rules. Be the typical secretary. I hated it! So I switched to accounting, and I liked it much more.

During this year I changed my mind and decided to go to medical school. I entered Ben Gurion University in Beersheba. Two-thirds were men – only fifteen women. I had boyfriends, but whenever the physical relationships became more intense, or after one or two experiences in bed, I became in my general relations much less warm. So naturally, I blew it every time!

At last I went out of the closet. I realized I don't like having physical contact with men, and if I do, I usually choose a boyfriend who looks more gentle than other men. Whenever I had a more masculine boyfriend, I felt repelled. I looked over my past, and remembered I was actually more than once in love with a woman. And when I was young, I was in love with my camp instructor. I thought: I'm attracted to women!

But I wasn't sure, and for a while I decided I'm an asexual creature – unable to enjoy any physical relationship at all. But after some time, I started to think hard about lesbianism, and found the more I thought about it, the more interested I became. I noticed every time there was a newspaper article telling about lesbian or homosexual life. And every weekend, I went out with David and his friends to gay places. I started to look around to see how lesbian women look. But it was all inside me – I didn't tell anyone. There was one club in Tel Aviv which once a week was open only for lesbians – Divine's. I decided to go once by myself and see what it is, because every time I was in Divine I was with gay men – I was supposed to be the straight friend! I didn't dare to try to look at lesbians. And on 'mixed evening' – ninety percent were gay men! You couldn't find lesbians, and if there were women, I didn't know if they were lesbians or not.

It took some courage to decide to go there by myself. [laughs] Several times as I got to the street I felt too much afraid and went home! I had an old radio club friend who worked nights in the international operator office of the phone company. She told me stories about how many gay women and men worked there, and that she was friends with a lesbian couple. I was very interested! Then I told her, 'By the way, did you hear there is a club open every Tuesday for lesbians? What do you say about going?' [laughs]

When we went there, I confided, 'This may be suitable for me,' implying I might be bisexual. After the second time, I felt ready to go alone.

That was very hard for me. First of all, Tuesdays I was supposed to be in Beersheba, not in Tel Aviv. I would sleep at a friend's so my parents wouldn't know I was in town. I went to that club many times, and left without talking to anyone! It's noisy, dark, and you feel the people are very distant. I began to feel hopeless.

At last, a woman asked me to dance and introduced me to a couple she came with. [laughs] The week after, we came there together, and started to be lovers! For me, I discovered that was what I wanted. But the relations with her were very hard. She was fifteen years older than I, married with two children. Her husband knew about her lesbian life, but he wanted her to be at home except for going once in a while with a friend, but not to avoid him or the family too much. He had his special demands which he didn't give up. Every Tuesday I came from Beersheba – I left at five after my last lecture and had to travel three hours. We would sit discreetly talking or watching TV until her husband went to sleep, then go out to the night club. She put the children in the parents' room, and I slept with her in the children's room. Then at five o'clock in the morning I went back to Beersheba to be there by eight. I don't know how I did it for so many months! She was possessive, too jealous. And she was paranoid – I always had to give excuses. At the beginning it was great because lesbian relationships were new to me, but as time passed I realized I'm loving her less and less.

In the meantime, I knew more lesbians. And during the third year in medical school, I decided to leave my studies. You see, being a doctor in Israel is hard work, long hours. It's hard to find a job. If you want to do a popular specialty, like plastic surgery, it's impossible. It didn't seem clever to continue to study medicine. After working for my uncle, a dentist, I decided to try dentistry and I was accepted to the dental school here. During that time I finished my relationship with this woman. We had many quarrels about her being jealous and suspicious about me. In everyday life, I don't share much about myself. I don't know why, but I don't. And she was sure that because I don't tell her whatever I did yesterday, that's surely because there's something I'm hiding. It was really terrible. Every time I tried to talk with her about ending the relationship she would react hysterically, even violently. I realized there was no way I could honourably finish the relationship. I had to cut it.

Before starting dental school, I went out with many groups, and I had fun. Because of the kind of relationship I'd had, I decided to not even try to have a new friend for a while. Then I decided I didn't want to live with my parents after so many years, especially because they didn't know about me. So I started to look for an apartment. That was how I met Gaby – she was the one moving out!

We had a long talk. I had bought a microcomputer and was trying to learn the computer language. Gaby said she would like to see it, and she was interested in the ham radio too. I invited her to my place to see them. I didn't feel interested in her in a special way – just finding her very nice. The second time Gaby came to see me, I started to be very much interested. Every time we met I felt I was developing special emotions for her. One day we took a walk, and I told her I liked her very much, and she told me she felt the same.

I found a place in Tel Aviv with a roommate, but after seven or eight months Gaby and I decided to live together. Since then I have been studying dentistry. When I finished the fifth year, a clinic year, I hadn't completed all the requirements – crowns and fillings, very strict rules. So I couldn't continue with my class. I had to just work, which was quite hard for me. Today I work every day from eight to six o'clock in the evening. I even am so busy with patients I don't use my break. Whenever I get home I'm totally finished! After this period I am going back to the clinic.

*

As a child, we had a lot of tradition in our home. It was more tradition than religion, although my parents believe in God. They used to go to the synagogue a few times a year, like at Yom Kippur. Every time my father went to the synagogue, he took me along. As a very young child, I liked these holidays, because there's vacation and good food and all the other advantages. The older I got, the less I enjoyed the traditions. I didn't understand what God is. As a child I started thinking about it. I did many stupid things, like, walking on pavements, I told myself, if I touch a crack God will punish me. And I saw nothing happened – it was like joking to myself about God and what God is. As I became interested in science, I started thinking about the world in a much more realistic way. I realized I never really believed in any power like God. As I became more involved with what was happening in Israel I started to less appreciate the Jewish religion. Religious people are too extreme – so Orthodox they can't let you enjoy the religion even as a tradition, not necessarily believing in God.

I now find myself an atheist – not only do I dislike any kind of tradition, I think it contributes to racism in the world. And I don't see myself as a Jew, although I know it may be hard to ignore the fact that the country where I live has a really special history. I don't find it unique, I don't feel proud to be a Jew. Maybe the people themselves were racist years before – even when you read the Bible, they told themselves they were the best, had the right God, and fought everyone else who didn't think the same way. Religion and tradition just make people more right-wing.

I'm lucky I was in the army many years ago – from 1979 to 1981. If I had to be in the army now, I don't know if I could make it. It's hard to live in a country where I oppose what is going on. I'm not at all patriotic, I never was. But now I do not feel proud of my country. It's not only because of the *intifada*; people are becoming more capitalist, materialist, selfish. You can feel it in the street – the average Israeli is so impatient. Most are becoming more right-wing because of the *intifada*. When I remember myself fifteen years ago, whenever I discussed politics with friends, they used to see me as radical because I was more left-wing than the average. But still, there were many things I could accept about this country, but today I really can't. I feel things are not only not getting better, they're getting worse. Gaby and I thought about leaving Israel last year when we were in London. But it's hard to leave a place where you know everything, the language and of course friends and community.

Living here, I try to do something. What you can do as an individual, to begin with, is not to take part in the *intifada*. It means if you are a soldier not to go and help against the *intifada*, as a citizen not to live or work in the Occupied Territories. For example, I told you I have to work in clinics. They can send me to Arielle or near Jerusalem, places in the Occupied Territories. If I am assigned to one of these places I won't go there although it's a better assignment than Kiryat Shemonah. This apartment was painted and remodelled before we moved in by an Arab from Aza. When he came and worked here, we felt we wanted to help him. We gave him a lot of stuff we don't need, we let him stay here, and even after we moved in, we let him sleep here a few nights, because we knew if he is out in the streets, the police would catch him. Arabs can't be here in the evenings without a licence. We feel very guilty about what is happening in the *intifada*, and we try to be as nice as we can to him.

Another thing you can do against what happens here is to be active, to fight for your own opinion, to persuade other people to think the way you do. But it's hard. Not only are people not being more reasonable, they are becoming more extreme. It's snowballing. When the *intifada* began more than a year ago, we had so much energy to go to Women in Black, in Dizengoff in Tel Aviv. We talked with many people before and after, and went to many meetings – we were really full of energy. But today I am feeling very frustrated. Still, we *have* to continue it. And even though you can't see results, it's important to show what you are thinking. If you can affect one or two people to feel the same as you do or make them feel more strong in their beliefs, this too can help. I don't know what really you can do else.

*

I didn't read much about feminism when I was young, but now I think I was always feminist. From the time when I was a teenager and started to go out with boys until I got out of the closet I felt awful, because I felt I had to play a certain type of role I don't like. One of the things about being heterosexual for me was I found it hard to act like a typical woman. I remember

my relatives always asked me what I was going to do after I finished the army, and I told them I might study medicine. They told
me, 'No! Medicine, that's too big for you. You should be a
teacher. That's very convenient for a woman.' I was angry inside
me about all these things. I felt I could never be what I wanted to
be. One of the reasons I feel much happier as a lesbian is not
being with men, because I feel that at least in Israel, most of the
men – 99.9 per cent – are chauvinists. And if not chauvinists, you
can find a bit of chauvinism in them.

Even before I got into lesbianism or feminism, I really felt as
a feminist. I always tried to prove myself not only as myself, but
also as a woman. Like seeking an important job in the army, and
then going to medical school. Afterwards when I got out of the
closet, my first girlfriend wasn't a feminist. I really felt very angry
about that relationship – that she had a husband, all that stuff.
When I met Gaby, I could read about feminism because she has a
lot of books. She took me to feminist lectures and activities, and at
the beginning I felt so ignorant! I knew I hadn't had a chance to
read about feminism, but in time I realized you don't have to read
to be a feminist.

That's how I got into CLAF. I joined a group that started to
have cafe evenings at the Feminist Movement for women twice a
month. We tried to have things about feminism, but there were
mostly lesbian social events. After some time CLAF began. And
now that I am an organizer of CLAF, I'm all the time learning more,
and becoming stronger inside, more decisive about what I think
about life and feminism, more complete about my decision about
being a lesbian.

When I was first out of the closet, I never thought I could live
as a lesbian couple. I was too much afraid of what people would
think. I didn't feel good inside myself. Being a lesbian was too new
for me. But then I went to a course about being in the Help Line of
the SPPR – what we call the White Line – and it strengthened me to
help other gay people. It also helps me to live with someone who is
strong, sure, and confident about herself. All these things are a
process that continues till today.

In myself I think more about what is happening in Israel –
the *intifada*, feminism – it's kind of a process happening inside me.

Maybe what is happening in the country is more good reason to think about it. It's all quite serious.

Note

1.   123,000 Jews, virtually the entire Iraqi community, emigrated in Operation Ali Baba.

גילה
Gila Svirsky
Edited by Gila Svirsky

• Gila Svirsky, born 1946

Gila is a tall, robust woman with a strong, pleasant voice and a mass of mostly grey curls. Her parents are Lithuanian Jews. Her father was a writer and dramatist before emigrating to the US on the eve of the Depression. He met her mother on a trip to Palestine, where she then lived. Both are ardent Zionists.

With her life partner, Lee, she has given anonymous interviews to the Israeli press about their lives as lesbians. For this publication, however, nearly everyone in her story has agreed to the use of her or his real name.

Since giving this interview, Gila left her job at the New Israel Fund to focus more on her writing, and has also deepened her political activism on several fronts, most publicly as Chair of the controversial human rights organization, B'Tselem.

FORTY-TWO years ago I was born on a chicken farm in New Jersey, the youngest of three children and the only girl. Both my parents were Yiddish-speaking and close to Jewish tradition. My brothers and I were sent to Orthodox Jewish day schools – yeshivot – though my parents' level of Orthodoxy was not as strict as that of the school.

My mother had strong convictions about everything, including me, and that ran to a strong distaste. This is hard for me to explain, considering I tried so hard to win her love. On the other hand, my father was passive throughout my growing up. In fact, I never had any relationship at all with him until I was in my thirties and he was in his seventies, because he had made such an effort to dissociate himself from what was happening to me. I should probably be angry at him for not standing up for me, but I'm not. I can't afford to write off both my parents.

One more unhappy element comes into the picture of my childhood: my brother sexually molested me about half a dozen times when I was ten to thirteen. He would play at 'wrestling' with me, and soon he'd take his pants off, pin me, and jerk off. I don't ascribe as much weight to this phenomenon in my psyche as my relationship with my mother. In my perspective of my family, my brother's deeds have diminished significance.

Life outside the home, on the other hand, was rather happy. I did well in school and had many friends. Even better were the summers, when my parents sent me to Orthodox-Zionist camp, where we spoke Hebrew and talked about going to live in Israel.

Not only did camp get me out of the house, but I excelled there: I was popular, a good athlete, and one of the ringleaders for mischief. Later, as a teen, I also loved the opportunity to be with boys.

At thirteen, I left the yeshiva for public school. Although being among non-Jews was new for me, junior high was a sheltered experience, as the kids came mostly from white, middle-class backgrounds. The real shock was the all-girls public high. About half the school was black and the rest immigrants from Puerto Rico, Cuba, Poland, Hungary – wherever revolutions were being quashed or ending. Very few Jews. There was hostility among the ethnic groups, and sometimes even violence – knives and guns.

My first Monday in high school, I sat down next to my deskmate. 'Hi, Audrey, how was your weekend?' She looked at me and growled, 'Shit, girl, we got busted holding up a bar.' Needless to say, academic expectations of the students approached zero.

My social life in public school was nothing compared to the yeshiva. In sixth grade, yeshiva kids used to hold Saturday night parties complete with 'heavy petting' between dancing to Paul Anka and Frankie Avalon. Weekdays after school – on the beds of our parents who were at work – we did everything but penetration: naked bodies, finger fucking, and gooey condoms to dispose of afterwards. The closeness was fun and the sex tolerable. But the public school boys scared me – as did non-Jews in general. So I had to wait for summers at camp to renew my socio-sex life. Winters were mostly a social wasteland, except for the occasional camp boyfriend who was horny enough to take a bus across the river to New Jersey to get jerked off.

In high school, I made enough mischief to amuse my classmates while avoiding big trouble. I excelled in sports, which – combined with false modesty – earned me friends. I was editor of the school newspaper, and we did some courageous pieces I'm proud of to this day. I was lucky enough to do well on the college boards and get into a good university, because my high school grades were nothing to speak of.

At Brandeis University, I was challenged with ideas for the first time, and I loved it – reading, lectures, even writing papers. Once I discovered philosophy, it became an obsession and I majored in it. I was also active in sports in college – captain of the girls' basketball and softball teams. I loved the physicalness, the competition, the teamwork. *The Boston Globe* proposed me for best athlete of 1966 as a way to disparage Bob Cousy and the Celtics who were having an off-season. Who cares why; I was thrilled.

A lot happened to me on the Jewish front in college. Through high school, my rebelliousness included moving away from Orthodoxy. But things changed at college. It began because I simply *couldn't* eat non-Jewish food. So I joined the 'kosher line' and that, of course, put me together with the religious students. I ended up returning to the religious fold I had left in the yeshiva.

I started to attend services in the Hasidic community near Brandeis. They were ultra-Orthodox – black-frocked men, long-sleeved women. I became close to the 'Bostoner Rebbe' and spent many weekends at his home. Living with the Rebbe and his family strengthened my religious convictions. Although there was some conflict between my studies and religion, the Rebbe preached *'na'a-seh v'nishma'* – just do it, and ultimately you'll get the point.

I went to Israel on a junior year programme. Hebrew University, 1966–67: what an exciting year. Besides the foreignness of the experience, this was the year of the Six Day War, which magnified all the Zionist conviction I already had. I went back to Brandeis briefly to finish my BA, and came right back to Israel. I think of my aliyah as dating from 1966, because at that moment I made the commitment to live in Israel.

When I moved to Israel, I started studying communications. I finally had my fill of philosophy, and wanted to try something in the real world. This is when I met my first serious male friend and also had my first all-the-way screw – after which I asked, 'Is it over?' Issy was an Israeli zoology student who took me to the desert to collect scorpion specimens. Issy was a difficult guy to get along with – he even slugged me twice during disagreements when he wanted me to 'come to my senses'. Nevertheless we decided to get married. As soon as I said yes, I knew it was a bad idea. But, having told my parents, it somehow felt too late to change my mind. Wedding arrangements were made, guests were flying into Israel and gifts were arriving at my door. I panicked and held a rap session with my roommate. 'You can have an unpleasant break-up

now,' Ilana wisely counselled me, 'or divorce down the line, with
joint property and children to complicate it.' I knew she was right.
The day before the ceremony, I got up the nerve to tell him. This
time I ducked before he swung and ran off to tell my parents. My
father's first words: 'This is the happiest day of my life.'

I continued graduate school, and had a series of affairs.
Playing the field again was fun. Sex also turned out to be better
with other guys, though orgasms were still confined to the private
domain of sex with myself. Still, I loved the arousal of being naked
with a man. Does it sound as if I was no longer Orthodox by now?
The paradox is solved: Orthodox in all but my sex life! My parents
were right: yeshiva was good training for life.

*

Then I met Shimon. I was twenty-four, he was thirty-six –
older, wiser, divorced, a man-about-town. I fell in love with Shimon, became good friends with his two teenage daughters, and was
excited to become part of a ready-made family. This started out as
an affair of the heart.

I began teaching philosophical aspects of communication at
Hebrew University and at Lifta Experimental High School in Jerusalem. The high school was more fun. Once I invited a woman to
lecture who was doing her doctorate about a lesbian commune in
San Francisco. We all thought it was fascinating, though it didn't
mean more to me in those days than hearing about a tribe in Africa.

Shimon and I had two daughters, and I enjoyed being a
mother. I even gave up teaching and my doctorate for a six-year
period to stay home and care for my younger child, Denna, who
had both arms paralysed in a bad delivery by a lousy obstetrician.
We did intensive physical therapy, and today she's fine: she has
some disability, but unless you know it, you wouldn't notice.

Being a wife was becoming less sanguine, however. I was
married for fourteen years, which breaks down biblically into seven
plentiful and seven lean years. The seven plentiful years were the
good relationship with my husband and my satisfaction with life as
a mother and a professional. When the good days ran out it took
me seven lean years to work up the nerve to separate from Shimon,

mostly out of fear I wouldn't be able to support myself economically.

I was only thirty-two when I first wanted to end the marriage, but he pleaded, 'Please don't, we can work it out.' I gave it a chance, again and again. I might never have had the guts to leave had I not found a good job. At thirty-eight I finally moved out. The separation was hard for him; for me it was nirvana – moving into my own quiet home, being able to say to the children what I wanted to say to them, having my own quiet life to come home to in the evenings. Paradise.

The job was Director of the New Israel Fund. That was about four years ago. I love being involved in progressive work in Israel – civil rights, women's rights, Jewish–Arab co-existence, and so forth. My task is to oversee the selection and fiscal monitoring of programmes we support and to advocate on behalf of these issues in Israel. I get to deal with issues important to me, to work with a terrific staff, to meet people who you read about in newspapers, to travel a lot, and to have a role in deciding how to spend an awful lot of money.

The only part of New Israel Fund politics that I did not feel in my heart when I took on the job was feminism. I thought then that feminism had nothing to do with me. It was men who opened my mind about this, because I didn't yet respect the opinions of most women. After that, sitting in the director's chair and hearing the feminist views of women's organizations, my own consciousness was raised. In fact, I would say transformed. Today I'm a committed feminist.

The only thing left out of this job is creative writing. Writing is an important part of me. Sure, I do political journalism and PR for my work, but what's important to me is writing fiction. When I think of the various components in my life – writer, lover, friend, New Israel Fund Director, mother – writer always comes first.

*

I never thought of myself as lesbian as I was growing up. I remember asking myself at relevant moments, 'Could it be I'm a lesbian?' And I would answer, 'Definitely not!' I've always had a great time with boys and later on with men, even though orgasms were not part of it. I used to think orgasms during intercourse were exclusively a male prerogative. Today, although I continue to find men attractive, I don't want to have anything to do with them sexually. I've had a number of men in my life, sexually and emotionally, and now I want women in my life.

But for most of my life, I was not with women sexually. I've always had close friendships with women, and I've always wanted to be close physically with those friends: to hold hands, put my arms around them, sleep next to and cuddle them. But not have sex. 'Making love' seemed different to me in those days, and had genitals attached to it.

I had a close friendship throughout my marriage with a woman whom I fantasized about in this non-genital way. I was madly in love with her – I tried to entice her into going to Europe or Eilat, anything to be together. I couldn't get her to be as physical as I wanted to be. Was this lesbian? I only wanted to hold her, not fuck her. Yes, today I think this is lesbian.

That was a special friendship, and the closest I got to an avowed lesbian experience until the turning point in my life, which came five years ago, when I was thirty-seven years old.

*

A woman friend of Shimon's from Germany came to see Israel. Sibylle was forty years old, a convert to Judaism, and breath-takingly beautiful. From the moment she walked into our home, I was smitten with her dark hair, blue eyes, and air of recklessness and independence. I was desperate to get away from Shimon but couldn't talk him into separating. Sibylle stayed with us, and she and I spent lots of time touring Jerusalem together, talking – me watching her eyes, her face, her skin, wanting to be closer with her. Finally, one night, as Shimon and I stopped by her bedroom door to say goodnight, I was overcome with desire. I went to her bed, lay down next to her, and put my arms around her. She put her arms around me, and I thought I was in heaven. Then I heard Shimon come over and say, 'Move over and make room for me.' 'No, Shimon,' said Sibylle firmly, 'let Gila and me be alone now.' I was thrilled. Shimon left, not happy, and I spent an unforgettable night.

I don't know what allowed me to do that. It was completely

unplanned. Sibylle and I had never talked about love or sex between us, neither of us had ever before been with a woman, and all this was in full view of my husband. It made me feel euphoric, powerful.

We spent the next few nights together, and I was utterly, passionately in love. Then Shimon demanded: 'I want equal time.' I didn't know what Sibylle wanted and she didn't know what I wanted, so we had a *ménage-à-trois* for a few nights. When I admitted to Sibylle, 'I don't want to be together with him, I want to be just with you,' she agreed! He was hurt and angry, and eventually tried to get back at me by collecting evidence of lesbianism to use in a custody battle. But that was the beginning of a great love affair, and I was too euphoric and defiant to worry about it. After she returned to Germany, I wrote passionate love letters. Six months later, I flew off to see her, but she no longer wanted me as her exclusive lover – she had fallen in love with a German man. Oh, I was very sad!

But Sibylle had broken the dam. After Germany, I continued to the States on business. I decided to find out what the women's world is all about, and I explored every lesbian bar I could find in New York, Chicago, Toronto, and Washington.

I don't know if I had a period of transition; it was more like an earthquake. It was discovery time, adventure time, time to unleash long pent-up forces, and I went at it with a vengeance. I went to bars, felt up women, and laid as many as I could – then went on to try to turn on all the straight women in my life. Like other born-agains, I was busy proselytizing, and I did convert a few. It was an exciting period, and there were exquisite tender moments. My trips to the States meant board meetings by day and gay bars by night. But then I met and fell in love with Lee.

*

I was exhilarated, knowing I could do anything I wanted with my life, and was no longer tied down to one person. Delirious with freedom, I allowed myself to try everything in the States. In Israel, however, the pursuit of happiness turned out to be more elusive.

In a closeted society like Israel, it's not easy to get in touch with women who are interested in relationships with women. The one lesbian couple I knew in Jerusalem put me in touch with some women, but there were so few. In the States, at least there were bars and discotheques to meet each other; what was there in Israel?

I learned the key question in Jerusalem for identifying another lesbian: 'Were you active in Kol HaIsha?' While not a lesbian organization, there had been enough lesbians at Kol HaIsha to make me hopeful if a woman said yes. Music was also a useful indicator, as in: 'Do you like women's music?' then tossing off the names of a few lesbian singers. But these techniques didn't always work, of course. Not every Israeli lesbian has heard of Cris Williamson! I often had to resort to turning on straight friends.

I met Lee by chance. My daughters and I were at a demonstration – planting trees in a Palestinian village – to protest the Israeli occupation. We spent the day planting and listening to political harangues. Towards evening, we hitched a ride back in someone's van. Just as we were about to pull out, a woman asked for a ride. As she was about to hop into the empty back row, she noticed a little space left in our row. 'Why not?' she said playfully, and hopped in beside us. I was surprised by how friendly that was – to squish into the middle seat when the whole back row was empty. I noticed what a beautiful smile she had. We talked a little and soon my antennae were up. I was interested – if only the sexual orientation would be right! Although chances were slim, I was hopeful. You'd need a lot of inexperience – as I had – to nurture that hope.

She'd said her name was Lee so I discreetly asked around about her, but her friends were even more discreet. My best informant said, 'As far as I can tell she's in a period of celibacy.' What did that mean? I hadn't heard of celibacy since my studies of medieval history! Finally I called her up one Friday night and invited her 'to come visit and have some coffee and talk'. 'It sounds great,' said Lee, 'but there's the problem of getting home.' Neither of us had a car and of course there's no public transportation in Israel on Friday nights. 'Yes I know,' I said slyly. 'If it's easier, you can stay overnight.' Ah, so cool. 'It sounds wonderful, but my parents expect me for dinner on Friday nights.' Sigh. 'However,' she continued – my heart aflutter – 'I'd really like to see you tomorrow night' – my heart now in heaven – 'and sleeping over sounds like fun.' Voila! A live one!

The next night Lee came for her visit. I was excited and nervous. I offered her a drink. 'Any herbal tea?' she inquired. I'd never even heard of herbal tea, so I sat drinking wine and coffee and she drank *hot water*. But the conversation was great. Finally when I thought it was late enough, I said, 'I don't know if the buses will still be running – why don't you stay over?' 'Fine,' she said. Then I said, 'You know, there are so many damn beds in this house now the children are away, but why don't you just stay with me in my bed? We can keep on talking.' 'Fine,' she said, and from there, everything was natural. The night was warm and loving. I was in Paradise. In the morning I was amazed to learn this had been Lee's first time with a woman and my initiative had come as a total surprise to her. My intentions had not been clear and her encouragement of me unintended!

That was it. I fell head over heels in love with Lee, and I don't think I waited more than a day to tell her so. 'And while we're on the subject,' I said, 'let's start a family together and raise children and would you like to move in and let's get going!' But she was not as eager – rash? – as I was; Lee would take more time about this. As for me, I had only one tiny request: I wanted a serious relationship, but I was not willing to tie myself down. 'Fine,' she said, and that's how we set it up. We spent lots of time together, but I was not monogamous, continuing to have affairs here in Israel and cruising the bars in the States. But I was feeling closer and closer with Lee, and I would always come back to her and be amazed at how good it felt to be with her.

You'd have to talk to Lee about how she was able to accept this lopsided arrangement. It would have been hard for me if she had told me she also wanted to be with other people. But early on, Lee said that equality is not necessarily the model for relationships. One has to have a relationship that's satisfactory to both parties, and needs are not necessarily equal. For me, it was a whole new way of thinking about relationships.

I did not cut down on my excesses, but something was happening to me inside. I noticed it on Lee's birthday, about five months after we began our relationship. She had a party to which I went, but – in the spirit of independence – left early to meet another woman. And I slept with that other woman, but it felt wrong. I woke up early feeling like a jerk. What was I doing here? I wanted to be with Lee. I showered, dressed, and took a bus to Lee's house. I tapped on the door – it was about six a.m. – and she opened it, all groggy and bleary-eyed, and let me in. Then she took me in her arms, and I loved the sleepy feel of her, and her trust of me, and her totally giving love. We lay in her bed and I held her as she went back to sleep, and all I could think of was how much I wanted to be just with Lee, to quit all this running around, and go to sleep and wake up with her every morning.

That's when I realized, to my surprise, that I wanted a monogamous relationship with Lee. Sexually, I wanted to be just with her. She said that was fine with her. It wasn't much later we made a commitment to each other. Nothing formal, just agreeing out loud that we were committed to each other for the rest of our lives. I told all my friends; she shared it selectively; and that was that. It felt *great*.

I have been monogamous ever since and it feels right. I love the security of the commitment, of having someone who I know will love me the rest of our lives, as I will love her. It's a combination of passion and the decision. I choose her because of the kind of person she is and I choose her because I choose her. And she chooses me for those reasons. It would take some enormous undermining of who I am or who she is for either of us to break off the relationship. We'll always work toward preserving it.

We don't have a set pattern in our lives. At home, both of us take part in all the 'traditional' roles: raising the girls, cooking, cleaning, household obligations, and also taking responsibility for earning enough money for us all. Our finances are completely joint. I'm amazed Lee wants to share all this, because, after all, the children add extra burdens on her life.

Lee and I have worked hard at figuring out what's good for us, but not everything is down pat yet. For example, I'd like to be more affectionate in public than Lee feels comfortable with. Or take my old crowd of friends from marriage, whom I've known for decades. At our get-togethers, I would love to put my arms around Lee and be physically close, but it's not surprising she doesn't, because some of them think this lesbianism is a weird trip. I'd like a group of friends with whom we'd *both* feel comfortable. I wouldn't want to confine it to only women or only lesbians, but I want it to be a group where it's perfectly fine to dance close with Lee or whatever I want that I would ordinarily do.

There are still glitches to work out, but the relationship feels great. I hope it lasts forever.

★

Let me talk a little about my children. Raising children in a lesbian home adds complexity to being a co-parent. Lee has a special relationship with Denna. They love each other and are affectionate with one another. Lee gives her a lot of things I can't give her because I'm a different kind of person. Mieka has a problem with Lee moving into our household. It's not simple for her. Maybe that's part of the reason she moved back in with Shimon.

When Lee and I first became a couple, Mieka was thirteen and she thought my affair with a woman was neat. She thought she had a really cool mum and in the beginning she shared it with her friends. But she got so many negative responses she started to keep it to herself. And she stopped thinking of me as cool. Now it's just 'Look, you have your shit and I have my shit and that's fine.'

School has been a problem of sorts. I always make a point of going to PTA meetings, but once I asked Lee to attend one I had to miss. Denna, however, said that would make her uncomfortable: 'What if someone asked Lee who she is and what child she represents?'

Don't forget, neither of the girls has friends who have a gay parent. We come from a typical Israeli background, where everyone appears to be straight. I'm sure my children feel isolated by the fact that their mother is a lesbian. They don't talk about it with their friends. They just have it deep inside them. They certainly can't talk to their father about it. He thinks it's disgraceful – an abnormal and unhealthy environment. I feel bad for them.

One Saturday I decided to open a discussion with Denna about lesbianism. 'I'd like to talk to you about something that's on my mind – my relationship with Lee and how you feel about it.'

'Oh, Mummy, again?' she groaned.

'Have I already spoken to you about this?' I asked.

'All the *time*.'

'So tell me how you feel about it.'

'It's *fine* with me, Mummy,' she said. 'You lead your life your way, and I'll lead my life my way. Lee's a nice person and I love her. Now stop worrying about it.'

Then I thought of something else. 'One more thing,' I said to Denna. 'I'm really uncomfortable with the word lesbian.' And she said, 'Oh, so am I – it's like a curse word! At school when you want to talk about some girl who's not nice, you call her a lesbian. And a guy's a homo. I don't like that.' And I said, 'I know. Neither do I. Besides, I don't feel like a lesbian. I feel awkward telling you this, but I want you to know something: I would feel comfortable being with a man, just as I would feel comfortable being with a woman. I choose to be with Lee because I love who she is, not because she's a woman. I'm open to either a woman or a man and that's called being bisexual, not lesbian.' And she said, 'Oh, good, I'm really glad you don't call yourself a lesbian. That's *much* better.' Maybe I should not have denied the lesbian label, but I wanted to make it easier for her, and what I said was theoretically true.

I wish there were some way I could help them feel supported in this, but I can't think of anything. At least they have each other.

★

I'm out to everyone except my parents. There's no way I could be out with them, but I am completely out elsewhere. I guess you can do that when you live in separate countries.

The New Israel Fund is one of the only workplaces in Israel where you can be out and it's perfectly acceptable. From the outset, I asked Lee if she would accompany me to social functions of the Fund. We were a little nervous about it, but it was fine for the American board members and eventually became acceptable to the Israeli board members as well. In the office, my relationship with Lee comes up in natural and not so natural ways. Recently there was a feature about us in an Israeli women's magazine. It was a serious article, but had highly provocative pictures – not of Lee and me, because we were anonymous, but of two naked women caressing each other. Ironically, in the same issue, there was a feature about the New Israel Fund. The day the magazine appeared, I walked into the office and found the staff reading the article about the Fund. 'Believe it or not,' I said, 'in the same issue there's another piece about the Fund.' 'Where?' they asked in surprise. 'Just a few pages earlier.' They turned to it and we all burst out laughing when they saw the article and especially the embarrassing photos. It pleased me that I could be so open with them, and I think they enjoyed having an outrageous director.

I don't give much thought to homophobia in Israel, just as I don't give much thought to my lesbianism. Gay rights are not as important to me as the peace issue, even though there is *terrible* homophobia in Israeli life. AIDS has raised some awareness to the existence of the homosexual community, but you still don't see gay couples walking with their arms around each other in Jerusalem – though you might see it here and there in Tel Aviv. I wish I would see it in Jerusalem, or even myself be a role model here. It would help everyone's morale to see it more.

I don't feel comfortable in any categories. There's no doubt in my mind that I identify more with women and I'm angry with men as a group, but I spend so much energy working with men, having good male friends, and striving together for a pluralistic society, that I can't be insular and feel exclusively woman-identified.

*

I'm politically active outside my job. For example, I go to every Women in Black vigil, and I believe peace demonstrations in Israel are effective. They raise public awareness and shift opinion, creating pressure the leaders must take into account. Fifty-four per cent of this country would not be supporting territorial compromise had it not been for Peace Now demonstrations and the like. Peace demonstrations tell the Palestinians they have allies in Israel. They tell [then US President George] Bush he can lean on Israel and there will be support from the inside. They tell Arab governments there's a movement inside Israel exerting pressure for peace. President Mubarak in Egypt said recently, 'The peace movement in Israel is what enables us to continue talking.'

*

To bring us full circle, I should explain how all of this fits in with an Orthodox Jewish point of view: it doesn't. Living in Israel, my religiosity has faded. Politics has become more and more important to me. My job is highly political and I spend much of my free time doing political work. Making grants is not enough for me; I also want to be on the front lines.

When I leave the New Israel Fund, it will have to be either to become a reclusive writer or for a political career. And it looks like the writer in me is winning the argument. Some of this decision has to do, of course, with knowing how difficult it would be to slog my way to political office, although I think I have the qualities required to get there. But what my heart wants now is to be a reclusive writer. So we'll never know how far I could have gone . . . until I change my mind again.

As for the longer haul, Lee and I intend to be together for the rest of our working and retirement lives, however long that may be. And to rethink our individual life plans and aspirations anew, whenever the spirit strikes us.

נעמי

Naomi Barach

Edited by Jenifer Levin

• Naomi Barach, born 1953

Naomi was thirty-five at the time of this oral history, a PE teacher by training, and lifelong resident of a kibbutz in northern Israel. Divorced, mother of a fifteen-year-old son, she had begun living with Michelle, her American lover of five years, about six months before.

Naomi's parents, both in their sixties, were two of the settlement's founders. Her father is Ashkenazi – blond-haired and blue-eyed; her mother is from a religious Sepharadi family from Iraq. Naomi, dark-haired and dark-skinned, identifies emotionally with the Sepharadi part of her family.

Despite her lifelong commitment to the communal ideal, preservation of individual difference is fiercely important to Naomi. She is quick to point out that both her parents were highly individualistic and rebellious in their youth.

At the time of this interview, Naomi had recently been appointed to a two-year stint as kibbutz mazkirah, *a difficult administrative position which only the most respected and responsible members of the kibbutz community are asked to occupy – and which many gladly avoid. As this is the first time she and Michelle have really lived together, they are still in the process of negotiating some of the day-to-day practicalities of their relationship. Michelle, who is younger than Naomi, doesn't quite share her lover's enthusiasm for communal life.*

I WAS a healthy, independent kid. My father says I was stubborn. But I always knew what I wanted – and I got it. I was closer to him, I think, than to my mother – although I wasn't too close to either one of them. My mother was more flexible and accepting; he had a lot of expectations.

When I started school on the kibbutz, there were only four kids in my age group – three girls and one boy. So we studied with my brother's age group – they were two years older, five boys and one girl – and a single teacher. That was our school: ten kids studying with one teacher, living in a little house with three rooms – one to sleep in, one to eat in, one to study in. We used to do everything together – there was no separation between boys and girls when we played, for instance. I remember it as a very, very good time in my life.

By the fourth or fifth grade, the boys and girls began to grow apart. I usually played with the boys – football, outdoor kinds of games – I mean, I was friends with the girls, but I preferred to play with the boys because it was more interesting, more fun, and it was mostly outside, which I loved.

I didn't find studying too difficult. I learned about things that interested me, and if I didn't care about it I'd say, 'So what!?' You see, at that time on the kibbutz, the attitude was that studying wasn't very important; but physical labour, working the land – that was important. As high school kids, we used to skip school, and on the kibbutz, if you don't go to school you have to work. Usually, grown-ups were glad to see a kid skip school, because they always needed more workers. This attitude is beginning to change now-adays; kibbutznikim see that if you don't study, you have no future. Even if you stay on the kibbutz, the community needs professional people. But, when I was a kid, all the work was very simple. I mean, we grew bananas, we picked fruits and vegetables, and that was life – that was the future.

After high school most kids go directly into the army. But a kibbutznik can choose to serve the country first, for one year, outside of the army, in which case his or her drafting is postponed. So for a year you might work in the Youth Movement, or work on a new kibbutz or in a development town.

In my case, I decided to work as a Youth Movement *madri-cha*.* This was great in a way, because it was the first time I'd lived outside the kibbutz. I was eighteen, and stayed in an apartment with five other people. But I also had time for myself, for hanging out at Dizengof,[1] whatever I wanted. Overall, it wasn't a difficult life. But it was difficult, as a kibbutznik, to talk to city kids all the time about kibbutz life – which is what I had to do. Youth Move-ment kids are supposed to at least try out kibbutz life. I worked with kids in the eighth grade, and being city kids they had a lot of things to do, they didn't really have the time to listen to me; I wound up having to go into their school to round them up. After six months I decided, 'Enough, this isn't for me.' I liked the city, but I didn't like the job. I returned to my kibbutz for a few months, and then I went into the army. I was afraid that in the regular army I'd be just a secretary – which I didn't want at all – so I decided to go into Nachal,[2] because as a kibbutznik in Nachal you automatically become an officer.

I'd met Avi before, in the Youth Movement. He's five years older than me, from another kibbutz. We began a relationship when I went into the army and then, after a little less than a year, I became pregnant and decided to get married. As a woman, you can't stay in the army after you're married. So he and I moved here, to my kibbutz.

At first, I tried to get an abortion. But the doctors told me, 'If you have an abortion now, you're going to have trouble conceiving

* Counsellor.

later on.' Well, I believed them, I accepted it without argument. I know now I just didn't have enough information about pregnancy or abortion back then; I was only twenty years old. And my mother really wanted me to have a baby! She said, 'So don't get married, just have the baby – give the baby to me.' And Avi really wanted to start family life.

With us in the beginning, before marriage, we shared a kind of love that was nice. Avi and I had never talked about my lesbianism. But it wasn't new to me. My awareness of it was there all the time – even when I decided to get married. I knew that, one day, I would have to finally let myself go, to accept what I felt about women. It was never my intention to get married and have children. I did it because I thought I didn't have any choice. But privately I told myself there were options; I mean, it didn't have to be forever.

I didn't like myself as a pregnant woman – although I had a very easy pregnancy, felt good, worked up until the last day, stayed in the army until my fifth month – but I just didn't like my body! I used to be thin, run and swim, do a lot of outdoor activity, and suddenly I was slow and *so* heavy. But then – the first day I had Ilan! – motherhood was absolutely the best thing in this whole mess. Before, I didn't even like babies at all! But with Ilan, motherhood just came naturally. I loved it.

Now, of course, I know that's partly because I continued to live my life – I didn't turn into a crazy woman who stopped working and going outside and living just because I'd had a baby. When Ilan was two years old, I began a three-year course of study at Wingate, near Netanya, to learn how to coach gymnastics and teach physical education. I used to visit home every Wednesday afternoon, and return to Wingate; then I'd go back to the kibbutz on Friday, spend Shabbat at home, and be at Wingate again in time for Sunday classes. So for three years, Avi was Ilan's only full-time parent. My mother helped too, of course; she always looked on Ilan as a sort of sixth child. He was not only her first grandson, but the first grandson of the kibbutz.

The fact that I was studying caused no trouble between Avi and me. He used to go to *miluim** for about three months of the

---

* Army reserve duty.

year anyway, because it was right after the Yom Kippur War; so I didn't feel conflicted about being a mother and a full-time student. In retrospect, though, I know Ilan had some trouble with me being gone so much. When I was home, for instance, I'd take him to the children's house at night to sleep, and he used to say, 'Sit with me until I sleep.' But he wouldn't go to sleep; he'd want me to stay with him all night. I knew it was because he missed me. And I felt guilty, of course; sometimes, I still do. A lot of professionals in the field would say it's not the right way to be a mother – to have a child, and just keep doing whatever you want anyway.

I've talked to psychologists about it. But, at the time, I didn't feel I was doing anything wrong. I still don't feel it was a crime! I mean, 90 per cent of the women around me wouldn't have done that – which I think is a shame. Here, the kibbutz can give you all the opportunities you need to have children and still study or have a career, because of the system of communal life. Yet women don't take advantage of it! Especially once they have a child. And I just couldn't be like them. Yes, I know it's not normal. But what other people say doesn't bother me.

During this time, Avi and I had some arguments, some differences. But even if we had problems, we didn't really have time to deal with them. The real trouble between us surfaced when I'd finished studying and came back home.

I must tell you, it was a shock for me. I had to start teaching little kids on the kibbutz. And the first year, I think every teacher will tell you, is the hardest. I felt as if all the studying had been a waste of time. But I decided to stick it out, and by the end of that first year I saw maybe the second year would be better; anyway, I felt I had to give it a try. I'm happy I did, too. Because I really like my job now; I love teaching, I love working with kids.

Also, after returning to the kibbutz, it was obvious to me where a lot of the particular problems in my relationship with Avi came from. The truth is that, during my time at Wingate, I'd had my first affair with a woman. Within two days of meeting her, I knew what I wanted. It was as if it had been waiting there all along; I just had to get off the kibbutz for a while, and there it was.

Still, for a whole two years I just didn't let anything happen. Finally, at the end of my third year, I had the affair. After I came back home, we only had letters, phone calls, that was it. At first, Avi didn't know. But he found out – I still don't know how – I think another woman told him, or maybe he read my lover's letters. This was traumatic and, for him, a terrible crisis. He wanted me to promise it would never happen again. I said, 'I can't do that, I know it will happen again – if not with her, with someone else.'

I was afraid to get a divorce then. Ilan was only five years old. I didn't know how he would accept it and I didn't feel secure enough about myself to be a single parent. So for two more years, Avi and I lived together. That whole time, though, he was checking up on me, asking where I was going. What's interesting is that, after two horrible years, we decided – together, without a fight – that we had to do something about us. Avi said, 'Listen, I want to take some time and go study, I need to clear my head. It's going to be very hard for me.' And we decided to separate. I know now that, if I'd had more courage, I would have insisted we separate as soon as he found out. But Avi was really sincere about trying to keep us together. I knew, though, that I couldn't give him what he wanted – because I knew for sure what I wanted.

Splitting up was the right decision. Because we worked things out together, most everything was all right eventually – about Ilan, about dividing up our belongings, who would stay in the house and who would leave. When we separated, Ilan was seven. On our kibbutz, kids don't get their own rooms until they're around fifteen years old; so for quite a few years Ilan would sleep half the week at my place and half the week at his father's.[3] There are times when I feel guilty, sure; but I can still live with it. To this day, Avi and I deal with everything concerning Ilan together. At school, for instance, we go to speak with his teacher together. If you have children, you really can't ever separate totally. And Avi still lives on this kibbutz. Now we have an okay relationship; we can talk. It's a relief to know if I have to leave for more than a day or two Ilan has another parent to turn to. So ... after our separation I was, as they say, free – but still very closeted, even to myself. In the beginning nobody else knew, except for Avi. I never even told my mother. My sister finally did that for me!

★

Now begins my coming-out story. I mean, it took at least two or three years to be out in the kibbutz. What happened was that I took a workshop course two days a week, near Tel Aviv, that trained you to be a group facilitator. Part of the course was studying group dynamics. We students worked on ourselves, on our own dynamics as a group.

I became very close to the people in this group because we worked together so intimately every week. By this time, too, I had a lover, another kibbutznikit. I was involved with a group that founded an organization in the kibbutz movement to deal with the situation of women on kibbutzim. At the 1982 feminist conference in Jerusalem, about thirty of us got together to talk about our special problems as kibbutz women. We chose a woman from kibbutz Gezer – she's originally Canadian, and a strong feminist – to lead the organization. Anyway, we started meeting once a month in Tel Aviv. That's where I met Chava. She and I were the only women there who identified as radical feminists, so we became friends. In the beginning, we didn't talk about lesbianism. And then she came to visit me with her lover, a woman from Denmark; at the time, they were close to the end of their relationship. Chava hadn't confided in me before, because all she knew about me was that I was divorced and had a kid – but, during this visit, she told me about herself. I just said, 'Yeah, me too!'

Okay. After a few months, we became lovers. This was my first real relationship with a woman. Chava and I were together two and a half years, meeting once every couple of weeks, either here, or on her kibbutz, or in Tel Aviv.

Anyway, towards the end of the first year of this course in group dynamics, I realized I had a lover, a real relationship, and I wanted to start talking about it. During our last meeting of the year, I decided I just had to speak. And I did! That was the first time I ever talked about my lesbianism with a group of people.

Then I took the second year of the course, and started working on it more and more. With this, it became easier for me to start talking about it on the kibbutz, with friends. The problem on a kibbutz is there's so much gossip; in one day, everybody knows everything – especially if it's really interesting. And my lesbianism was interesting, so it became a hot topic for quite a few months. But you know, that was okay. Because I was able to just use it after a while – by not denying anything – and it helped me to come out.

Before this, I'd felt sure if I wanted to live openly as a lesbian, I would have to leave home. It didn't seem possible to live on the kibbutz, near my family, near all my friends, and still be a lesbian. This was a very difficult situation for me, because I really wanted to stay. I love this kibbutz; it's my life. And then, I mean, I was twenty-seven or twenty-eight; I felt I was at the beginning of my real life – and I didn't want to leave.

So I had to work on myself. I don't really know how it happened, but after a year, I began to feel life would be possible here. It was a process for me; and for the kibbutz, too. At first, it was just gossip – I mean, a good story to pass around, behind my back. But then, when they found out I wasn't trying to hide anything anymore, the attitudes started to change. I had a lover, and she visited me. So now everyone knew Chava wasn't just my good friend, but my lover.

For a while, then, the attitude was just 'Okay' – it wasn't an issue the way it really is now. Now people can come and ask me questions, or talk with me about it. Now it's not only an issue; it's something people can discuss. And if they have stupid questions, so what? That's just because they don't know anything about lesbians. On this kibbutz, it's not as if you can *just* come out to your parents, or *just* come out to a couple of friends; here, if you come out, you come out all at once, to 300 people. And, you know, I feel that 300 people went through this coming-out process with me.

I know it sounds frightening. Many gay and lesbian kibbutznikim – most of them, in fact – choose to leave home when they deal with their homosexuality. They go to a city, maybe leave the country altogether for some place like Los Angeles, just to get far, far away. But, I mean, you have to make your own choice. I decided I wanted to stay here. So, I had to deal with that.

On kibbutz, you can't really hide. People always know exactly what you're doing. Or maybe you can hide – I mean, maybe some people can – but you have to put so much energy into it that I know I just couldn't.

For instance, here's a story to illustrate: Michelle was in an ulpan here the first summer we met. She wasn't out, so she told people one weekend she was going to a feminist conference in Jerusalem. Now, on this kibbutz there are many Anglos who read the *Jerusalem Post*, and in the *Post*, the following week, it was reported that 'The first lesbian conference in Israel was held in Jerusalem last weekend.' So people would just stop Michelle and say, 'Oh, so you went to a lesbian conference, eh? – not to a feminist conference!'

On the other hand, people here know me – they know how I am at work, how I am in public, how I was as a kid – they know so many aspects of my life. And then they find out I'm a lesbian! Well, that doesn't just erase my entire personality. And if they like me, if they know I'm okay, I'm good at this, good at that, they're not going to be influenced only by stereotypes. They have to deal with *Naomi* as a lesbian – not with some abstract lesbian stereotype. And that's good. That's what educates people here, I think – that someone they really like, and think is a good community member, a good woman, a good worker, good mother, good teacher, happens to be a lesbian. So they have to really deal with it. They can't say, 'It's because she's ugly' or 'It's because she couldn't find a man.' I mean, it breaks down all the lies. And I think that's good for the community.

As for homophobia, it depends on what level you are calling it that. I mean, homophobia is all over. But it's hard for me to pinpoint it, because whatever I've done, whatever I've wanted and asked for, the kibbutz has had to deal with. I know there is homophobia here, of course. But maybe I don't feel it as much because I don't expect this community to be without homophobia. It's a small community, a conservative community, but I can see how they deal with this issue every single day. And they live with it! They let me teach their children!

As far as the effects of all this on Ilan, I don't know. He doesn't tell me about any problems, and I don't know of any. But I don't think there are any, because, you know, I was the teacher of his age group. So I still have a lot of connection with the kids in that group. I'm not just 'Ilan's lesbian mother'; I'm Naomi – they've known me for a long, long time.

With my brothers and sisters, there's no problem. I mean, my sister was the first one I told; and I talk with my brothers about my personal life all the time. Michelle does, too. My parents are another story. With them, I've never spoken about it. I asked my sister, who is very close to my mother, to come out for me. She's different from me, very emotional, very open. So she spoke with my mother about me. So, after the entire kibbutz knew about it, my parents were the last to find out. My mother told my sister she'd known all along; but it was still hard for her to accept. As for my father, I don't know what he feels – and I don't intend to find out!

In a way, the situation now is almost perfect – partly because I don't feel I want to speak about it with my parents. It's my life. I don't feel comfortable taking on the issue, openly, with the whole family. And throughout my life I've made it clear I have boundaries. Even though we live very closely together, my house and my life are my own. On a kibbutz, with all the intimacy of friends and family, you have to maintain your boundaries.

*

When I met Michelle, I was still involved with Chava. It was summer, five years ago [1984], and a group of Jewish students were here from the USA for a three-month ulpan. The woman in charge of the ulpan came to me and said, 'There's one feminist woman in this group, from Berkeley; she wants to meet other feminists in Israel.' So I invited her to my house. Chava was there, and Michelle knew from the first that we were lovers, not just 'friends'. That evening she told us she was a lesbian. The three of us became friends, and spent a lot of time together.

Michelle and I felt a strong attraction for each other; we didn't know what to do about it, but we felt we'd have to do something. So we decided we'd make love once – that would end it, we thought, and we could be friends afterward. Well, we've been together ever since! And the attraction is still there.

This was the first time I really fell in love. Chava and I had become lovers over time, but I'd never been in love with her. With Michelle, in one night, that was it! I got together with Chava and told her, 'Listen, I think I've fallen in love.' Chava was very, very hurt. Five years later, she still won't speak with us. She was very involved in the feminist community in Israel but left it all, because she said she didn't want to run into me. She's moved away from her own kibbutz; she has another lover now, and lives in Haifa. For me, this doesn't feel right. Israel's a little country, and I know we'll see each other again sooner or later. Some day, we'll have to meet and resolve things.

After the ulpan, Michelle went to Haifa University. Then she decided to go into the army, into a three-month military course of service for new immigrants. It took us a while to see that things between us were too serious just to let go of. She eventually decided to return to the States for a while; and then I came up with the idea of taking a year off and going with her. I had never been away from the kibbutz for that long before. But I wanted to show her she was really important to me.

So here I was, principal of the school, and I was going to leave my job, leave my son, leave my community, and go to another country far away. I didn't know what I'd do there, but I wanted to be with her. She didn't believe, at first, that I'd actually do it. But I'd thought about it a lot and I really had decided. I didn't want to lose this relationship – it was too strong. For me, it was the first relationship I really put energy into. I mean, Michelle and I are so different. She always thinks about the future, and I hardly ever plan more than a year ahead, I just live in the moment and don't like to worry – maybe because I live on a kibbutz and I've never had to. She needs so much I'm not used to giving: like attention, sensitivity, noticing the little things. I've been working on it for five years, and I still have work to do!

But I felt – for me, for us – that we needed to be together. So we went to the States for a year. It was a great year for me – difficult, but great. Michelle has enough energy for five people; she studied and worked, and I worked. Living in Berkeley was like heaven: all the coffee houses, all the women! I don't mean only the lesbians, but the whole feminist environment. Also, I travelled, with and without Michelle. We drove from California to New York together. It was a lot of fun. After this, we decided we'd come back to Israel.

Michelle went into the Interns for Peace programme, where you work with school children in an Arab village for one year and in a Jewish area for the second year. During the first year she lived about forty minutes away from my kibbutz, so we could still see each other a lot. Then she decided she didn't want to stay another year in Israel, she wanted to return to the States. Neither of us knew what would happen. Because if we lived separately, so far away from each other – what then?

She left for a year. That separation caused a crisis between us, because she had another relationship. I knew, too, if she did decide to come live in Israel, it would be on my back. For a lesbian feminist to leave Berkeley and immigrate to Israel is a bit strange! I told her, 'Listen, you have to decide, you know what you're going to miss out on. I want you to come to Israel because, this time, I can't leave my kibbutz; I don't feel I want to.'

Anyway, after all this time of being in a long-distance relationship, Michelle returned last August with a group of new immigrants. We'd decided that, if she made aliyah, we would join a group, the New Wave, that was going to build a new kibbutz; they had decided to accept gays and lesbians in their community. But my kibbutz offered me the job of being *mazkirah*. I told her, 'It's very important for me, I want to do it.'

At first, she didn't want to come to live here. She'd say, 'It's too much yours, I won't feel comfortable, everybody will treat me like Naomi's lover.' She's right – that's true. But she also wanted to be with me. Then she found a job working in a programme called *machonim tsioniim* – they give courses to high school kids about democracy and Zionism, and about what's going on now in Israel between Arabs and Jews. She could work in that programme three days a week, for a good salary, and spend the rest of the time here.

So I went to the kibbutz *mazkirut** and I said, 'Listen, I want my lover Michelle to come live here with me.' After discussion, the mazkirut brings important issues to the *asefa†* for a final decision. Before bringing this issue to the asefa, the mazkirut had a very good discussion. I remember one man saying he wanted to let Michelle come here, because he wanted to know that, on this kibbutz, all kinds of people could live, including lesbians. So, in dealing with issues around homosexuality, this was an important part of the community's process.

---

* A committee of ten that deals with various issues of communal life.
† The kibbutz general meeting, in which all adult members may participate and vote.

Because Michelle's not a kibbutz member, and she works outside and earns her own money – which a member of the community is not allowed to do – she had to be given a really special status. It's a status that, with a man's wife, is called *eshet chaver*. Here, in our case, it's two women, so it has to be *eshet chavera* – wife of a woman member. This status isn't written in the books, but it's the same. It was created to let me have her here. I mean, she *is* the wife of a member. Yeah!

I think now the kibbutz really accepts us. I feel comfortable here. Michelle wants more; she wants to feel comfortable hugging me in public, and I don't feel right about that. But we have a good family life. We have a son, we have two cats, we have a lot of guests. My mother treats Michelle as a member of the family. In the beginning, there was tension between them. But now she invites her to everything, she brings her a present for Passover, or for Rosh Hashanah. And the kids love Michelle. They know she and I live together; they refer to us as 'Michelle's Naomi' and 'Naomi's Michelle'.

Usually, Michelle and I meet after work, around four or five in the afternoon, and we're together for the evening and the night, every day. Sometimes I have meetings during the evenings, and once a week she goes to teach dance at a nearby kibbutz. It's nice; I like it. I mean, I have to get used to it, because for years I lived alone. But family life on the kibbutz is wonderful, it's very peaceful, you don't have to worry about a lot of practical things, you have time to deal with your own personal problems if you want. Our life is really an everyday life, like the life of any two people who decide to live together and then do. If you had told me three or four years ago that this was going to happen to me, I wouldn't have believed you.

Ilan doesn't seem to have a problem with Michelle; he's never mentioned any. They sit, they talk, they play. I think he feels comfortable being with the two of us. At first, things were a little tense; now, though, it's okay. My son has his own life, too – he decides when he'll come and go. Sometimes he won't show up for days. There are evenings I don't know where he is, and I don't see him at all. Sometimes he comes in and sits, and stays. If he's here, even if it's 'our' evening, we don't ask him to leave.

Michelle and I go to feminist events, we go dancing, we go

out to parties. We have quite a few friends now. Most of our friends are couples, and we like that. In the past year, we've had many visitors here, lesbian friends. This kibbutz is a very nice place, and we really encourage them to come see us, because we like spending time with other lesbians. Although I know that, as a kibbutznikit, I expect them to act a certain way, in keeping with the way people generally act on kibbutz; I don't want my guests to be – how do you say it? – demonstrative. In my house, okay; but outside, or in the dining-room, I prefer they don't show physical affection. And I think my friends understand this. People know most of the women who come to visit me are lesbians; it's not a big deal any more.

There's a gay man who lives here, too. He has a lover, from a moshav nearby, so they spend three days a week at the moshav, and the rest of the time they stay here. They're out, everybody knows about them. I don't feel as much support from him as I would with a feminist woman – I mean, he is a feminist, but it's not his issue. We're still close, though, and that's good for me. And I think it's great for the community.

*

You know, as a kibbutz kid, I was raised to have a negative attitude towards religion. And I was ready to say, until the age of twenty-four, that I was Israeli but not Jewish. Later, when I took the course in group facilitation, we studied about the history of the kibbutz movement and about Judaism. It was the first time I'd ever studied it – I mean, saw a religious text, opened the Talmud, read.

Our studies were very liberal, in the Reform mode, where you read the text and understand it in your own way. That was the first time I ever found a religious text interesting. All the history, and what people said, and thought – it was fascinating to me. I studied for two years, and it opened my mind about my Judaism. I became very much against the *dati*,* but very open to alternative thought – like the Reform, some of the Conservatives, the Reconstructionists. And then, when I met Michelle, we found we think alike in this area. She came from a Reform background, and we just clicked.

* Ultra-Orthodox religious Jews in Israel.

On kibbutz, you don't deal with the issue of Judaism – it's amazing. At least in our particular movement, we study the Tanach as kids; in the kibbutz artzi movement they don't even learn Tanach at all! And this is a problem, because when we have weddings or celebrate holidays, we copy what religious Jews do on those occasions, and we don't understand why. We're very secular, yet we think only the religious Jews have the right to be Jews! We accept whatever they tell us! We've given the *dati* the right to interpret all of Judaism! We get married the way they say, we get divorced the way they say – everything, all our lives. And we think we don't have any alternative, because it's law in Israel. I think it's absurd. I hope the Reform movement in Israel – through the kibbutzim of the Reform movement – will work very hard on this issue.

You know, the people who built the first kibbutzim came from religious families in Europe. They left partly because they were anti-religious. So they abandoned everything; they decided to work the land and forget about the books, they wanted to create a new kind of Jew in Israel. Only now, when you see the first and second generation of people who grew up on kibbutz – you know, I'm second generation, and my son is third generation – you see it's created a great emptiness. I mean, you can't live in Israel without roots to your own Jewishness. Well, you can, but it leaves a big hole inside you.

Not many people think like I do, though. Or maybe they do, but they're scared to say anything. We'll see. I believe this issue will arise on the kibbutzim – slowly.

*

I think Israel is really two countries right now – not just politically, but mentally. I see progress in issues of feminism and lesbianism. But if I look at the other part of Israel – at the very conservative people who vote Tchia and Likud – I don't see progress at all. So it's hard to say there's progress in Israel, overall. The point of view is so different between people who believe Arabs are human beings and people who think the Arabs are animals you should kill. These two different points of view can't co-exist.

What will happen? War, between the Jews in Israel? I don't like to say it, but I think it could happen, yeah. The opposing points of view are too far apart for there ever to be a bridge between them. If Israel decides to give back the Territories, I'm sure the *Gush Emunim** will start a war. They won't go quietly: it's too important for them; it's their life. I mean, I can understand in a way. I don't accept it, but they believe in dying for this purpose, so that's what they're going to do.

I've always been proud to be Israeli, and in some ways I still am. But I can't live with the things my country does to the Palestinians. And it's not *just* to the Palestinians; slowly, the rightists are turning against Israel itself. They're turning against people who favour peace. They burn their doors and their cars.

I won't fight them. If this is going to become a fascist country, I won't live here. I don't think I could be part of an underground – I just wouldn't stay.

On the other hand, I still think Israel is the place for the Jewish people. I think we have the right to have a state here. We just don't need the Territories, that's all; and I need to know that Arabs who are citizens here get treated the same as Jewish citizens. But I don't see anyone in government, now, who can effect this – even the Labor party. I mean, there are some very right-wing members of the Labor party. So I don't know what will happen, but it won't be good! It might be okay if the state decided to speak with the PLO, and give back the Territories. Even then, though, there would be war – if not from outside, then from within. So, even in the case of a good decision, the result's going to be bad for Israel.

Also, if the right wing wins in the next elections, it's true this could very easily become a fascist country. But in the long run, if Israel lost half her population because of that, and if people lost faith in what they were doing here, I don't think the country could continue to exist. Israel exists only because the people who've gone to war to defend her with their lives had faith they were doing the right thing, that they didn't have any alternative. That's the only reason! I mean, the Arabs are millions around us. We have the best air force in the world, but that won't be enough forever.

Oh, this is so sad. Let's not talk about it.

*

* West Bank settlers.

To me, 'Lesbian Community' in Israel means, first of all, *feminists* – I mean, activist and political – not only lesbians. A community of lesbians who are just lesbians – that's not enough for me. I need to be part of a community that deals with women's issues, political issues, Arabs in Israel, Israeli issues. One issue of concern to me is that I believe there are *big* problems for women on the kibbutz.

In short, I think the kibbutz is like a traditional family. So all the women work in service positions – with kids, laundry, in the kitchen – work the kibbutz doesn't make money from. The men work in the fields, the factories, the places that bring in money. We have the framework here for a very liberating society, but the women and the men don't know how to make it work. It never was right, from the very beginning. And it's important to me, because kibbutz used to be the leftist, socialist, alternative society in Israel; but it's become the conservative society in Israel on many levels, even the political.

*

As far as things stand with me and Michelle, there have been tensions lately. We've had some problems; we've had some fights. But we try not to leave it. At least we deal with it.

My job is very demanding – it takes almost all of me. I have to deal with complicated, sensitive issues that require a lot of thought, all day, every day. I meet with people, I cope with their problems, I know they have a lot of expectations of me, and I want to do well. Then I come home and I want to nap, I want to read the newspaper, watch TV, and that's it. But Michelle comes in and says, 'Come on, I want to talk with you! We don't talk any more.' And it's true!

It's going to be an issue between us until I finish this job. But it's going to be an issue whenever I do any job I have to put myself into. So I hope I can learn how to reserve and budget my energy. On a kibbutz, you know, you don't just lock the office and go home and not think about work for the rest of the day. At least three times an evening, the phone will ring and somebody will want to talk with me about things.

When Michelle got back to Israel the last time, we sat down

and wrote out a long agreement – five pages! We spoke about all the things that were going to cause problems, and decided what we'd do. So now, I know what she wants from me, and she knows what I want from her. When she says, 'We decided Thursday is our evening, and you scheduled a meeting that evening and I don't like it,' I know I blew it. So, when we make decisions together, we talk a lot.

After my term of office is finished, we may live together somewhere else in Israel, or maybe try America again. After two years here, Michelle has definitely decided she wants to study again. We're sure it's going to mean another year apart – and that frightens me. But I know if we decide to stay together, we'll stay together. It's just a matter of deciding how we're going to handle the time. I feel a responsibility to the community. And to Ilan, too – he's part of the plan. So, it's complicated.

But the truth is it would be difficult for her in Israel. In fact, when she told me she'd decided to study again, my first thought was: 'That's it, she won't stay.' Because whatever she wants to do, she can probably have an easier time doing it in the States. Here, she'd have to work very hard to build the kind of community she wants. If she's willing to fight, if she's willing to work that hard, she can try. But I don't know. It opens up a lot of difficult questions for us.

Notes

1.   A centre of shopping and activity in Tel Aviv.
2.   A special division of the army that sends groups of first-year soldiers to kibbutzim to work and learn first-hand about kibbutz life, philosophy, and management procedures.
3.   The institution of communal children's houses had, by this time, been abolished at Naomi's kibbutz.

סרון
Saron
Edited by Amy Gilley

• *Saron, born 1940*

A counsellor for an agency in a small town near Jerusalem, Saron did her graduate work at Chicago's Eastern University Without Walls in 1980. Although she returned to Israel in 1982, she and her American partner, Rebecca, maintained their relationship until 1989 by making long visits to each other's country.

Saron lives in a stone house that she and her former lover, Na'ama, purchased and remodelled in the early 1970s. It's famous as the site of many big dancing parties for lesbians and gay men.

Forty-eight when recounting her history, Saron is a handsome and witty woman, with shining dark eyes and a rich Greta Garbo voice. She shares her house with her dog 'Cookie'.

I REALLY didn't have a name I liked until a very close friend of mine, Na'ama – who was also my partner – started to call me 'Saron'. I adopted this as my real lesbian name. I was born in Morocco, and my first name was French, Germaine. When we came to Israel my mother re-married; I was adopted and received my step-father's family name. Later, when I was close to eighteen, I almost changed my name to Yael. I wanted, I think, an identity of my own. But I changed my mind when I went into the army. In the army, you make a close circle of friends and because they know you by one name, you don't want to change it. Most of the people in Israel know me as Sara Ganon. But if you ask me, I am not Sara Ganon, I am not Germaine Dabuda, and I am not Sara Gaanon, the way the Americans say it. I feel the most that I am *Saron*.

It started as a joke. Na'ama is Ashkenazi, and I am North African, what we call here in Israel, Sepharadi. In the 1950s the differences between the Ashkenaz and the Sepharadi were very harsh. People were changing their names, from Sepharadi to Ashkenaz – especially the endings. Na'ama called me 'Ganonchik' in order to sound Ashkenaz! Then she started with 'Saron Ganon', and the Ganon was dropped, and it stayed Saron.

Na'ama and I: we are still in close touch. She's like a sister, a good friend. Actually part of this house belongs to her. She has a daughter – she is a single mother. And since I am discussing names, I should mention that I was the one who was asked to choose the name of Na'ama's daughter, and I chose Yael. What luck, finally after years, to name someone the name that really means so much to me. Yael is like my daughter, in a way.

Na'ama and I were together for five years, from 1970 to 1976. When I moved in with her, it was the first time I left my house – I was almost thirty years old. It wasn't far but my mother acted as only she could act. She said, 'If you leave, don't come back any more,' and she didn't talk to me almost ten days! She didn't understand it was time. I just wanted to be completely independent.

This difficult relationship between my mother and myself, I think it is due to the fact that I was born to an unmarried woman. In 1940, for a Moroccan Jew to have a child without a husband was something very special. She had been married and had had my sister eight years before, but by the time I was born, she had long been divorced. I wouldn't know anything about my father even today if I hadn't twisted my uncle's arm. She wouldn't tell me even when I was very sick and told her the doctor needed a family history.

Until I was six years old, I stayed at home. Fatima, an Arabic Muslim Black woman who worked in the house, took care of me. My mother was afraid the Arabs would take us, so she placed us in a convent in Casablanca. I was perhaps too young, but my sister was fourteen – an attractive age for marriage according to the Arabs.

In summer of 1947 we came on a visit to Palestine – and we never left. We had relatives in Palestine who had immigrated in the Magreb Aliyah, a hundred years ago. Things then happened fast. My mother believed the move was fated. She said, 'Maybe this is what has to happen to save my daughters.' We stayed here and abandoned everything in Morocco! The only resource my mother had was some gold jewellery, and she sold a piece whenever we needed some extra food. Ironically, two months after all this happened, the statehood of Israel was declared. So I was here in the time of Palestine. Now if people say, 'Are you sabra?' I say, 'I feel like a sabra but I'm not.' My uncle helped us settle in – all at once we had everything, even a house in the German Colony, a very Orthodox area. I was placed in a religious school. Suddenly I had to speak a different language, and pray! I didn't know what they wanted from me! But my mother said, 'You will learn, it will be

OK.' It took me a year or two but I learned Hebrew. In fact, I taught my mother Hebrew.

I don't know when I knew I was lesbian. Until I joined the army, I considered myself asexual. I'd had two close friendships with boys. In the 1950s, when I was a teen, we weren't as open and free like today's teenagers. If we liked each other, it would only be acknowledged when we were in a group – he would sit by me, but no kissing, no touching. So respectable, so secret – all these little games! In the army, I had my first relationship with a man – he started it. I liked him so we went out. I didn't take it seriously; I didn't fall in love. When he wanted to go to bed and I refused, he left. However, I was a sergeant in the army and I had to train the women. I remember now how many times I would pay more attention to one or another of the women. Not physically, but emotionally, I would try to be close to them. Perhaps here is the beginning of my consciousness as a lesbian.

When I was about to leave the army, I went to the director of my boarding-school to ask for advice about my future. He said, 'Listen, you were good here as a student, so maybe you want to be a counsellor.' That is how I got into counselling as a career.

In the school course there was a woman who had graduated from my boarding-school two or three years before I had. I didn't have any idea she was a lesbian until she started to 'make a pass'. After the first month, she arranged my move to her room. She was the first woman who touched me sexually, and taught me how to touch her. I was very upset, very resistant. For four or five years we were 'friends', but for me it's a bad memory. I don't deny I was a lesbian – I *am* a lesbian – but this relationship was the ugliest. The jealousy! The first year we were studying together, I was frightened someone would discover our relationship. Also the psychology books showed me something was wrong with us. I was lucky my second relationship was so *opposite*. Na'ama is from another planet as a lesbian. Really, she was so patient with me, I flourished back. That's why when I counsel a lesbian couple, I'm conscious of the possible distances. If one of the women came out very early but the other just recently realized her identity, there is a gap there. The power is different. I know every lesbian has her own story about coming out – I just wish no one will have one like mine.

When I met Na'ama, I had also been involved in a relationship with a married man; he was more a friend for me than a lover.
I met him in Allenby Bridge when I was a policewoman there. He
was in *miluim*, army duty. He just bought my heart, because up to
this time, every man who saw me wanted only one thing. I hated it.
But Chaim and I talked a lot, we had fun, we hugged, we kissed, but
that's it! There was a point though when I no longer felt positive
about our friendship. Chaim was fierce, he didn't understand my
ambivalence and then I told him, 'I think I am a lesbian.' This and
my growing friendship with Na'ama were the real moments of self-
recognition for me.

We bought the house together; we worked hard. I was lucky
she had the patience to cope with all my attitudes: I'd become
afraid maybe I shouldn't be with a woman, maybe yes, maybe no,
and I love Chaim but I love Na'ama. Finally I realized that it's OK
that I enjoy being with a woman. I don't need to feel guilty or ugly,
or when I go outside that everybody will look at me, thinking who
knows what. I didn't care when people visited that they saw how
we organized the house. It took a lot of time, a lot of talking with
Na'ama.

Unfortunately one day, when I returned from a trip, I discovered Na'ama had had an affair during the weekend with a
lawyer friend. I couldn't accept it. I was very square at that time; I
said, 'If this could happen, then there must be nothing between us.'
I broke off the relationship immediately! Oh yeah, I was very, very
tough. And I know why! I thought this sort of deception can happen only between men and women.

I've grown up since then – I don't think it has to be this way.
I am very North African. I am very proud. I am tough, a stoic. Even
if you get hurt, don't show it; so the problem continues, but life will
be OK. Until I met Rebecca this was a big part of my personality.
Na'ama also has her toughness. After all, I know Na'ama loves me,
and I love her too. We even tried to go back to each other, before I
met Rebecca. It didn't work, not because we didn't want it to but
because we are both stubborn, proud.

After I left Na'ama, I was working in a poor neighbourhood
with street gangs. I was about thirty-eight or thirty-nine by this
time. I wanted to be a counsellor for all different ages but I had

started my career as a counsellor of children and teenagers, so I gradually moved over to work with the street gangs. One year we had a visitor from Chicago. Joe was a professor in public health at the University of Illinois. He worked with addicts – and most addicts are street gang members. Because I was the senior in this job, he observed my work. At the end of the month, he asked me about my education. I told him that professionally I was a teacher. I didn't have the advanced degree you really should have as a counsellor on the street. When he asked me, 'Would you like to do an advanced degree?' I said, 'Yes!'

Joe explained that there is a university in Chicago called Eastern University with a 'University Without Walls' programme that will accept older people as students. It took me a year to apply. While Joe was checking about the chances of my acceptance in the university, we kept in touch through cassettes and letters. At this time, I was involved in a difficult relationship with a woman I will call Zofi. Zofi was very possessive; she was constantly testing me. I had to prove my love twenty-four hours a day for five years.

It was difficult to decide about going to America. I was afraid, and I had just started therapy – I was almost an alcoholic. For almost four months, I have to admit, Na'ama helped me. Luckily, I was good at work so they didn't throw me out even though I could barely function. Through the counselling I understood that my relationship with Zofi would have to come to an end, but I didn't know how. Her cousin even told me, 'Save yourself. I know her.'

I received a letter from Joe on my fortieth birthday. Joe was actually inviting me to come to the United States. He wrote, 'I talked with my family and everybody wants to know you. You can definitely spend the first three months with us. At the university, the papers are ready. All you have to do is have an interview, and you have to send your curriculum vitae.' I couldn't believe it. Na'ama said, 'I will take care of everything, I will buy you a ticket, and you are going!' I was so *frightened* to leave, but I did it. I even received a year's sabbatical from my job. For me it was like a dream!

I finally arrived in Chicago during Chanuka in 1980. Joe, his wife, and Rebecca, their only daughter, met me. Rebecca had graduated from Oberlin and had just returned from one year biking all around Europe.

Meanwhile Zofi decided to come to New York, to start her master's in television communications. She wanted me to transfer to New York and work on our relationship. But she really wanted to go back to our claustrophobic relationship, to disconnect me completely from Israel and my friends. She came to Chicago, and spent – as 'a friend of mine from Israel' – a week in the house. Joe and his family were wonderful – Rebecca even had a crush on her. We didn't tell them anything about our relationship. Only at night we put the twin beds together. Then something important happened. We were walking on the street and a Black woman turned around to look at me and Zofi decided I was watching her or, I don't know, staring after her or something. I said, 'You are starting again. I didn't look at her any more than she looked at us. That's it! I'm not going to destroy my only chance. I have a family here, I have everything here.' We fought a *lot*. The day Zofi left, we didn't talk for twenty-four hours. But I was free.

Rebecca told me about her life at Oberlin, and her relationships with women and gay people. She asked me about my life, and I was very, you know, talkative about everything *except* about my real life. She was in between two important times in her life, finishing Oberlin, and then after this long trip, running away from the idea that she has to deal with coming back home. We became friends and she thought of me as a sort of big sister.

Two or three weeks after Zofi left, I was accepted to school. Rebecca said, 'We are going to celebrate.' I said, 'What do you mean?' She said, 'I will take you out for a dinner, and then we will go dancing. Do you like to dance?' I said, 'Very much. Where?' 'Don't worry. I know a place that you don't need a man, it's a woman's bar.' In London, I was in a woman's bar for the first time so I knew she meant a lesbian bar. I thought, 'Oh my gosh, this little girl, what's going on with her?' At the bar, I played the coolest, the toughest. I was drinking a lot of beer. I stood near the bar, and let her dance and do whatever she wanted. My heart was jumping when I saw all the women. I thought, 'Oh God, where are you, all the Israeli women, to see where I am!' I was laughing inside and Rebecca didn't know anything. As I stood with my back to the door, Rebecca came over and said, 'Is it nice?' I said, 'Yes, but in a way, I am missing home. It's weird for me to be in a public place and nobody knows me, nobody calls to me like they do in Jerusalem.'

As I finished this sentence, somebody yelled, 'Sara! What are you doing here?' I turn, and who do I see? The dean of the school who had that morning called Joe and said I was accepted. She is a lesbian! She said, 'I am so glad to see you here.' She *meant* that if you are here, you are a lesbian. Rebecca is listening to this! I grabbed Rebecca and I said, 'Let's dance!' We danced for an hour, because I was afraid to go back and stand near that woman! Some of the songs were slow dances and here I am, holding Rebecca, and dancing slow. Close, far, she came close to me, I pushed her back, and then I pulled her back to me because I started feeling good, and my emotions were up and down.

She asked me how I felt. I said, 'Wonderful! Well, the way your parents talk to me, it's like now I am a member of your family.' Then I asked Rebecca if we could leave, because I was afraid that now Rebecca knew that I am a lesbian that she would tell her parents and they would throw me out of the house.

We walked to the lake. I told her about myself then, and my relationship with Zofi. I told her not to take what happened that night seriously because I didn't want a relationship with a woman in the United States. I felt I had an obligation to myself and I definitely didn't want any relationship with her, not after her father had brought me to America.

Rebecca said, 'Don't worry, my father and mother know about me. They accept gay people, they are open-minded.' I said, 'I don't care. Now listen, you have to promise me not to tell your parents, because if you don't I am going to leave on the first plane.' Then she said, 'But it's not fair. I want you. I want to be your friend.' I said, 'Well, I don't think it will work. How can you be my friend when I don't love you?' I even told her I was still in love with Zofi. She said, 'I don't care. I like you very much and let's start, from here. And you know what, let me think if I am going to tell my parents; it's hard because all my life I am very open with them, but let me think about it.'

On Friday, I was very low – school started on Monday, and look at what has happened during this first day of the weekend! I decided I had to leave, and maybe this is God telling me I should go back to Zofi. Rebecca followed me, though, and convinced me I was about to do something foolish. She said she didn't care if I didn't love her but she would like to be involved with me. 'Stay here and we will tell my parents, and you will see, we will work something out.' I said 'No.' She said 'Yes.' We argued until Saturday noon. She said, 'Now that my parents are back from temple, we are going to talk with them.'

I couldn't believe she could so easily tell her parents and that her parents took it so well. Her father said, 'Mazel tov!' But then her mother said, 'Wait a minute.' She asked Rebecca if she understood the hard life she has chosen – not just being lesbian but that I was only studying here and would probably want to go back to Israel. She was worried too about what to say to Rebecca's brothers. Rebecca said it was *her* duty to tell them – she knew her family wasn't against gay people. They stood up, hugged and kissed me and said, 'We are happy for you, we love you, we know you are a good person, and we know you will never do her any harm.' I didn't say *a word* – nothing came out from this mouth! The same day we moved into the same room.

*

When I was twenty-five, thirty, my friends and I would often discuss why we were lesbians. Most of them – I cannot say everyone – felt it was connected to a poor relationship with their mothers. It was the opposite with me. I thought I had a good relationship with my mother but I had no father. My mother was the one who called me 'my tomboy, my son', because I had many practical skills. I knew electricity, carpentry, all the skills that, according to my mother, a girl cannot do. I was perhaps playing unconsciously the role of the absent father. For instance, why I didn't leave my mother until I was thirty? In therapy, I tried to understand the core of this relationship, and realized it's more complicated than I thought. Now I think there is a connection between my relationship with my mother and my identity as a lesbian. The more I dealt with the issue, and learned about it, and was open – and it cost me a lot of pain – I realized this 'great relationship' wasn't so great. Now that she is very sick, I still can't give her up. I try to keep her alive. Intellectually, I understand, but emotionally, I can't give up. I'm in denial.

For her I am the 'good daughter'. My sister is also good, but unfortunately, she got married and divorced three times. For me this is good, because when any of the family asks me, 'Why don't you get married?' I can say, 'My sister did enough for both of us.' I've still never directly come out to my mother. She never asks me about myself. She didn't know when I got my first period! I had a closer relationship with a nurse at my boarding-school. The nurse asked me how come she never saw me with pain, or asked about pills or whatever I needed, and I didn't know what she was talking about. I wasn't prepared! I was completely on another planet. I was athletic, playing sports with the boys until I was eighteen or so. Finally, about a month before I went to the army, the nurse came to me and she said, 'Tomorrow a doctor will be visiting here and I want you to see him.' I discovered I should have had my period and so the doctor had to prescribe hormone treatments.

My mother has met all my partners – I always brought them home to meet her. When she visited Na'ama and me, she saw how we shared the house. Even when we bought the house, she didn't ask any questions. Once in a while she will say, 'How about getting married?' And I reply, 'You know I am not going to get married.' And she will say, 'OK, but you know what, how about children?' And if I say, 'Yes, I do want children,' she will respond, 'You know what, get married, have a child, get divorced.' This is my mother! You see?

When Rebecca visited me during the winter she asked me, 'Do you sleep with Rebecca?' and I said, 'Sure.' She said, 'Very good, it's cold at night.' [laughs long] It's cute! I mean, it's very my mother. She's not sophisticated; she's illiterate. She understands from her intuition that I am different but she doesn't know the terms 'lesbian' or 'gay'. But I have a feeling that she *knows*. She never fought me, or put me down, or my friends, my partners. Na'ama is like another daughter to her and she considers Yael as a niece. It's amazing! Although she never confronts me, deep down I believe she knows I am a lesbian.

רינה

Rina

Edited by Jenney Milner

● *Rina, born 1959*

Rina was born in Canada in a family with Ashkenazi, working-class roots. With her parents and her sister, she came to Haifa in 1964, when she was five years old.

Thirty years old at the time of this narrative, Rina chose not to use any real names here. Rina lives in Haifa still, with her partner, Ella. She works as a physiotherapist.

MY parents chose to live in Israel for reasons of Zionism. My mother's father came to Canada from eastern Europe as a child, around 1910, with his parents and nine siblings. He was a tailor. My mother's mother was a big, tough woman. She used to carry a hat-pin on her coat so she could stab men who bothered her. She was emotionally, if not physically, abusive of her daughters, and perhaps of her husband as well.

My mother is a very special person; I like her a lot. I don't know too much about her childhood, except that she worked for her father making waistcoats. Her mother made her quit school and go to work at age sixteen, despite her own and her teachers' pleas. She made her way to success on her own terms. She met my father when he rented a room in their house. She decided she'd marry him and see what would happen. He was a very shy guy and she had to take all the initiative, but in a subtle way. Women weren't supposed to be active in a relationship then. Once she told me she married him because she knew he wouldn't hurt her. What a world!

My mother doesn't have good feelings about herself, especially because she doesn't feel very intelligent, and my father reinforces that, because he thinks he's Mr Rational–Homo Sapiens sapiens. But he's very dependent on her. The closest he comes to a friendship of the heart is with my mother, and he can't even tell her he loves her! And it hurts her, his being so superior.

My father's family are from eastern Poland. They're

religious – Hasidic Orthodox. After my grandfather came to Canada, my grandmother stayed behind with their daughter until he sent for them years later. My father, born in Canada, grew up in a very religious home, but their neighbourhood wasn't even Jewish. As a boy with *payot** and skull-cap, he had to deal with a lot of anti-Semitism.

My father decided to leave religion after spending high school in a *yeshiva.*† He was – still is – principled in this way: he would not keep the *mitzvot*‡ without the faith. He still is fond of Judaism, reads and studies Bible and Gemara, loves the Sabbath songs. Throughout my childhood, we went to the Reform synagogue because my parents wanted me to have some contact with Judaism. It didn't really connect me to Judaism. Still, being Jewish is important to me, although growing up in Israel meant not looking at it very often. In some religions it's enough to believe, but Judaism seems like a religion where it's important to *know*.

Ignorant as I am, maybe it's easier for me to choose what I like about Judaism: the part about choosing life and choosing joy, treating others with respect, and the *brachot*, the blessings – thanking God before eating a fruit, or after going to the toilet. It's a wonderful blessing, that one about going to the toilet – thanking God for making us full of holes, and if they got blocked we wouldn't be able to live. What other religion would thank God for making holes?

A couple of years ago I thought I would look at the synagogues around Haifa to find a community I liked, to get a little closer to Judaism. I had an aliyah l'Torah at a Reform synagogue, and I was so excited. I thought: it's mine too! But I went back only once or twice after that. Feminism hasn't influenced my Judaism in a daily way, because I'm not a practising Jew. I like knowing about the Jewish women who are trying to create a women's sort of Jewish religion – our way of thinking about it, interpreting it. All the violence in the Bible: horrible bloody heroes that we had! It would be nice to be with feminists who are aware of these issues

* Sidelocks.
† Hebrew school.
‡ Commandments.

and have their own readings of things. I'd like that: to reclaim parts of this heritage.

As it is, I like the holidays even though there's this painful side, the parts of the history or the blessings that seem 'off'. They may be acceptable when you're the minority, but not when you're the majority.

There's that whole other side of what being Jewish means: having the burden of a strange history, and having to cope with what it means now. I think a lot of Israel's political behaviour has to do with thinking the Holocaust hasn't ended. Of course anti-Semitism hasn't ended. But people confuse them. To them, *everything* is anti-Semitism, and the Palestinians are the *enemy*, and [Yassir] Arafat is *Hitler* – really confused.

But even in myself, I know I've had a lot of fear to work through. When I started thinking about a Palestinian state as a possibility, it was really scary. I'm not surprised a lot of people aren't willing to look at the possibilities. It is scary for Jews to trust, but we have to, if we are to make peace.

Going to the Women's Conference in Nairobi in 1985 got me more interested in being active about issues of the Occupation and peace. I participated in founding the group Israelis and Palestinians for Non-Violence. One of our actions was planting trees in a Palestinian village, on the Jordanian side of the 'green line', whose trees had been uprooted because the authorities said they were planting them in no-man's-land. We went over there one Shabbat, on Tu B'Shvat. That was my first experience organizing political work; I was amazed it was so easy to get press coverage, perhaps because at the time this was still a creative kind of action.

*

I'm not really part of mainstream culture here. Even though I consider myself Israeli, not Canadian, my closest friends aren't Israeli born. Although my English is pretty good, my Hebrew is better. It's easy for me to fit in either place. Yet in Canada I don't always know what's going on, and I can ask people the wrong questions, like how much they paid for something. I am proud when Canadians do wonderful things, and there are things about Canada that touch me. But I'm clearly more Israeli.

When I was young, I was a very good girl – quiet, shy, polite. I always had a best girlfriend. I was falling in love with this boy and that boy, but I had very few close or romantic friendships with them. Being scared was a big part of it, though I wasn't aware of the fear at the time. I thought something was wrong with me, that I couldn't get close to boys.

In the army it became easier. I had a few good relationships with young men. Later, as a student, I met a man in Tel Aviv, and we were together for a couple of years – a relationship that I think now I wouldn't be interested in at all, although it was really good for me to have that closeness. He was quite a good person, really. Now I expect much more, but it certainly wasn't *bad* for me, which is something to say for it, considering the powerlessness I felt all those years.

Then we broke up and I met Avram, and we lived together for four years. There were things I just couldn't figure out – like how we never really talked about the relationship! Another thing made it harder to stay with Avram. I was starting to have memories of sexual abuse as a very young child. I now have a clearer picture of what happened: a male relative raped me in my mouth when I was a few months old. It hurts less now, but then all this fear was coming up and I couldn't get close to Avram at all. It was hard for him, too, but he took it well. He didn't even complain. In fact, it was hard to be around him, because he didn't stand up for himself.

After him, and dealing with the memories of sexual abuse, I decided to be alone. I called myself celibate. I had my little place to live and my nice little job, and I spent a lot of time thinking, 'What do I want to do now? What do I want to eat today? How do I feel? What kind of music do I want to listen to?' I was trying to build my life out of little pieces that were good for me. Figuring out who I want to be with, trying to choose my friends – it felt really good, a healing experience.

About then – nine years ago – I started noticing my fear of rape. There was one horrible rape and murder in the Negev and I was talking about that story a lot and realizing how terrified I was just about all the time. A bit later, I noticed they were looking for volunteers at the Rape Crisis Center in Haifa.

I've been volunteering there for about seven years now. As a volunteer organization it really gives you room for initiative. There are basic requirements, like staffing the hotline – but then you can develop in any direction you choose. I helped start the Arabic hot line. I and another woman went around talking to Arab women all over Haifa to figure out whether to start something separate or to do it within the existing hotline. We found the two women who started the hotline in Arabic – our first Arab volunteers. That was an exciting thing to do and we were hopeful about the co-operation as Arab and Jewish women.

I also studied the area of child sexual abuse and incest and brought information to the Rape Crisis Center. We are still giving talks to all sorts of groups of adults about it – raising consciousness, helping parents and teachers figure out how they can talk to children about it and how they can help if something has happened.

My mother wondered about this work I do. The way I ended up telling her about my relationship with Ella started with her asking me if I was abused as a child. I saw she was willing to ask hard questions and to hear hard answers, and I wondered whether she asked because she was sensing a secret. I thought, it's a sign I can tell her more about my life; I wasn't ready then to share about the sexual abuse, but it was a good time to share about Ella and my commitment to her. Just recently, I did speak with her about the abuse. She believes me and is willing to help me confront this man, who is still living, if I should choose to do so. That has been a healing experience and we are now closer than ever.

Remembering and working through the sexual abuse has made a big difference in my life. I haven't finished, but it's made everything much easier. I used to think something was wrong with me. Now it makes sense, in light – or in the shadow – of what happened.

★

About lesbianism: around 1982, when I first went to Isha l'Isha, I took out *Rubyfruit Jungle* from the library. I really liked it. It helped kick out some of the prejudices and homophobic stuff I grew up with. I even gave it to my mother to read. But I didn't tap into anything personal until I had a crush on a friend at the Rape

Crisis Center. I would do anything to spend time around her: we did a few joint projects – boring statistics – but just spending time together was wonderful.

One day out of the blue she told me she was in a relationship with her flatmate, and that was why she wouldn't become more involved with me. It took me time to figure out what she was saying. It hadn't occurred to me to put our friendship in those terms at all. At first I was surprised and then I felt jealous and rejected.

Then another friend – that's funny, these are the first two friends I felt I really *chose* – told me she was a lesbian. I was so excited about her as a person, and she too about me. And by then lesbianism seemed really natural to me. I considered getting closer to her – maybe getting sexual and seeing what it was like – but she started a relationship with somebody else. But it really seemed *possible* – except, of course, I was celibate! For so long I hadn't wanted a sexual relationship because it was hard to get close to someone while holding onto myself. I had this big, big confusion about sex in general, having to do with all the hurts. It just didn't seem worth it.

When I met Ella, she was looking for a relationship with a woman. She tried to ask around about me, and didn't get any clear information, except I was celibate and that doesn't tell you much. She found excuses to get together to do her work, and we talked. I thought 'Aah, this is somebody I want to make friends with.' But then I didn't even have a *chance* to do anything because she invited me over, and I stayed that night! I panicked ... but not about her being a woman. I thought, 'What's going on?' and 'It's a sexual relationship!' and 'I can't do this, I'm going to disappear!' and 'Who am I?' It took a *long* time to get to a place where I thought a commitment to this relationship made sense. But I've learned there are things worth coping with, for being together with somebody. I've learned I don't have to be so careful about myself, I'm not so fragile. I don't have to close myself away in a little house alone.

First I started sleeping over at Ella's on weekends, then sometimes in the middle of the week. Then one day I moved my newspaper subscriptions over (laughs), because I needed them for my work as a press reviewer. That was a symbolic act! It meant I had to wake up there every morning or go over really early to get the newspapers. I was shocked – not only did I easily abandon celibacy, but soon I moved in.

★

It wasn't just my relationship with Ella that was a shock – all of a sudden I was co-parenting Ella's two adolescent daughters. As a lesbian family in Israel, issues that come up are around the girls. K., the older of the two, goes to a real 'freaky' high school. There are a couple of teachers who are homosexuals and everybody knows it, and the children whose parents are still married are in a minority. For her, it's not such a big problem, but still she chooses who she brings over, who she tells. In the beginning she would tell everybody, 'Hey, my mum's a lesbian' – showing off – until she figured out maybe it wasn't such a good idea to flaunt it. She's very mature: she knows what's going on between me and Ella, she knows what's hard for her about it, and she talks about it.

N., the younger of the two, doesn't talk about it much. When she does, it is in very defensive terms: 'It's OK, lesbians are like everybody and should be treated like everybody' – she defends the ideological side. But how she *feels* about it, I really don't know. It limits her life more than her older sister's and certainly more than ours. For us it's our choice; for her it isn't.

With both of them I try to remember I'm not their mother – they have a mother around, and a good one. I can be an older friend. K. is full of life and energy, and she's really excited about things, and it's great when I can be around when she comes home, to listen.

My relationship with N. is different. She's trying out new ways, but she still behaves a lot like a child. She's still cuddly and warm. She, too, enjoys having somebody around to tell her stories to. Ella works long hours, K. is out a lot, and I can be home sometimes so N. is not alone quite as much.

My commitment to the part of the relationship that's hard for me is to remember *me* – to keep thinking about what I need, and what I need to do for me. But it seems like everything is possible. Ella and I have a process. Things come up, so we talk about them. I don't know where we'll live in another year or ten years, what each of us will be doing. I don't know what we'll be like; we might change. But it's a partnership. Sometimes I think of it like we're each on our own voyage and we're supporting each other on it, we're co-travellers.

Our relationship is long term, although I think there might be a time when it will take on a different form. Both of us have to cope with stuff about relationships with other people. It's important for me to make friends, to keep meeting all sorts of people who are different from me, including men, and not shrivel into this one relationship, which is great but can't be everything.

As for my identity as a bisexual woman, being with Ella, for me, is first of all, being with Ella. She's a woman, but it was a choice of the person, not a decision in principle about women or men. But it is certainly much easier for me, and much more comfortable, with women. I'm more relaxed around women. With a man it would be an enormous project of breaking through where I'm stuck and breaking through where he's stuck, to start meeting in some sort of a common ground.

I don't place relationships in a sexual framework. Sure, sex is important – it's part of a relationship – but the choice of Ella is not who I'm choosing to have sex with. My choice of sexual partners doesn't seem central to my identity. Possibly some of this has to do with the ways I'm still struggling with the question of sexual relationships at all, although I have a sexual relationship and am enjoying it a lot. Maybe in some ways I am really celibate.

And what I'm going to say now, about relationships with men, also isn't a question about sex. In principle, I think I, and women as a group, will have to step out and make allies, if not love-mates, of men, if we really want to change the world and make a better place for women – for human beings. It's really healing to see some men making an effort to change and deciding to do better. I feel I have to get close to men, and to help them change, even though it's their responsibility.

I think part of my personal power is waiting to be reclaimed in conducting powerful relationships with men. That is, making friends on my terms, requiring that they change in a way I'm sure they're dying to but haven't figured out. Not letting the oppression come in to separate us.

This doesn't mean anything about the nature of those relationships. It doesn't mean getting married with a man, or having a long-term, or romantic, or sexual relationship. That's not the point, and that's connected to the point about my identity not being connected to the sexual. My identity isn't bisexual, perhaps it's 'bi-relationship'.

★

A few days after I came out to my mum, she called me on the phone and cried for fifteen minutes about how she must have done something wrong as a mother – so guilty, oy! Since then, she treats Ella like a daughter-in-law, and K. and N. like granddaughters. My mother told my father; that's the way it goes in my family. My mum asked a *lot* of questions right away, like who was active and who was passive – and I didn't realize she was asking about sex! I gave her a wonderful answer about depending on what kind of things, what each of us likes to do better, and does better, and feels like doing. Then I asked her, 'And you and Dad, who's active and who's passive?' And then she gave me an answer about sex, so I realized what she had asked me.

She asked me questions about the girls, about my future. Maybe she hopes someday I'll get married and have children – but she's very gentle about it. And I don't want children of my own. I have children around me, I'm participating in a family. I wouldn't be able to adopt under existing laws. There's room for my time and energy in children who have already been born and are not getting what they need. Poor Earth is overpopulated as it is.

The whole thing about family and children is a heavy trip in many cultures, but is said to be somewhat heavier in ours. It's hard for me to compare, but it's nice to think there are other places where it's easier to choose not to have children. It hasn't been *such* a pressure on me, but I think in other places I wouldn't be so unusual in my choice. It's one side of being Jewish. People are really hard on each other – Israelis and probably Jews in general. And of course having children is considered part of survival.

I've never spoken directly with my father about being in a lesbian relationship. But last year, my brother had a big fancy bar mitzvah for his son. When I told my sister-in-law Ella and I were coming, she freaked out: what would her family think? My father –

who never stands up for anybody or for himself – told my sister-in-law, 'Don't you know the most important thing in life is a loving relationship?' Then he said if Ella and I weren't invited my parents weren't going either.

In the end, the bar mitzvah was fine. I didn't introduce Ella to my sister-in-law's family, but she knows enough of my side of the family to be OK. Ella didn't feel uncomfortable at all. Unfortunately, Ella and I can't dance together at these events; it's not that we dance so much, but we probably *would*. Maybe when we're twenty years older, two nice old ladies dancing together: 'Isn't that sweet!' Maybe I can dye my hair grey and not wait so long! Or maybe things will change. Who knows?

All the same, it seems to me there's something about our culture here that is much more tolerant than the US, at least about women being with each other, if not gay men. There is less uptightness about anything having to do with sex. An example that seems related is the whole question of child sexual abuse being introduced into schools by the Ministry of Education, not by feminists who are fighting to get it in, like in the US.

*

Feminism means a lot to me. It broadens how I think about the world in general, people, relationships. It has everything to do with my political work on other issues, too, because for me all oppressions are connected in a fundamental way, and as long as someone else is oppressed, then I am not free. I think that's really what feminism means: stopping people from hurting people. It's especially important for children; it can't be left to children to defend themselves against oppressive adults. People have to change inside. Everybody. Including me.

I still don't know how to make a difference on a large scale in the world. It's been a transformation from feeling like nobody to actually feeling I can make a difference, but I have yet to learn how to be effective. And in terms of restructuring society – I don't have a clear idea of how things would look: would a state be with or without police? with or without prisons? – all these questions.

One thing I do on a larger scale is Rape Crisis Center work. And I've also been doing consciousness-raising with a group of

Ashkenazim – figuring out together who we are, why we behave as we do towards *Mizrachim**, and how to change. This work is precious and interesting to me, and I hope we can find a way to make it more widespread.

I believe I *can* make a difference in a personal way, one person at a time. On the one hand, I think that is very important: just building strong relationships, good friendships, helping particular people I like live a life that's more where they want it, be stronger for themselves; for example, in the lives of the two young women I have at home. On another level, I think we're up against faceless powerlessness – especially for women, who have been trained into not knowing how to make a real difference in the world around us. We need to figure out ways to organize, to change things politically.

I'm up against a place where I don't know what more to do, I don't know how to do it, and it's going to have to be done. I don't think the things we're doing are enough. On the other hand, maybe something good will come out of it, and maybe somewhere along the line we really will make a difference.

* Eastern or Oriental Jews.

בת מרים

Bat Miriam

Edited by Pamela Gray

• Bat Miriam, born 1950

Thirty-eight at the time of this interview, Bat Miriam was living in Jerusalem with her husband Uri HaLevy, who is gay, and their daughters, four-year-old Madesch and infant Hodaya. Because Uri HaLevy is observant, Bat Miriam keeps a kosher home. She speaks an idiomatic English flavoured with the accents of several languages, and laughs frequently while recounting her exploits.

MY mother was a Holocaust survivor, who hid in a small village in the south of France. Her oldest brother was in the Resistance and was shot by the Germans in a public market-place in France. My mother came to Israel when she was eighteen, and her family later moved from France to Brussels.

My father's father died in the 1930s before the war, and when my father was thirteen, he was deported with his mother from Mannheim, Germany, to French concentration camps. From there, they separated the ones for Auschwitz and the ones who could work. He watched his mother be dragged off to Auschwitz. My father and a friend escaped and crossed the Pyrenees by foot. He was hidden in Spain by a farmer and then with an underground organization that brought Jews to Palestine in 1944. My parents met in 1948 on the Kibbutz Neve Ilan, my birthplace.

For the first three years of my life, my mother was the kindergarten caretaker, which was difficult for our relationship. She had to take care of the whole group and I wanted her special attention. I had to wait until four o'clock when all the children went home with their parents for my mother to finally be 'my mother'. At night, I slept in the kids' houses. When I was three, we moved to the German Colony neighbourhood of Jerusalem.

In 1956, my mother took me, my older sister, and younger brother to visit her parents in Brussels. I was six years old, and I remember me and my mother standing with our suitcases in the Brussels airport, ready to return to Israel, being told the plane wouldn't depart because the Sinai War had broken out. I don't have many memories before that, but this one I remember with such a shock.

My mother had been through the Shoah and she said, 'I'm not going to return to a place of war.' Back in Israel, my father sold everything and joined us in Brussels. We stayed for the next two years. My father had a difficult time trying to find a profession in Brussels, and finally decided to take us to Mannheim, the city that had deported him. He said, 'At least there I know the language.' Before the war he'd been wealthy – and then of course, the Nazis, the Holocaust – they lost everything. Now he was returning poor and unemployed. He sometimes found factory work, but I remember many moments when he came home without any. We lived in the socially poor areas, but we always had enough food.

I attended school in Mannheim. There was a Jewish community and there were Jewish lessons for children. I became close friends with a girl named Edna. She was also a *sabra* – born in Israel. We didn't have a name for our relationship, but we were friends and lovers right from the beginning – from the age of eight until eighteen! I was her family's 'schabbestochter', because spending every Shabbat with them made me like another daughter. I would sleep over, and we shared a bed. Her family called us *Busenfreundinnen* – 'bosom buddies'. Edna's mother walked in on us a couple of times, but she didn't say anything. Edna and I weren't aware of 'it' – that this was lesbianism. We just were very best friends. We used to play Prince and Princess, and I always got to play the Prince!

*

When Edna was eighteen, she had a boyfriend, a drummer in a band. It was so traumatic – she wouldn't look at me anymore, and needed me only as an ear for her problems with her boyfriend. Socially, it was very difficult after Edna left me.

Edna and I had been involved in the Zionist movement, but I didn't want that involvement anymore. The early 1970s in Germany had incredible counter-culture movements, which attracted me very much. For a while I lived in a commune called Socialist Patients Collective, which involved Communist consciousness-raising and a commitment to equality among its members. When the police banned the organization, we formed a new progressive group – the Psychotherapeutic Institute for Students.

In this environment I came out as a lesbian. It was 1975, and I was in Heidelberg to study social work in a politically radical school. I was working as a social worker at the Institute – that's how I became involved with German feminism, leading a women's consciousness-raising group. I was drawn to the lesbians – I kept reading the chapter about lesbianism in Simone de Beauvoir's book over and over, but I still wasn't making connections between being a lesbian and my relationship with Edna! I knew my relationships with men were terrible, and I went to therapy for that. I always had this 'problem' – I was too dominant; men wanted a woman to be weaker, to fit their needs. I didn't know what an orgasm was, or how to masturbate. A friend taught me, and I felt so liberated. It even helped me separate from this man I was involved with at the time – a therapist who would fuck his clients, just like Phyllis Chesler said in *Women and Madness*. That book really made things click for me.

The night I came out as a lesbian, I went with the lesbians from my women's group to Amsterdam for a demonstration about abortion rights. I met a woman, Gudrun, from Frankfurt. I knew she was a lesbian, and I found myself attracted to her. It was becoming clearer and clearer that when I'd be listening to music and daydreaming, having romantic feelings – it was for a woman. I could barely sleep for fantasizing about Gudrun. Gudrun's friends were all grinning – they encouraged me to tell my feelings. So I told Gudrun, 'I really have some nice feelings for you,' and by the time we were on this bus going back, we were hugging and kissing. Here I was born a lesbian!

Gudrun and I eventually lived together. She was a painter, a little tomboy who spoiled me, cooking for me, doing everything for me. She was so cute and so good to me. In 1976 we went to an international conference about 'Violence Against Women' in Brussels. There we met other lesbians who wanted to live together, and we created what we called the 'Lesbian Nest' near the Castle in Heidelberg. We ate healthy food, picked herbs for healing, used menstrual sponges, and had full moon rituals.

Once a week, the basement bar in the university had a lesbian night. We brought our own drinks and music, danced, and listened to this wonderful lesbian band from Berlin called 'Flying Lesbians'. I still dream about those magical evenings. One night at the bar, a butch/femme couple was sitting near us and my friend thought the butch was a man. She was a lesbian named Chip, and I was so attracted to her. I loved watching the way she was courting this other woman. I asked Chip to dance, and found out she was in the US army. I didn't have the nerve to ask for her phone number, but eventually, I found Chip again and invited her to my house.

Chip was closeted, terrified of the army finding out about her. It was consciousness-raising for me to see the difference between a closeted dyke and an out dyke. We became lovers, but after a couple of months, suddenly one midnight Chip told me, 'I'm signing out, I'm going back to America.'

I was devastated. Chip was a very disturbed woman, but I was so blinded by the attraction I didn't want to see it. After Chip left, she wrote me crazy letters telling me to come meet her in New York where she'd be stationed. I saved my money, but the day before I was leaving, Chip called and told me not to come, once again afraid of being found out by the army. I already had my tickets and went anyway – I found her somewhere in New Jersey! Luckily, I knew some women in New York and stayed with them. I was madly in love with Chip and put up with her craziness, but our relationship never worked out.

I went to see friends in Los Angeles and then went to the Gay Pride parade in San Francisco. I met some Jewish women going to Wolf Creek, women's land in Oregon, for Jewish women's week, so I went along. I was absolutely *crazy* there. I was walking around wearing only pieces of cloth! I painted my face with berries, did Shabbat rituals, and got back in touch with myself.

Back in San Francisco, I stayed in homes designated 'Women of Colour Houses'. It was 1977, a time of increased awareness about race and class. I reconnected with women I had met when I went to women's camps in Denmark called 'Femøe'. These camps were so fantastic! Afterward, women calling themselves 'wild women' set up giant army tents in Wales. They wanted to be connected to nature, doing all kinds of rituals with fires burning on the beach, but many were on drugs. Anyway, I met up with some of the Femøe women who were now calling themselves the European 'tribe'. Several groups of women were forming tribes, including one in Mexico and one in Guatemala. I called myself the Jewish tribe!

A rich American lesbian donated $3,000 to the tribes, and mine was given $500, which I was supposed to carry back to Israel. Instead I used it to join the tribe of women in Tepotzlan, Mexico, high on a mountain with a pyramid on top. It was a spiritual, wonderful retreat, even though there was some tension between the women, and Mexican men used to bother us and steal from us in the middle of the night. In the day, we would play music, smoke marijuana, go to the market-place, and feast on delicious fruit. We participated in peyote rituals, listening to reggae music on a little tape-recorder.

My friend Cypress and I rented a little house high on the hill, near a field. The house was too low to stand in; we had to crawl to get inside. We would shop in the village, collect our own wood, make our own fire. We carried water up the hill but eventually a little boy with a donkey carried it for us. There were scorpions and spiders, no running water for showers, and enough privacy to walk around naked.

Cypress was a writer who inspired me to write. She gave me a blank book and said, 'Here. Now you're going to write.' We stayed in Mexico for a couple of months, then returned to San Francisco – to one of the open women's houses. At that time I identified as a woman of colour, although the Black women didn't see me that way. I am Jewish, I am not middle class and, being born in Israel, I feel Middle Eastern.

I was influenced by a Black Hebrew woman I met there. I had this very spiritual ritual where I pierced my nose, and I wore turbans, big shirts and skirts of Indian fabric. The Black Hebrew woman and I, along with a couple, Makar and Kahikine – everyone had given herself her own name – those names! – decided to take a trip around the world. Makar belonged to the European tribe, and claimed that her Gypsy parents didn't want her so they'd put her on the doorstep of an Italian family. Kahikine, born in Arkansas, had olive-coloured skin and said she came from Transylvania. Who knows, maybe she did! Makar and Kahikine weren't Jewish, but spiritually, we belonged.

In 1978 we decided to travel to Egypt, Sudan and Mozambique, with India as our final goal. With our turbans and pierced noses, we were an unusual sight. None of us had suitcases or backpacks or cameras. My bag was a length of cloth over my shoulder. I carried everything in it – money, passport, writing book, tarot cards, a few pieces of clothing. We decided not to speak English on the trip; we wanted to disappear underground, leaving civilization behind. We developed our own language to use around people, and when asked where we came from, we said we were rich girls who had run away from India. It built a sort of protection around us.

I was getting tired of the women, but I was too afraid to tell them. I was also feeling homesick for Israel; I was twenty-eight and hadn't been there since I was eighteen. This was a very spiritual time for me. I did rituals, washed myself in the river, and played emotional Israeli songs. I felt a renewed connection to Judaism and Israel. I decided to return to Israel permanently.

When we were camping by the Pyramids, I ran away in the middle of the night. I went to Cairo, through Athens, to Israel. I had the address of an American couple, Bea and Etti, who had a kindergarten near Kibbutz Ramat Rachel, and they befriended me.

In 1981 I entered the live-in ulpan, Ulpan Etzion, in Jerusalem. I'd forgotten my mother tongue, and had so much rebellion inside of me! I couldn't relate to the young women in the ulpan who weren't very committed, and were there just to check out whether they wanted to return. For me, this was a serious decision. In the morning I was in the ulpan, but in the afternoon I connected with a lesbian feminist community with meetings, festivals, and Kol HaIsha. Slowly I started to feel I was reconnecting to myself.

After the ulpan, I took a course to help social workers from other countries get oriented to Israeli jobs. The course was in Tel Aviv, where I met Shura, a second-generation Holocaust survivor whose mother went through Auschwitz and whose twin uncles underwent Mengele's experiments. We became lovers, and our relationship lasted for five years.

After the nine-month course, Shura and I moved in together in Jerusalem and became part of a lesbian community. When I met Shura, I had fantasies and dreams of settling down with children, and was starting to think about ways to become a mother. Bea and Etti were our close friends and were a role model for me. Bea became pregnant by a friend through artificial insemination, and I got information from them about the process.

I became close to Bea and her baby, and got a lot of support from her about becoming a mother. One day I said, 'That's it – I can't wait any longer.' I was thirty-four years old and it was time to act. I made an appointment with a gynaecologist who was willing to do artificial insemination even after I told him I was a lesbian. But before the day of the appointment came, Etti said, 'Wait a minute, we know someone for you.' It was a Dutch gay man named Uri HaLevy, who was also a social worker. He was willing to be a sperm donor, and after a serious discussion, we drew up a contract.

The first time I did artificial insemination, Etti transferred the sperm into my vagina and showed Shura how to do it. The second time, in March 1985, Shura did the transfer and I became pregnant. I remember the *exact* feeling of getting pregnant. That night was Shabbat and I'd gone to services at Beit Knesset Efrata in order to pray for my mother, who was ill.

Uri HaLevy and I went to a feminist lawyer, making it clear he was donating sperm, but I was the caretaker with custody and legal responsibility for the child. The child would have my name, and Uri HaLevy would not be responsible for child support. After signing the initial contract, we decided to marry for a time and divorce afterwards so the child could be born legally. We had a formal wedding – *chupah** and rabbi – on the roof of a house in the old city. I was very pregnant, and Etti was our only guest. Afterwards, we had a joyous party with around forty gay friends, including Shura.

The divorce proceedings, six months later, were *terrible*. The rabbinut constantly said, '*Shalom bayit, shalom bayit*' – make peace in the house! But I had to keep insisting, 'No, this is a *gehenom*' – this is hell! I had to bring other people to prove the divorce should be granted. My father was one of the people who was interviewed.

By then, my father was living back in Israel. My mother had

---

* Canopy held over a couple during their wedding.

died in Germany after I became pregnant. Before she died, I was able to tell her she'd be a grandmother, something she desperately wanted. When she was on her deathbed, I told her I had found a father for my child and I was sure she was going to like him very much. That was her last smile.

Madesch was born December 1985. A month later, Shura left. There'd been tension between Uri HaLevy and Shura, and her leaving was somewhat of a relief to me, but also painful. I had decided to be a single mother. I was the one who wanted the child. Shura had been at the birth, not Uri HaLevy, but my life and Shura's were heading in different directions.

As a single mother, it was difficult going to work when Madesch was five months old; of course, I had to put her at the *metapelet*. Fortunately, Uri HaLevy became more involved in the parenting. We were getting closer, and he wanted to share more responsibility. Through the first year of Madesch's life, he and I got to know each other, to be parents together, sharing fears and hopes, seeing our child grow up. My self-image as a single parent began to change. I wanted to have a sibling for Madesch, and knew I wouldn't have the strength to raise a second child by myself. Uri HaLevy, who was willing to have a family with me, was the ideal partner. We moved in together.

For my second pregnancy, Uri HaLevy wanted us to sleep together. For him, there was a relationship between the act of intercourse and fatherhood. We already were lovers sometimes, because we'd gotten so emotionally close around Madesch. I hadn't expected to be able to have a sexual relationship with any man. I'm not in love with Uri HaLevy – he's not a woman. Our primary commitment is to our family, and our special relationship feels like *matanah mehashamayim* – a gift from heaven.

When I became pregnant with Hodaya, I was in love with a woman named Millie (see page 248) and it's funny, because I think Hodaya resembles her. But I realized when I was lovers with Millie that it was difficult for me to be involved outside of my family. Family life takes up so much time and energy.

Uri HaLevy and I got remarried before the birth of our second daughter. The children have both our family names. Hodaya was born on the same birthday as me – both my Hebrew and Christian birthdays, something that only happens every nine-teen years. I feel that for the sake of the children, it's easier to have a mother and father around. Uri HaLevy and I don't know what will happen when one of us gets into a serious involvement with a lover.

I had lost interest in the lesbian community, but recently another single mother encouraged me to go to events, including a lesbian mothers' group. I had some hesitation – I was afraid of being judged because I'm living with Uri HaLevy. For myself, I know I'm lesbian. I'm just so matriarchal, and I feel it with my two girls; I feel like the three of us have this special bond. Once Etti asked me, 'Do you consider yourself lesbian?' I said, 'What am I going to do, just deny the last twenty years of my life?' My reaction to her suddenly made me realize how sure, how secure and how strong I feel about being a lesbian. No one can really come and say to me, 'You're not.'

The lesbian mothers' group consists of about twelve women from different lifestyles, such as a newly out lesbian who was mar-ried to a man, a recently divorced woman who's still open to living with a man, a long-time lesbian with teenagers – we are such a rainbow of cases! I feel accepted there. The group tries to meet on a regular basis, and we discuss issues such as how to come out to our children.

Uri HaLevy and I sometimes have tensions about our differ-ent religious beliefs. He believes in a traditional Orthodox male God, and I believe in the Goddess. When Uri HaLevy wanted to send Madesch to a religious school, I felt threatened. Another mother, Nurit, warned me, 'Your kids will say, "Hey, why didn't you light the candles on time?"' So I refused to send her, and we dropped the subject. I don't feel synagogue expresses my religious feelings, and I'm passing on my spirituality to my daughters. Madesch will say, '*Ima*, it's a new moon.' I teach her about nature, birds, and trees on Tu B'Shvat. Our connection through nature has helped us through some of the difficult adjustments we've had to make. Recently, Uri HaLevy said, 'I don't want Madesch to go to school without knowing she is Jewish.' He got all emotional about this, and I was able to understand his side better. We're trying to find a way to work on a compromise.

My dream for ten years from now is that I'll find myself in a relationship with a wonderful woman. I hope Uri HaLevy will also find a lover, and the two of us can remain partners in parenting. I hope we don't have to go through a traumatic separation the way other partners do, especially for the children's sake. For now, I must say I'm happy. We're a little family – my dream come true.

מילי
Millie Ben David
Edited by Marla Brettschneider

Nitzan, family friend Sue Kahn, Corey and Millie

• Millie Ben David, born 1960

*Millie's husky voice, pigtailed short hair spiked with purple,
Latina colouring, and usual jeans-and-workshirt garb only
partially communicate her identity, which is also observant Jew,
mother, and at the time this oral history was recorded, wife. Soon
afterward Millie began the process of separating from her
husband, eventually moving with her daughters to Los Angeles.
There she founded 'Lesbian Mothers and Our Children' and is an
activist for lesbian and gay families. She works as an apprentice
union electrician and serves on the Women's Committee of her
union, the International Brotherhood of Electrical Workers.*

I AM twenty-nine years old, born in America, married with two kids. I'm a carpenter, working with wood for eleven years. I studied engineering and industrial design, and now I'm making lyres. For the past three years I have been living in Jerusalem with my family; we have been in Israel for six years altogether. I am Ashkenazi, Israeli, Puerto Rican-American. The languages I speak now are English and Hebrew, since I have no one to speak Spanish with. English is our basic language at home, and the kids speak Hebrew. Culturally, our household is a nice mixture between Israel and America.

My husband, Menashe, and I have kept a firm traditional base at our home. I want my kids to grow up in a religious atmosphere. We don't keep Shabbat but we keep *kashrut*,* and we go to services. I love even the most traditional things, like the laws of nidah, *mikveh*.[1] Very feminist women look at going to the mikveh as something women shouldn't be doing. I can understand how things have become so twisted: women are pushed into a position of no power, are ignored or have the most mundane and unrewarding position in Judaism. It's so easy to get confused in all this. The advantage of being a convert, however, is you don't have that mucked-up feeling – growing up and seeing this taking place with your parents and with your mother especially. For example, for me the mikveh is a spiritual renewal and it's also tied up with sexuality. To me sexuality and spirituality are the same. In order to have a

* Kosher; following Biblical dietary laws.

renewed sexual relationship, it's like your spirituality has to meet it, prepare for it and enjoy it. To enjoy that, God willing, if you want a child this is a renewal and a cleansing of your soul and spirit to prepare for a new life. When observing the laws of nidah all of this becomes very conscious and up-front.

*

Both my parents are from Mayajues, Puerto Rico. They came to the United States, where they were matched by my father's mother. My father was in the Air Force and my mother was a housewife. We moved around a lot ... they just happened to be in Tampa, Florida, when my mum gave birth to me. We then settled for eleven years in Brooklyn. We lived in Park Slope, and I studied at a local parochial [Catholic] school. I have a sister one year older and a brother eight years younger.

I came from a strict patriarchal home. My dad had the last word on everything. My mum was submissive; loving, but quiet. I was beaten up by my father and sexually abused by my uncle when I was eight up to age twelve. It became very damaging later in my relationships, my sexuality and my relationship to men. In these early years I had very little encouragement. I always wanted praise, confirmation, acknowledgement and recognition from my dad – which I never got.

I was an achiever, fairly bright, but people assumed I was stupid because of my nationality. Then I started meeting people who were interested in art and music. I began going to museums, plays and concerts – all within walking distance. I was a real tomboy, loved sports and playing with the boys.

*

How I came to Judaism is a story. I converted to Judaism through a Reform rabbi when I was twelve. This was a time in Catholicism where they wanted to expose kids to different religions, so we had an introductory week on the world's major religions. Things clicked for me. I began reading some more and I started having very strong dreams about Judaism – I saw myself reading from the Torah. It was too powerful to ignore. I kept waking up tranquil, peaceful – it was a feeling I hadn't felt in anything else. I was certain Judaism was what I wanted. From then on there was no decision-making, there was just studying.

The first time I told my parents I was sitting on my father's lap. I was trying to be very serious with him, using big words, asking if it was OK while I lived with him if I could be Jewish. He threw me off his lap and told me I was crazy! From then on I was very careful. Sometimes I would sneak out of the house and go to Hebrew School. After a while my parents knew where I was going. Every Saturday I went to services and every Sunday, instead of going to my regular Sunday School, I went to the synagogue and took courses there. Later, when I finally left my parents' house, I was free to keep all the *mitzvot* – or whichever ones I wanted to – and I was free to practise what I believed.

Surprisingly, I was received at the synagogue with open arms. I guess that's why it was so easy to follow through – I had a very understanding rabbi. It was a wealthy congregation with few young people. To have a new face was something. I remember there were six to ten kids in the class, all very wealthy and four years my senior. There were so many new things! Judaism just kind of elaborated on basic feelings I already had, so there was very little disagreement, and nothing difficult to digest. It was just a matter of absorbing the words.

We moved from Brooklyn to Las Vegas, Nevada, when I was fifteen – my second year of high school. It was a big shock. I wasn't used to such a small place where everything was so spread out and everyone was very laid back. I was a real New Yorker – knew all the subways and was very street-wise. For example, my relatives lived in Spanish Harlem and I would go there by myself! I loved it in Brooklyn; I loved the adrenaline. In Las Vegas you needed a car for everything. My mother didn't drive, so I just stayed at home. Really suburban. We all got into a major depression – until my sister finally got her driver's licence! She became our chauffeur.

★

Every stage in my life was somehow linked with my lesbianism because it has always been such an important part of who I am. The first time I started having any sense of my sexuality was when I was eleven or twelve and I found myself attracted to my girlfriends. I had no idea there were lesbians; I had no idea there was women's love. So I always interpreted my attractions in terms of my dream to be a boy. Since I was four or five I wanted to be a boy because my dad wanted me to be a boy. I never really valued being a woman ... it was a fault, rather than a benefit.

I didn't have any attraction for boys, but in Las Vegas I found out *I* was attractive to *them*, and had a lot of dates. The first time I kissed a boy I was fifteen and I had my first serious boyfriend at sixteen. I knew I was starting to be sexual, and I was constantly being approached. At sixteen I had a couple of flings. Because I was afraid of being used, I was the user.

It was then I met a very gentle soul: a brilliant and talented Jewish boy a year older than I. We became very good friends and liked each other for a long time. He was shy and I didn't want to put him in a position where he'd feel funny about me approaching him. Finally I sort of elbowed him about it, like 'Nu, so when?' He got very nervous and so we had a serious talk.

He told me he was scared about being with girls because he fantasized about being with men. I accepted his fears: it didn't threaten or hurt me. I also told him about my fantasies. In our whole existence in Las Vegas there were so few people we could feel open with. All of our crowd – there were five of us – in the end turned out to be gay. Although it wasn't obvious then, five or six years later we realized the common tie between us.

*

I left my home in Las Vegas to go to college in Socorro, New Mexico. I ended up studying for two semesters, taking a break, then going back for one semester for engineering. Some friends in Albuquerque had a really nice *minyan* – a *hevrah** – that I would go to. There was no separation between men and women. Most were academics, well educated in Judaism and at least a third were keeping the *mitzvot*. This is where I met my husband Menashe. There were only three religious Jews in Socorro, so we shared a kosher kitchen and prayed together in the morning. Menashe is Israeli. At the time he was tutoring me in maths, Judaism and Hebrew and I was helping him to adjust to American life – how to function with the administration at school, the language, shopping, cleaning, cooking. It was a mutual exchange of needs and help. He became a second father for me – the ideal father. For whatever it's

* *Minyan*, the ten Jews required for community prayer; *hevrah*, a group.

worth, it helped me get out: he supported me and helped me to grow.

I drew away from my family. I had always hated my father: hated the very idea of him being my father. Now, as a grown-up, I can't excuse him for the things he did to me, but at least I can accept him. He's my father. My father came to accept Menashe, not because he was a good man who was loving and took care of me, but because he had a good job. On the other hand, my father had no respect for me as a cabinetmaker. He told me I was wasting my time. 'Why do you have to have a man's job?' he would ask.

*

The decision to marry was the same kind of feeling as my Judaism; it just hit me. I was nineteen. After we got married I went back to college for two years, for cabinet-making and computer science simultaneously. Menashe had convinced me to come to Israel with him. Although I had talked about making aliyah since I was a teenager, my mum was very angry with Menashe because she felt he was responsible for my decision to move. She could've relaxed, though – we didn't end up going for five years! We decided it would be foolish not to go back with some money so we could take advantage of my rights as a new immigrant. At that time we were making about $350 a month between us! He took a job in Los Angeles. We saved, I worked in a cabinetry shop, and then we had our first child after three years of marriage. At that point it was time to go. We were living in a very small apartment and we knew if we moved to a bigger, more comfortable place we'd stay there longer than was healthy for us. And I had worries of my own, because long before we left LA, I'd begun getting involved with women.

*

I had told Menashe about my lesbian fantasies even before we became lovers. He knew I wanted to experiment – I think he kind of got turned on by the idea. In fact, Jeannie, Menashe's secretary, was gay, and he became our matchmaker. It took me about two months to realize she was gay. At a party she mentioned she had broken up with somebody. I asked, 'Who?' and when she named a woman I said, 'Oh, your roommate.' Everyone looked at me! Then I finally got it.

I ended up going to Santa Barbara with Jeannie for my

twenty-first birthday. What I expected to be an innocent outing turned out to be my first contact with a woman. It was so natural, so easy, I found myself initiating it! What bothered me then was that I was feeling more comfortable with her than with Menashe, more trusting, safer. It was really scary.

At first Menashe wasn't jealous at all. He saw it as a game until one day she joked, 'I'm taking your wife away for the weekend.' That's when the shit hit the fan! He didn't want me to see her again. He said he hadn't intended it to be like this – he just wanted to fulfil my fantasy. He had no idea of the strength – *I* had no idea of the strength – of lesbian love. Surprisingly, I also wanted to stop it because I was scared. A few weeks later I got pregnant. I guess we both figured this would be the beginning of the rest of a normal life. I think Jeannie wanted to stop too – she didn't like the idea of breaking up a marriage.

But going to have a baby confused me. Menashe was ignoring me, but I wanted to be fondled and to connect with my pregnancy. I felt womanly for the first time in my life, and I wanted another woman around. Even though I thought having a child was a healthy return into heterosexual life, after Nitzan was born I found myself struggling to meet lesbians.

I started going to the LA clubs. I was so awkward, always in the corner! I would end up having a couple of drinks, leaving and never meeting anybody. I didn't know other places beside clubs.

I was very lucky though – a woman with a baby the same age as mine moved in downstairs. At this point I insisted on being identified as bisexual, and she was bisexual too. We became friends in about six hours. Both of our husbands went on business trips and we supported each other. Whenever we wanted to visit, we just banged on the floor or the ceiling. It was seldom we didn't eat dinner together. They were poor, we were better off, and I got such pleasure by helping her out. We did become lovers ... but it didn't last very long. I was nervous and so was she. But we still remain friends. In fact, after I moved to Israel, we got pregnant again at the same time and without knowing we named both of our babies Corey!

When I started going to therapy right before we came to Israel, I didn't even tell the therapist about my lesbianism. She picked up on it, however. It was difficult for me to deal with; I felt guilty, really disgusted with myself. I didn't know what to do with it! Finally, I made a vow to myself not to sec anyone again. It was horrible. I was suppressing all my sexuality – with my husband and with women.

Part of that fear had to do with being identified as a lesbian. Being 'straight' I was aware of what everyone thought about lesbians – weird, abnormal, lewd, repulsive. You just don't have gay teachers, or gay this or that. They're the weirdos, the fringe society can't fit in. I wanted to be close – within boundaries – to the mainstream. They told horrible jokes in our woodshops. Even though LA's got a strong lesbian community, it was scary.

I thought it would be even worse in Israel. That's why I decided to stop. I figured there'd be no gay scene in Israel anyway.

*

By the time we moved here I was no longer sure why I had wanted to come. As predicted, I'd gotten used to being comfortable. But still, I felt committed to aliyah, and I didn't feel I could back out. I couldn't just say, 'I can't leave my health club!' I also knew I was missing something solid. There was this five-year hole that had been filled with money and achievement, but there was no personal growth in a deep sense. Things had happened – I finished school, had a profession, and had my first child, but ... something was missing. I was very depressed, but when I came to Israel it was even worse.

I experienced deep culture shock. I had trouble with everything from the language to dealing with the movers. Menashe's mother didn't accept me because I was American, because I was a convert, because I'm Puerto Rican – because of everything about me. She hadn't talked or written to Menashe in the five years we were in America. His parents had expected Menashe to marry this nice girl from a Polish family!

*

When I look back on it, how I was feeling makes a lot of sense. Before my first child I was very sexual, very free, and I could express myself sexually without any guilt. In Israel, I realized my role in life had changed. Instead of being a lover and a wife, I became a mother – which for me was totally non-sexual. Everything became more important than sex and myself – I was totally self-denying. I felt dreary and almost hopeless. It changed when I started horseback riding three hours every morning. It was just then, when I started making that break to my own life, I got pregnant with Corey.

It was just this big 'again'. It was less than three years since the first child. I couldn't accept it. I wanted an abortion, but it's difficult to get one here. You go from one quack doctor to another because it's illegal except for certain reasons. I didn't know the tricks. I remember sobbing for days and feeling like I was being controlled by men, by society, and not having any choices in my life.

Only after six months did I reluctantly start accepting it. I had to, really, because you get so dragged down with the weight. What changed was, I found a midwife and decided to do it in a private hospital – the way I wanted. The hospitals here have no desire to have natural childbirth. Corey ended up being born at home, which was absolutely wonderful. The fact it was a girl – I wanted a second girl and Menashe did as well – helped also. She turned out to be a wonderful baby too.

*

Even though I now had two kids to take care of, I think Menashe was jealous of the idea of him working and me 'playing', because he gave me a challenge. He said, 'I know you can't do cabinetmaking because it's such a low-paying job in Israel. Why don't you look for something new?' I can't turn down dares. I applied for Bezalel, the famous school of art and design, and against all odds I was accepted. That's why we moved to Jerusalem from Kfar Saba.

That was the beginning of another crisis because I wasn't ever at home! I left at 8:30 in the morning and came home at six in the evening, somehow managed to wash or change – or maybe not – sometimes feed the kids. Menashe would come home at eight when I was leaving for the studio. At Bezalel I was studying industrial design and was barely passing in the majority of the work. Everything was in Hebrew, and the things I specialized in – especially furniture – were just a small part of the programme. At least I learned I can draw, that I have a sense of colour and a lot of

talent that before was never explored. It was during that year at
Bezalel that I decided to come out about my lesbianism.

★

In spite of my fears and the vows I'd made, I still wanted to
be with women; there's no competition, there's a lot fewer power
games. I'm not saying there aren't any. It's just less complicated
because I can get rid of that threat – the threat of being over-
powered. I can start to relate to another human being. I had a
bisexual friend in Tel Aviv who introduced me to a lesbian in
Jerusalem. It took about an hour chatting before I got enough
strength to say, 'Here's what I really wanted to talk to you about
…' I was at a point of desperation, but to actually do something
about it was a big jump.

Through her, I got involved with somebody on and off for
two years. This was around my second year of Bezalel and I became
very promiscuous. It wasn't such a pleasant time. I figured I'd be
staying in this marriage the whole rest of my life, satisfying only one
need. So I ended up cruising – and getting very sick of it. I was not
meeting such nice women and I realized I was being very hurtful to
myself. I was also just tired! I was leading three incredibly different
lives. I got very sick: ulcers, pneumonia. I spent a month in bed and
I realized I had to stop.

I quit school. We bought a new apartment in Bakka, where
most of my lesbian friends lived. I became closer to them – their
neighbour as well as their lover. I had a lot of parties in my house
when Menashe was on trips – a dance or a potluck. This was in part
because I thought I had to be accepted, like there was this membership. When I realized I could have my own ideas about politics,
family, or anything else and still be lesbian – as soon as I could just
be comfortable with who I am and what I am – I started finding the
people I wanted to meet.

I'm very conservative and traditional. This can be awkward
because often when political discussions come up I'm the only one.
I can feel a bit ganged-up on and out of place. But if I came this far
– breaking all these ties – and then went to another group and just
followed their ideals, then I hadn't achieved anything. The problem
is, in Israel the lesbian community is very small, I mean compared
to America. I think in America lesbians are spoiled. Here in *Eretz*

Yisrael, you have to fight for every scrap you get – and then you have to be grateful for it!

Around this time I met Bat Miriam at a party in my house. She was also a mother, and we became lovers. I realized then that motherhood was something I wanted to keep – I got rid of the idea that being a mother wasn't a great lesbian thing to do. Then Bat Miriam got married and this helped me to ease up about Menashe as well. I began inviting Menashe, not to parties and stuff, but to friends' houses. I started making it obvious that I was married to him, part of a couple. I brought him to lectures so he could learn about women's issues. For a long time I had tried to keep him in the dark about my life; finally I just started uniting the two halves.

So far, he's been very accepting of it. I realized he's a very important person in my life and whoever didn't want to accept it wasn't a very good friend anyway. Those who did accept it, in the end, became our friends. Eventually, instead of trying to be accepted by the whole of the lesbian community, I began to be able to let go of stereotypes and roles. This was the beginning of being whole in myself and working on my marriage, being healthier, closer with the kids and calmer.

Although I don't think the changes are over with, the one thing I've learned out of all of this is to follow the inner voice. It can be a very small voice and very weak. But if I listen to it and take a few steps at a time, I know it will lead me where I need to go.

Note

1. The laws of nidah, 'the laws of family purity', include, among other things, the Talmudic laws governing the timing of sexual intercourse between husbands and wives, based on the wife's menstrual cycle. For example, during menstruation any physical contact between husbands and wives is forbidden. At the end of her period, the wife purifies herself by immersion in the *mikveh*, the ritual bath. The mikveh is also used for other ritual purposes, including the process of conversion to Judaism.

ברברה
Barbara Becker
Edited by Mary Ellen Carew

Sharon and Barbara

• Barbara Becker, born 1944

Barbara Ann Conrad Abu Becker, forty-four, is a lively Capricorn originally from Buffalo, New York. Barbara is the only non-Jewish participant in this book. After growing up in a wandering military family, she joined the Navy Reserves, had a baby which she gave up for adoption, studied broadcasting and theatre in college, and decided to do a world tour before settling down to a career. She hasn't lived in the States since.

In recent years, Barbara has been active in the movement against violence against women, volunteered at Jerusalem's Rape Crisis Center, and earned a black belt in karate. Her latest career is as a real estate agent.

YOU could say there were a few prefiguring influences for my coming to Israel, like reading *Exodus* when I was sixteen or my best friend being Jewish. There were quite a number of Jewish girls who went to the same Catholic girls' school I went to in San Diego. My mother's a real anti-Semite, but she's anti-everything: blacks, browns, yellows – anti-Barbara too!

The pattern of my life has been that I've always moved around a lot, since my father was in the military. I learned to read maps at an *early* age. I went to thirty-six schools before I went to college, and about half of them were Catholic. The education was OK but socially it was much more difficult, having to readjust every time. There were some schools where either I didn't have the energy or I just couldn't adapt. I was often lonely, the outsider. And then there were other schools where it was just the opposite, I was popular and would have many friends. I learned how to look a place over, check it out; I've used that skill here, too, especially when I was first becoming involved with my lesbian identity.

I just kind of *ended up* in Israel. After I had been around Europe and Russia and Persia for a couple of years, I was tired and bored with travelling, didn't have any direction or desires. I felt I was at a point of no return – you know, as far to continue forward as to go back. Returning to America wasn't really a consideration. The unknown in foreign places was more alluring. Finally one day in Athens I said I'd take the next boat, wherever it was going, and it was going to Haifa! And that's how I arrived: 1 September 1967.

I never decided to stay, per se. I just stayed. First I went to a kibbutz – part ulpan, part work programme – for eight months. When the ulpan ended, there was some talk of my staying on the kibbutz because I was such a good worker. But I'd done only indoor jobs – kitchen, children's houses, dining-room – and I couldn't stand it anymore. I wanted to be in the fields, in the orchards, in the carpentry shop, *anything* else. They were saying, 'This is the kibbutz, you work where you're needed and not where you want,' but I just didn't buy it. I got myself appointed *sadronit avoda*,* arranging the work for everybody including myself. But the kibbutz is not easy to conform to. I started travelling every weekend to Jerusalem, Tel Aviv, Eilat. It was just at that time that Israel TV started in Jerusalem. TV was my ticket out of the kibbutz. I got a job as a camerawoman.

That was an exciting time. First of all, we had the euphoria of the years directly after the Six Day War. Israel was really a fun place to be. There were very few cars, but you could travel any-where – people picked you up within five minutes. Sexual harass-ment was practically unheard of – and everybody travelled by tramp [hitch-hiking]. It didn't matter if you were going down the road or to the other end of town or to Eilat! You tramped.

People invited you into their homes, to their weddings, to their funerals – it was very open-hearted. All the myths about Israel as an incredible place seemed true. People seemed so warm and genuine, with a great sense of equality. In Jerusalem I had no trouble finding places to stay. I lived with a Persian woman for a couple of weeks inside the train station where she was in charge of the cleaning detail.

Then I got the TV job and there was plenty of money, and I found a place to live in the Petra Hotel, inside Jaffa Gate.[1] A motley and flamboyant assortment of people gravitated toward the Petra. The Old City was *empty*, like in the curfew now, but then it wasn't because of a curfew. The Arab population was completely in awe of what had happened in the Six Day War. They didn't know the rank and file Israeli – they knew Israeli soldiers, from afar. They were just plain afraid. Soldiers patrolled the streets, but not with the

---

* Person who assigns the work details in a kibbutz.

tension and fear and aggressiveness that they do now. It was relaxed – there were attacks, but few and far between.

So this hotel rented out rooms by the month, and we felt like we owned the Old City. All the foreigners got to know each other, and the Arab shopkeepers living nearby got to know us. We walked through the Old City *every* hour of the day or night. We knew all the furnaces where they make bread at night. The soldiers we kept away from because we didn't like soldiers anyway. Drank millions of cups of Turkish coffee.

I think most everybody was Jewish. There was one woman who was a holy-roller-type Christian. My not being a Jew usually came out – I seemed readily identifiable as a non-Jew. Nowadays, I almost forget I'm not Jewish. But at the time it wasn't given any great consequence, although the Ministry of the Interior wasn't interested in renewing my visa all the time, but once I was in TV, it was no problem. There were a lot of people in their twenties: two students – a mixed Arab/Jewish-American couple I still know today, both lawyers; two artists; a scholar translating the Koran. I think the oldest person there was in her sixties.

The camera work was irregular. I'd be gone on a feature story two days, back for a day of news work around the city, followed by days when I didn't work at all. At the station were a bunch of foreigners with experience and education in TV and a bunch of Israelis who didn't have either but were definitely after it. Everybody was enthusiastic about what they were doing and making a good salary compared to other people, although the important thing was just to have enough to live on. It was a very unmaterialistic society.

Jerusalem, you must remember, was really a village, very tiny. Bakka, where we live now, was close to the outskirts. And Kiryat Moshe, where the entrance to Jerusalem is, was like the other end of town. It was very quiet. There was Jaffa Road, that was all – those dinky shops, a few movie theatres – really not much social life, so we made our own. Everybody who was young was either at the university, which I didn't know anything about, or at the TV. So there were always parties. Few people had phones; we'd just drop in.

There was one *tremendous party*. The guy in charge of the

graphics at the TV – some David, from the States, very outgoing – made a big party in a house that was out at Sharfat on the way to Ramala. He invited all of the TV, all of the Israeli establishment, and all his Arab neighbours – hundreds of people. The chief of police, the muktar of the area, Armenian priests – everyone was there. He hired his neighbours to cater the party, and they were sending the food, the pitta, in by donkey from over the hills. It was *quite* incredible. It went on for two days. I met Hussni, my husband, there.

He was teaching music, clarinet and saxophone, which he had learned in the Jordanian army, which was still very English. They would take kids, ten, eleven, twelve, and teach them a profession. It's like the Israeli army has a military high school for boys – the Jordanian army had the same thing, specially for musicians. I saw him as the most handsome and wisest man I'd ever met! He wanted to get married very much, so not thinking there was any reason not to, I did. We got married in December of 1969 and my son, Udi, was born in the spring of 1971. We were married about seven years.

We lived in the Petra for a while, and then we got an ancient house inside Jaffa Gate, sort of at the edge of the Armenian quarter, a little pocket called the Syrian Quarter – it's not really a quarter, just a few Syrian families – near the youth hostel. Life continued much as it had in the Petra.

But there began to be changes. First of all the TV started getting organized, and they ran tenders for all the jobs. Everybody had to reapply for their job or any other. A political conflict between the infant television and the radio broadcasting system in Israel resulted in most of the foreigners or anybody who knew anything about TV getting shafted, and a lot of radio people sliding in. At the time I didn't know enough about the society to push my way back in.

So I left TV and got a job in a bookstore, part-time. I was making a lot of furniture, doing stuff with the house. I was pretty happy, but compared to the action of the last couple of years, I was much more alone.

The next big watershed was: Hussni and I got busted. The police came up with a matchbox full of marijuana, which wasn't in the house before. It really wasn't. We *did* smoke, but we kept the house very clean. After that things got very hard. Both of us were fired from our jobs. We were acquitted, but it took three years. We were in court seventeen times, it cost us a fantastic amount of money which we didn't have. For the whole time Hussni didn't have his identification, without which he couldn't work, because he was Arab. And I had a baby! To make ends meet, I modelled for the art school – mostly in the nude.

Hussni began to be a serious drinker. It was heartbreaking. Now I'm in a whole different consciousness and have had years of therapy and so on. But at twenty-seven, I wasn't very wise in interpersonal relationships. I was also cut off from all the changes taking place in the States. I 'd left during the flower generation, civil rights, and Vietnam was just beginning. So I missed the later part of the 1960s.

And I hadn't prepared for motherhood in the *least*. I was still floating around on a cloud. The real world of economics and so on had just sort of thrown itself on me because of not being regularly employed – plus the court case hanging over us all the time, and Hussni's drinking. I didn't know myself very well.

Having a baby scared me. I didn't know what to do with it! I felt extremely isolated, home alone with a child all day. Udi would cry and fret and sleep only sporadically. And housekeeping chores are deathly boring. I felt trapped. Not to mention I was probably into this whole dependency/co-dependency pact with an alcoholic! I felt captured in this strange house, which I'm sure lots of young wives have felt all over the world – it's probably how my mother felt.

I started sewing to supplement our income, and sometimes my husband and I would dance for openings and fashion shows. And then one of my girlfriends opened a boutique called The Gypsy and Esther offered me a regular job there. She wanted to teach me to cut, and she knew I could sew. Eventually, a core group of five women ran the boutique – me, Esther from Texas, Reggie from Switzerland, Jackie from the US, and Jenny from England. It was in Nahalat Ziva, a very old area of old houses, pubs and restaurants. It wasn't in the Old City, but it was in the old part of the new city. Now it's a trendy mall, but we were there first.

We had a wonderful time, and we had gorgeous, gorgeous

clothes. It was *the* place to buy clothes. Even today people remember me from the boutique – just like they remember me from parties on the top of the Petra twenty years ago! It was in operation for ten years, and I was with them for five. Here my feminist consciousness began to develop. First of all, my marriage is deteriorating, I'm doing something vital with other women, and we're all very close. Nobody's gay, but I was getting for the first time a lot of the sensitive and emotional support one needs, from The Gypsy and all it involved – customers, too.

And I was going home to a drunk husband and a child I couldn't deal with. I turned Udi over to my mother-in-law, who was happy to have him. I was a workaholic – anything to get away from home. But then I got sick with hepatitis. It's a mind-bender – anything connected with the liver affects your mind. Suddenly I had to be home, because the only way to get well is to rest. So after not being home at all, here I was, home!

One day, Udi was playing with my wallet, picking things out, spending time with me, and he said, 'Didn't you use to have a pink money in here?' I said, 'Yes, it's in there.' And he said, 'No, it's not in there 'cause daddy took it out.' It came out that all the years I had been supporting the family, Hussni had been stealing money from me. That's when I decided to get a divorce.

Of course, first I had to get my health. Being at home I was reading a lot, books and *Ms*. magazine, and the women who visited me were supporting me, and all of a sudden I was getting a feminist perspective. By the new year I started divorce proceedings, and I also took Udi for a vacation to Greece for six weeks.

Greece was very important from several viewpoints. First of all, I'd become very fat, and I *felt great* – a major breakthrough in feeling good about myself. I'd become closer to my son, and I was beginning to discover myself, to direct my life the way I wanted to go, to feel big and powerful.

And then started the play! A Gypsy customer got me involved with five women putting together the first feminist play in Israel, *Nishim Odot Nishim* (Women about Women). It started out with about twelve people and boiled down quickly to five: Miriam, myself, Gaby, Nitsa, and Ruti. Two were actors, one was an art student, and the other was from the university.

The play was really great. We put it together organically, we *built* it. It's never been written down. It was made up of sections, tableaux characterizing women's lives – Childhood, Adolescence, Motherhood, Death. It began with Waiting. And Love! First you have to love yourself, then you can love other people. That was a great piece, a body sculpture.

We had the top floor of the Jerusalem Theatre – a giant empty space, bare concrete. People came! We played to audiences of sixty to eighty. It was very innovative for its time, certainly in Israel. In the beginning we were on stage, but by the end we were in the audience, passing out fruit, talking with the people. A real matriarchal production. Altogether, we gave between forty and fifty performances over two years. By then, we'd evolved out of it, and it ended.

For perspective, when I came back from Greece, I realized I was interested in women for more than just emotional support. I was almost always in the company of women, and I realized I was getting from women just about everything that was keeping me alive, except sex. For that I was going back to the male world – for *sex*. How ridiculous!

There was one woman I was *very* attracted to. I realized she had been making passes at me, and I had never responded, not recognizing what they were. Then when I *was* ready, I searched her out. We were both virgins as far as women were concerned, and we decided not to be virgins anymore.

We decided we needed a weekend together to see if we could have a physical relationship. We were so excited – about this experiment, our courage, each other. We'd laugh and make love, make love and laugh. I've been pretty high in my life, but I don't think I was ever so high as I was that weekend. I was *sure* I had found the promised land. I was in such a good mood I was telling everybody, 'I have this new friend, and guess what, it's a *woman*' – just bubbling. And all my friends accepted it, and were happy for me too. Yeah, I didn't lose anybody.

We were together for a very short time, physically for an even shorter time. She woke up one morning and said she was *not* lesbian, and this was *not* for her, and that was that! *I* on the other hand knew this was my direction, I *was* lesbian!

My divorce was finally just coming through. I was pretty fed up with the legal system here: I'd been through the whole drug thing, I'd just gone through the whole divorce thing, and now I had one to go: custody. And I hope I am *never* in court again!

From then I kind of backtracked. I felt I needed to conserve the energy I was putting into my relationships. They were butterfly relationships anyway, flitting from flower to flower. I opted for my own company for a while, and went to therapy. As hard as the therapy was, my determination to stop living my life with one foot nailed to the floor was even stronger. I went to group and individual therapy once a week for three years. One of my smarter moves.

I got divorced in 1976, which was the end of the play and more or less when I stopped Gypsy. Then I studied carpentry for a while through the Ministry of Labour. They have vocational courses, and I was the first woman they put into carpentry. It worked out very well, but I didn't stay with it. I had a family to support, and I could do much better with the sewing machine. So I freelanced, sewing for factories and boutiques or making costumes for plays – but it was very hard. I don't know how it is in the States, but here you are *always* running after the money. Getting the money afterwards is *not* easy. Sometimes it just never came through at all. And the worst part is you never come home to relax, you're always coming home to work.

Meanwhile I made another smart move in my life and bought this apartment – a major, major thing. That was 1978. And I'm realizing the girl who moved fifty times before she was fifteen has been in one city for more than ten years! I always find it amusing when I hear the common question, 'When did you decide to make aliyah, what's your motivation?' Sure, I know where it's coming from: if you're Jewish, you have a background and a connection with Israel. And most people don't leave America to come here without deciding to do it!

But having no obvious connection to this place whatsoever, it wasn't something I decided consciously to do, ever. I really think I must have been here in a prior lifetime. And things just seemed to keep me here. First of all, in the late 1970s there was a feminist political party. Then in the early 1980s there was the Jerusalem women's centre, Kol HaIsha. I found myself gravitating towards it, as someone who had more or less by herself found she was lesbian, without knowing there was any community. But when you run out of resources, you go to where the corn is growing! Kol HaIsha had a library; I read it *all*. I watched who was there, and every now and then I went to a meeting, but I preferred the fringes.

When I was a child and moved around so much, I got good as an observer. Very often I would simply decide how I wanted to be before I got there. I'd decide whether I wanted to integrate or join the fastest crowd. Sure, the new kid in town is always intimidated. But this wasn't just another bunch of kids, right? There were women who were also interested in women! I wanted to watch and see what other lesbians look like, how they talk, how they relate, what's going on here! I never really got into Kol HaIsha. It seemed too cliquey. Cliques frighten me.

In 1982 I decided to take a trip home, to America. My mother was the one I was after – to confront, connect, know. I wanted to show Udi the States. And in America I had an affair, which was *lovely*. When I came back, I was really looking for a relationship with a woman. I'd finished going back and forth, checking things out. I didn't see men on the street anymore – only women.

So whenever there were parties, gatherings, I was there. First, I was with an Israeli woman half my age – very exuberant and extravagant and loving and immature. We partied a lot. There was also a man involved: a *ménage à trois*. Then some weeks after that bubble burst, I met an American visitor. I was *not* in good shape when she left. I had made a bigger investment in it than I realized, even knowing it was going to end. After a one-night stand or two, I put sex on hold, and gave some real thought to what qualities I wanted in a partner, what kind of relationship I wanted, and things I wasn't willing to tolerate – now all I had to do was find the woman. It took all of a week to find her, to find Sharon. There's nothing like timing!

The first time I saw Sharon, she was bubbling with enthusiasm, urging people to get off their inertia and play some games at an International Women's Day outing in Sacher Park. That night there was a party. I arrived on my 12-speed bike, in a wonderful mood, looking forward to the company of women and dancing. It was not crucial if I went home alone – the sexual Barbara was on hold. I don't think I sat down once!

Towards the end of the party, there she was, dancing in front of me again and again – Sharon is an excellent dancer too. I met her on the dance floor, just like I met my husband. And they're both Leos! Still, I was surprised when she asked for my phone number. I gave it to her on condition that she use it.

Two days later we got together, and within a week Sharon bought a bike – one kind of commitment! Only four and a half years later did we begin living together, when we decided that was the next logical step to expand our relationship. Right now, I'm very involved in the process of living together – a giant step for me. I'm pleased with what we've been able to accomplish, not only Sharon and I, but also with Udi, who lives with us. I hope we will always have the courage to make those changes.

I'm happy. We have lots of fun times and we struggle with the hard times, using them to learn and grow. I'd like this relationship to last a long time. I feel I've built a kind of security – an overused word in this country – but it's something that gives you a place to come from. Still, there are no guarantees in this life, and the best we can do is to live it fully, one day at a time.

Note

1.   One of the four gates in the wall around the Old City of Jerusalem.

ליל

Lil Moed

Edited by Sarah Jacobus

• Lil Moed, born 1927, died 1991

Lil Moed[1] made aliyah at the age of fifty-eight and lived for six years in Israel. A working-class American, professional psychologist, and life-long activist for progressive political causes and world peace, she was involved in Palestinian–Israeli dialogue and women's peace groups, and was a founder of Shani, part of the Israeli Women and Peace Coalition. She travelled yearly to the States to do peace education workshops. Her youngest daughter, Julie Moed, a lesbian, lives in San Francisco; her elder daughter Leah became an Orthodox Jew and lives in Israel with her husband and children.

I GREW up during the Depression in the East Bronx in New York, a working-class, mostly Jewish, neighbourhood. My own nuclear family and my parents' circle of intellectuals and friends were all socialists. It was *all* Jewish, *Yiddishkayt*.* So in my formative years, I had a highly developed sense of social justice within the framework of being Jewish.

The issue of the day was unemployment. People were just scraping by at subsistence level. The idea of women's equality never even came up. Then came World War II, with a typical war economy prosperity for many people. People were going off to the army or finding war work, so the emphasis then became fighting fascism – fighting Hitler, fighting Mussolini. My parents were part of an anti-fascist movement.

But it was the dropping of the atomic bomb, the thought that America could drop bombs on two cities and kill millions of people, that was most earthshaking. To me, it was as big as the death of millions of Jews in the Holocaust. From then on I became involved in peacemaking.

I later lived in upstate New York, where the most progressive thing was working for the United Nations. I thought it was wonderful to be part of something so big. I think it had to do with being Jewish and coming from a home of immigrant parents, where I never grew up with a strong Zionism or strong American patriotism. We were not apple-pie Americans, so this became a comfort-

* Jewish customs and culture.

able place for me to hang my political hat: that the world was one and needed social justice, that you couldn't think of peace only for Americans, that there had to be peace around the world.

Then I got involved with groups that protested nuclear testing, women's groups such as Women Strike for Peace and the Women's International League for Peace and Freedom, where we took up campaigns on what testing meant in terms of children.

When I was living in Philadelphia, I spent about five years working intensely on civil rights. This was in the mid- to late 1950s and early 1960s. We tested housing discrimination in teams, going in as a white couple to rent a place after a black couple had been turned down. I remember a group of us, mixed black and white, testing a roller rink where blacks had never been allowed. It was a brave thing to do, skating around in mixed couples, but we did it.

I joined a choir deliberately because it was mixed black and white in a city that didn't have any kind of integration. When the civil rights movement really got going, we white supporters sent money and material aid to black groups that were working in the South. We were with CORE, (the Congress of Racial Equality), which was more left than the NAACP (National Association for the Advancement of Colored People).

My civil rights work was an incredible personal development – really knowing what other people were going through and what injustices meant in a personal way. When I was married, my husband George Moed and I chose to live in black neighbourhoods, and since then I've continued to. There are few integrated areas; you either lived with whites or blacks. Those of us who were in these integrated or predominantly black areas were privileged to see another slice of American life.

*

I got involved in feminism in the late 1960s and really took off. My marriage broke up, a lot due to my new consciousness and being able to get over some of my fears about losing a husband and having to be a single parent. I had stayed married for over twenty years. We had worked at it; we had kids and all that.

I grew up with a mother who felt that if you just had bread

on the table, clothes on your back and kept a clean little apartment, you had it made in America. So in some ways I bought that – don't ask too much of life, because if you don't die in your twenties or something horrible hasn't happened to you, you have a charmed life. So I didn't really think I should be *happily* married. After all, he didn't beat me, he didn't drink and he wasn't terrible, so we stayed married.

But the most marvellous thing with feminism, unlike all the other movements I'd been involved with, was a discovery of myself as a person. I really found out something about who I was and felt good about myself. For the first time, I was living for myself and my kids. I had lived a lot for my family, but this was a whole new thing.

Around 1968 or 1969 I was finishing a doctorate in public health at UCLA [University of California at Los Angeles], a hotbed of women's activities. I was meeting feminists and thought they were a bit off the wall. With all the things going on in the world, women's liberation seemed a hell of a thing to be concentrating on. But as tends to happen with feminism, it touches you in a deep way as a woman. I helped found the women's studies programme at the University of California at Riverside and started teaching. My feminism just took off from there.

There was so much going on, all emphasizing women's liberation. We did consciousness-raising groups and radical therapy groups, developed women's studies, and worked with women's centres and collectives. I think at one point I was part of three or four collectives at one time! I would move from meeting to meeting to meeting. It was exciting – tiring but nourishing. I was flying high most of the time, because my life was changing a lot.

I had never met lesbians before. I went with a friend and a colleague to a women's dance at the Women's Building in Los Angeles, which had just opened. I freaked out at this dance. I'd never seen a whole room full of women dancing close and holding each other. Some were kissing. I tried not to look. I remember how uncomfortable I was. I thought, 'Oh God, this is *so* abnormal.' I said to my colleague, 'I'm leaving.' I took my friend, who was straight, and left. I could not handle that scene. I was so overwhelmed by it.

Actually, I was first aware of really loving a woman when I was about nineteen. I was very much attached to a woman, Lucille Saner, who was my best friend at the Fordham Hospital nursing school in New York. The truth is that I was in love with her. When she got married, I married soon after. I remember feeling that if I couldn't be with her for the rest of my life, I might just as well get married. I married George, her husband's best friend.

Because Lucille and I had some kind of falling-out over George, we couldn't continue our relationship. Years later, we reconciled, but it had pained me all that time, the kind of pain you have from a love relationship, not just the kind from an ordinary friendship.

Then I buried my attraction to women; I just buried it. I continued having friendships where we talked endlessly and about everything, deep relationships with women, but I never again had that feeling of falling in love.

Not long after that women's dance where I felt so over-whelmed, I got involved with one of my colleagues, Marcia Keller, who was a philosophy professor at UC-Riverside. Marcia and I were working together on this new women's programme in the university. She was married, and I'd been separated for a year.

Marcia and I spent a lot of time together. She had a house in the mountains, where I'd go and visit overnight. There was an *incredible* intensity. When I think of Marcia, I don't think of physical attraction, even though we were lovers for a year. What happened to me was feeling that there was this other person I had such an attachment to, in a way I had never had with my husband or male lovers. It was deeper than sexual attraction. I loved her enormously. I think I was her first woman lover and we were both very, 'Oh my, *this* is what it means?'

In some ways it was exciting, because there were so many women coming out. But it was scary too, in that I was changing my identity in my middle years. I went through a denial stage for a year or so of not calling myself lesbian. I wouldn't even say the word to myself, and I continued a long-term affair with a man.

But at some point, I started a love affair with another woman, Gerry Clark, and began to identify as a lesbian. That's when I gave up men. It just didn't work for me anymore. I would compare the men to the women and wonder what I was doing with men. Sexually, I was still used to being with men, but emotionally, being with a woman was so superior. I was with Gerry about five years and with her, I learned how to be sexual as a lesbian.

By the mid-1970s, I was deep in the LA lesbian community. This was my new social network. I identified with all the lesbian women in the community. And I finally learned that it was great to go to women's dances! There was a part of me that was very proud, because I was coming out at a time when it was such a politically right-on thing to do. I was working for the LA County Department of Mental Health and was in the closet at work, as many of us were. But in the women's community, it was a badge of honour to be called lesbian. I still saw my old friends, my straight friends, but that was not my community any more.

I started coming out to some of my straight friends and told my kids too. I was a lesbian when my older daughter Leah moved out of the house, moved here to Israel, and it was okay with her. But it was a time when it was okay, especially in southern California, to be living a different kind of lifestyle.

My younger daughter, Julie, was fourteen at the time and still at home. I had a lot of trouble with her. She had the hardest time with my first relationship, the one with my colleague, Marcia. She was jealous of Marcia and really gave her a hard time. Julie was angry, but when I look back, a lot of it was my own discomfort and hiding. I wouldn't sleep with Marcia in my house because I thought Julie shouldn't be exposed – even though I had told her I was a lesbian.

With Gerry, I finally got comfortable enough. I think it was because she looked at me and said, 'Are you kidding?' Then I could see how ridiculous it was to worry about Julie knowing her mother was in bed with someone. And by then, Julie had had at least a year to absorb my being a lesbian. She was also crazy about Gerry. Gerry happened to be a very playful, sort of joyous person, who liked Julie a lot. They got on marvellously well for the five years she and I were together and to this day are good friends.

When Julie was in high school, she had a boyfriend, but some of her girlfriends were lesbians. I didn't know which way she was going, but by the time she was about sixteen, it seemed to me that she was a lesbian. She was never open with me. She would talk to Gerry, tell her everything – to this day I don't know what their secrets were. I really respected that confidentiality and never pushed to get from Gerry what was going on. But, lo and behold, when Julie was about eighteen, she started a relationship with one of the women in my lesbian community. And there she was, out!

I used to test myself, saying, 'Okay, if there's some homophobia within me, it should come out around my daughter.' Like, 'Oh, my God, my daughter's gay!' or something like that. But I felt really good about it. To this day I do. I feel proud of her; I think she's doing the right thing. Why would she want to burden herself with some man?

Julie is thirty now. She lives in the States. When we're together, we talk about our lives. There's an ease in our acceptance of each other. She talks about her girlfriend. She doesn't get into talking about lesbiansim as a political phenomenon. It's just her life, the way it is.

Most of her friends say, 'Oh, wow, are you lucky your mum's a lesbian,' because all her close friends are gay. But she'll come up with, 'You know, I've got my problems with my mum.' What she's saying is, just because your mum is lesbian doesn't mean that makes everything okay. Because it hasn't been. Both being lesbians, we have a lot to work out. It's a big part of our mother/daughter relationship problem. Our relationship is packed with love, but it's not easy.

My mother, Rose Weissman, also knew I was a lesbian. She would never have understood the word; my mother's English vocabulary was limited and we always spoke Yiddish with each other. But she knew about Gerry. My mother lived with me, and Gerry often spent overnights. My mother saw us in bed. She was very old by then and I have no idea what she was thinking about.

But I do know that she received enormous love and caring from my lesbian friends for years, and she recognized it. They did everything a family would do. We would take her to many of our lesbian parties and to every celebration, especially around the Jewish holidays. She seemed to fit right in! People would always ask me, 'Where's your mother?'

My father, Morris Weissman, had died long before her, and

she had lived alone for five or six years before she came to live with me. She lived with me six years. When I came here in 1984, I put her in a home in Los Angeles. She died a year after that. I think she was disturbed about my coming to Israel. She was in her nineties by then and had had a stroke. I don't know how much she really understood. But it was hard for me. My intention was to bring her here, but her doctor asked me to think hard about that. After I was here a year, I more or less said, 'Well, I'll go back and get her,' but by then she was so sick, she really couldn't do the trip. Frankly, I think it broke her heart that I broke up our home. She probably would have lived another few years, but I had sort of had it, too. I had been six years taking care of her and was feeling like I wanted to make a change in my life. I just didn't want to stay in the US any more.

My daughter Leah had become Orthodox and moved here. I wanted to better understand her choice and the community she was part of, so I had come each year to visit. And I had shifted into Middle East peace work after the invasion of Lebanon in 1982, which absolutely floored me. How could Jews do this? Sabra and Shatila – it was like trying to understand what happened to Jewish justice.

By then, I had been in the feminist movement for at least twelve or thirteen years and I'd done a lot in my local community, teaching and counselling. I was ready to step into non-lesbian work, to bring my feminism into the world. Working with the Middle East task force of the LA chapter of New Jewish Agenda, I'd established an environment of men working on their sexism and women being assertive and taking leadership roles.

Doing that work with New Jewish Agenda, I was one foot in and one foot out of the closet. If anyone ever confronted me, I wouldn't deny that I was a lesbian, but on the other hand, it never became an issue unless somebody brought it up. But I was definitely much more out there than here.

Since I've been here a number of years as an immigrant, I've been very careful about telling anyone I'm close to that I'm a lesbian. My closest Israeli friends are lesbian and I think of that little inner circle as my family, although I do have blood family here. I see my lesbian friends once a week or so. Then I have another circle, where there are a couple of gay men. I'm out with a few straight friends. Beyond that, I'm pretty much in the closet.

I'm not out to people I work with politically. It would never occur to me to tell them. I wouldn't feel safe at all. I think with some of the people I deal with, it's obvious that I'm a lesbian. They know lesbians in the community and know they're my best friends, so I'm just assuming that's how they know. But I haven't felt comfortable or trusting enough with them personally to come out, though I may trust them on a political level. With people who get to know me well and are willing to open a door by asking a question that tells me they are sensitive and observant, I would never say to them, 'Oh, no, I'm not.' But that doesn't happen very much.

Here, I never thought much about feeling isolated as a lesbian, because I feel isolated as an immigrant. I feel isolated as an English speaker in a Hebrew-speaking country. I feel isolated as a staunch peace worker, a minority person in that political arena. Putting lesbian on top of that feels like the least of my problems.

And yet in many ways it feels like the *most* of my problems, because being lesbian adds such another queerness to the whole syndrome. I'm a minority in a minority in a minority in a minority and that feels like too much for me. So I have my own psychological defences where I just push it away. Being an older woman and having no partner or love affairs here, it's easy to just say, 'Forget it, what's the meaning of all that?' I have no *need* to identify as a lesbian. I don't have to explain living with a woman in the same house; I don't have to explain any of the things that I used to explain to some degree in the States.

So I have to answer that question, 'What *does* it mean that I'm a lesbian?' Because it's the core of me. I see the world through strong feminist lenses and to me, going to the edge of feminism is being lesbian. My analysis of what's wrong with the world is that men have always run it and do run it and women are an undercaste, a lower class. That awareness *never* leaves me.

It's a little strange to be so deeply involved in such a core way and then go around in the closet. To not be able to say to people I'm in contact with, 'I am not a heterosexual person.'

With straight people here, much more than in the States, I don't trust that they have dealt with the issue. I feel they wouldn't have the foggiest notion and would be patronizing to me if I came out to them. I don't want to go around feeling I have to start educating them. I feel Israelis are like all people, better on a one-to-one level. If I were living with children in a lesbian relationship and my neighbour got to know me, that would be fine. But that same neighbour could march in an anti-gay protest or want a law that prevents gays from coming into the country. I absolutely believe that coming out is the best thing a gay person can do as a political statement. But emotionally, I don't have the courage to do it, so I don't.

My life is full here, with lots to do and enough good friends and closeness that I don't feel a heaviness about that. Leah knows and accepts me for what I am, which is enormously important to me. We have always talked freely on the issue of lesbianism. If I couldn't do that with her, it might be more difficult for me.

The driving force for me here is making the political situation right. That sounds presumptuous, I suppose, but the way I see the situation is that Israel has conquered land and people and resources and is oppressing Palestinians. I can't live with that, so I do whatever I can to correct it. That means ending the Occupation, going beyond that, seeing what kind of just peace we can have for both peoples. I dream of Palestinians and Israeli Jews being able to live together in harmony and co-operation.

Jews and Arabs are so segregated now, and many Jews talk about 'the Arabs' in some sort of abstract way with a lot of fear behind it. I found myself with some of the same fears and stereotypes when I first went into East Jerusalem and the West Bank. But having had this whole background in civil rights work, I could at least recognize that I was having an attack of fear because I didn't know who these people were. In some sense, they became dehumanized from the stereotyping. I worked a lot of that stuff out around blacks. Once you live in a neighbourhood, you lose that. I really miss that interaction here.

I'm not a Zionist. As a Jew, I do not particularly see the need for a Jewish state. My parents weren't Zionists and I don't have an emotional tie to Zionism and a Jewish state. Intellectually, I don't have the answer to what ends anti-Semitism. Being a socialist, I have always believed that the end of exploitation will bring the end of many of the isms, though as a woman, I know that's not true, because we've seen the place of women in the world of revolutions. I recognize that sexism, anti-Semitism and racism are very deep things that are learned. Just because you get rid of the economic reasons for those isms doesn't mean you get rid of the psychological garbage people carry in their heads about anti-Semitism.

But I don't see that the Jewish state answers the need for preventing another Holocaust. In fact, I worry a lot about a nuclear holocaust in this entire area. I think that's much more likely than another Jewish Holocaust anywhere else in this world.

If I think of the Middle East and my love for the Jewish people, Palestinian people, and people anywhere in this area, I would say that the safest thing to do is build a state where both peoples can live in harmony and equality – with its problems, of course, as every nation around the world has.

What I think is possible and good enough for now is a two-state solution. The way politics in this world goes, we have to see just little steps and that's one little step. At some point, if and when both peoples see they can live together in a bi-national state, they'll make it. But it's not my programme now to push for a bi-national, secular state. It's unreal as far as I can see. I'm comfortable thinking in terms of a two-state solution, a Jewish state alongside a Palestinian state. I'm not into fighting windmills!

Another important part of my life here is my family – my daughter, son-in-law, and their kids. I have developed a close relationship with my grandchildren and I want to integrate myself well with that family. So I spend time with them; sometimes my grandkids will come and stay with me at my apartment. These family relationships get in a hard place from time to time, like any relationship. There are stumbling blocks and you have to work at it.

I'm also developing my spiritual side now, which has come late in life for me. This is almost embarrassing to talk about, because I've been a life-long atheist. There's something about being here in Israel and the land; maybe it's even more about Jerusalem. Having close friends who are religious, both Jews and Christians, and being around religious feminists, I've started re-evaluating that issue. I never thought there was an open door for me here. But I've opened those doors for myself and I want time to reflect on that. That feels scary, exciting, difficult, and ridiculous. But I'm doing it.

It's almost like being in the closet! I don't tell anyone about it, except the same little core of friends, people I can say 'I'm a lesbian' to. I think where the embarrassment comes from is immediately thinking of all my Marxist friends who say, 'Come on, the opium of the masses' and all that bullshit.

But my feeling is that there is certainly something more than the materialism of this world. It makes me feel good to think that somehow there is a spirit, there is a soul in every person that's more than our cells and the chemistry and all that. The souls of people are meaningful and beautiful to me.

I've started asking myself what all this means for me. I feel like there is something to letting go of the idea that you can control everything, that *I* can control my life. It makes more sense to me to say, 'I can give up this control and there is a higher power working in some mysterious way, but that I *feel* is working with me.'

I don't think I could have come to this without feminism. Feminism made me face my own detachment from myself. I had been detached because I was living through a man, so none of my experiences had validity. I didn't even see them as *real*. It was feminism that validated my experiences as a woman. Once they became real, I could own them and gain a better handle on who I was and know that I was important just for myself. That extends into the spiritual side of me, which is also there and important. I don't have to deny that. I have a right to pay attention to the personal side.

I've been reading a lot about liberation theology too, which is a good mix of Marxism or socialism and theology. Somehow it fits together and makes a lot of sense.

I've never been religious. The word Judaism connotes to me some understanding of the religion, which I have never understood. From time to time I read Torah, yet I can't connect with it. It feels patriarchal, these Bible stories with women who are so incidental. Everyone begets someone who begets someone. If this is the word of God, he gave it all wrong, as I see it.

But of course, I view the Bible as having been written by men and this is the way they saw their history. So when people talk about the 'holy word' and the 'learned rabbis who passed this down', all I can say is that a bunch of guys handed this down and it was not meant for me!

But I did grow up feeling Jewish, with Jewish parents who had no other identity. They came from Europe, but that was just a coincidence. They happened to be Russian, but they never felt Russian. They felt *Jewish*. I grew up with the idea that *this* is what I was. It's what I sucked in with my mother's milk. I threw it over in an attempt to be accepted by the American Christian world, but I never got rid of it.

It's at the core. If you peel layer upon layer upon layer of me, like I was an onion, you'd get to the core! And there's the Jew and there's the lesbian, or at least the feminist, because I became a lesbian much later in life. But the lesbianism has been very powerful, like a rebirth. The lesbianism became a rebirth, but I have remained a Jew.

Note

1. Out of concern for her security, Lil recorded her oral history as 'Malke', giving pseudonyms to the people she mentioned. Many of those people have elected to restore their full names to the narrative in the interests of historical accuracy. At first mention, the use of only a first name reflects the person's desire to remain anonymous.

אמה
Emma Gilbert
Edited by Lisa Edwards

● *Emma Gilbert, born 1948*

Emma's Parisian accent dominates her English, which she projects with energy and verve. Forty-one at the time of this narration, she lives in Tel Aviv, a city she loves, where she works as manager of a travel agency.

A more recent step in Emma's coming-out process was being the lesbian in a panel on differences in identities among women at the 1993 Israeli Feminist Conference. By policy, panels contain Ashkenazi, Oriental (Mizrachi), Arab and lesbian women. Emma's presentation allowed her to relay her experiences and identities as a woman, a Jew, an Israeli, a French person, a radical feminist and a lesbian.

MY father came to Israel in 1962 on a holiday because we have relatives here. He came on one of those fancy boats and by car, a Citroen – you know, that old French car which goes 'bub bub bub'? He made an 8-millimetre film and I thought, 'I'd like to see that place.' I read about Israel, and two years later I came here alone on a holiday – I was sixteen, having been born two weeks after the State of Israel.

I stayed six weeks. I went to the beach, started smoking, and went to discos with boys for the first time. It was the big life! People said to me, 'You should come here, we need young Jews to build the country.' I thought, 'Me – a Parisienne – in this desert? It's so primitive, what would I do here?' The place was so backwards compared to Europe. There was nothing to buy! We used to bring soap, toothpaste and even toilet paper because it wasn't soft here. Nothing was good and everything was very expensive.

When I went back home, I started learning Hebrew as an optional language at school. I even took Hebrew for my baccalaureate, which is the very tough high school final exam. Then I took Hebrew at Ecole Nationale des Langues Orientales, where people who want to work for embassies and things like that study languages.

Then in 1967, the Six Day War broke out. I was among the few people my age who had been to Israel. You probably know that many Jews 'discovered' Israel during the Six Day War, because it gave them this idea of strength and pride. I ran to demonstrations and collected money, and was *very* worried; we listened to the radio all the time. I wanted to volunteer to work on a kibbutz for the summer. But my mother said, 'If you go I'll die,' and my father said, 'Don't go because she'll drive me completely crazy,' and I gave in. [laughs] Instead I came on a three-week holiday. I could speak Hebrew, I could manage a little.

In May 1968 we had our revolution in Paris. I was right there – a student at the Sorbonne. In April I had come to Israel with my mother on a holiday. She wanted to stay for Yom Ha'atzmaut. I said, 'We can't because I have exams,' so we went back. A week later riots closed the Sorbonne. Ten million workers on strike!

I was in the streets. That is, when I could prevent my mother from locking me in, *then* I was on the streets! I was active on the student committees opposed to the system of forcing students to cram for exams, while the semester's work counted for nothing. I was one of two representatives of my class who negotiated the changes.

I was also a member of the Union of Jewish Students. One day we got to the Sorbonne and saw a PLO flag and stand. The PLO was not what it is now. Just today Arafat talked in Paris about recognizing Israel. At that time they said, 'We'll destroy you. We'll never accept Israel.' I heard some guys from Algeria saying, 'It took us 132 years to become independent and get rid of the French. It will take us whatever time it will but we will get rid of you!' It was *very* scary. So we organized to try to answer them. What was really incredible was that you had this big strike and nothing was working – no banks, no gas, garbage piling up, the cobblestones removed from the streets, people wounded and in hospitals. And right there, in one of the main areas, what were people discussing? The situation in the Middle East!

I think this is what pushed me to my final move here: when the word 'Israel' became taboo. Many Jews among those leftists have since become 'better Jews' – today my old Maoist friends are studying Yiddish! What gave me the last push was hearing non-Jews say, 'Why are you talking about the War all the time, and genocide? What's the big deal?' I thought, 'I cannot stay with people who say such things.'

★

The first year in Israel I could just sleep all day if I felt like it, without having my mother start the vacuum cleaner, washing machine, and coffee grinder all at once to make sure I wouldn't stay in bed. I didn't do *anything* because I couldn't get myself to do things without somebody telling me what to do. I had been dreaming of being free, but once it happened I didn't know how!

The second year I registered for an MA in English. I *hated* Tel Aviv University. You know, coming from the Sorbonne when things went upside down – here they're so, I don't know, so *rigid*. They didn't hand out one political tract in three years! People are not encouraged to *think* here.

Anyway, people would always ask me, 'Are you going to stay?' And I'd say, 'I don't know.' And then after several years I realized I kept saying 'I don't know,' but I was still here and didn't feel like leaving. So I stayed!

Then my parents said, 'If you're going to stay, we're going to buy an apartment.' I said 'OK, that would be nice!' My parents rent, like most people in Paris. They never bought anything before. My father got some money together, I got a mortgage from the Jewish Agency, and I bought this very apartment. That helped me settle down. This was three years after I came here, at the end of 1972.

★

I had wanted to be a travel agent since the age of fifteen – the dream of my youth. I began working in the travel industry, and my life began to take some shape – in this field anyway. On the emotional level it became one big mess. But I'll get to that.

When I was thirteen, I fell in love for the first time – a day I'll never forget. School started in September, and there was Anna, surrounded by a bunch of groupies listening to her stories of what she had done during the summer holiday. I took one look and thought, 'That's that!' It was love at first sight – and I realized it *then*, without a qualm. Anna and I became best friends, and then it became stormy because I was so jealous and possessive. There was nothing sexual – just *sooo* romantic. You know what teenagers are: extreme. I didn't want her to have any other friends or to talk to anybody except me.

I had this pure, unstained vision of life that there's nothing wrong with being in love, whatever the person's gender, as long as the person is OK. If she's mean or doesn't act nicely – like I often thought of Anna because she didn't pay me enough attention! – then there's something wrong. Also I believed love is not necessarily a cause of joy and pleasure, but causes suffering – the romantic idea of love connected to death and despair.

I tell you the truth: I had her in my head for twenty-five years! Even now, sometimes I dream about her. Anyway, she was not Jewish, which didn't matter except it would've been more acceptable if my best friend had been Jewish.

Now, on the other hand, I had another friend, Karen, who was very Jewish. We three were a triangle, but triangles often don't work. They were both a year and a half older than me, and there was a lot of competition between them. I was like a little sister. I was never very 'feminine'. They already used make-up and wore small high heels. I never did that! With Karen I had a sexual experience when I was fifteen, which she initiated, and I was rather passive. [laughing] I may have been passive, but I had very good orgasms! When we studied for exams, this is how we rewarded ourselves. [more laughing] We joked when we were doing it, but we never discussed it. We just *did* it as if it was something we'd forget about once it's done. She was a friend of mine for many years, and we never, ever talked about what we did.

With Anna I initiated the sexual relationship, and whatever we did, she was passive. We spent weekends together – her parents had a house in the country – and we slept together at night. I knew if I tried to ask how she felt, something bad would happen. It was like walking on a mine-field.

At the same time we started going out with boys, but didn't sleep with them. In the society where I grew up – Jewish girls mostly – it was a very bourgeois upbringing. We had internalized this idea that good girls don't sleep with boys until they think they're going to marry. So we'd go out with boys, but end up together afterwards.

One time the school social worker called my mother and said there was something wrong with this relationship, and we shouldn't be allowed to see each other outside school. My mother freaked out. I promised we wouldn't see each other, but we did.

And just my tough luck – Paris is a big place – one time a friend of my mother saw us and told her. Now, Anna's family didn't like me very much because I was Jewish, noisy, and didn't have nice manners. [laughing] But neither family could stop us. Even at twenty, and dating boys, there was still the connection. But then I came here, and a year later she got married.

Now, I spoke of this whole thing because I think this was a good relationship. But just after I moved here, I began the most fucked-up relationship I've ever had, or ever will. I was doing the first year of an MA when I noticed a girl in my class. She spoke perfect English and perfect Hebrew and looked mysterious.

We became friends quickly. We spent a lot of time at my place because I didn't have a roommate. I remember one morning in April 1970, it hit me, as if the sky had fallen over my head: boom! 'I'm in love with her!'

But I didn't want her to know. Why? Because my fear was she'd run away and I'd get hurt. But after some time, I couldn't restrain myself so I made timid moves, which she didn't resist. So I became bolder and bolder, and again I got into the pattern where I was the initiator and she was passive. We had a few months which were good, and then this power relationship started, which destroyed me, little by little, but surely.

She thought what we were doing was wrong, and we should go to a psychiatrist – or *I* should go, anyway, because I had dragged her into it. I felt I should go, not for the reason she thought, but because I couldn't handle the isolation. For about three years I was totally dependent. There would be desperate conversations: she would say, 'If you do this again, I'll leave you!' And I would say, 'Don't leave me, I can't live without you!' Very dramatic, but unfortunately not drama. I was miserable.

At some point, we started going out with men. She had a bad marriage, and we continued the relationship. A little after her second child was born, we had a big fight, and I decided, 'That's it,' and put an end to it. Also I had done the travel agent course, I had met other people, and I had found a group called the 'Feminist Movement'. But the wound was very deep.

★

By the fall of 1976, my involvement in the Feminist Movement became a major thing in my life. I became an active feminist, and met lesbians for the first time. I don't know what I would have done otherwise. I didn't define myself as a lesbian yet – in fact, I had men lovers – but meeting them broke through barriers of isolation, even though I was still very closed. I didn't talk about it except on an intellectual level.

A short time afterward, we opened a centre, and there were lots of activities. I sometimes went to four meetings a week, and I *loved* it. I'd come home from work, change into jeans, and go to meetings until one or two in the morning. We discussed intently, took votes, and then at the next meeting somebody would lobby everybody to have the vote reversed! At the beginning I was in two consciousness-raising groups and also on some of the organizing committees like public relations, money, etc. We also had social evenings.

One CR group was in English, because of so many foreign women, and one was in Hebrew. The English meetings were open, loose. Shoshana – now one of my closest friends – was among the first lesbians I met there. She was twenty-two and living with Moira, an Irish woman. We were going around the group one time, and women were saying things like, 'I came here, and I met this guy, and I married him, so I stayed.' When it was Moira's turn, she said, 'I met this Israeli woman, we fell in love, so I came here to live with her.' It was cute, and everybody laughed. I told that couple, 'You were the beginning of my salvation.' I realized lesbians were just like anybody else.

At the time I didn't have all the responsibilities I now have at work, so I could devote a lot of time and energy to my feminist activities. Also, my energy kept increasing! I felt dormant parts of me finally coming to life. Things like demonstrations, writing leaflets, giving interviews, and having discussions gave me an outlet for my anger, my sense of injustice, this desire to change the world. There were times when I was so elated I felt I *could* change the world. I have become a little more sceptical as time has passed.

At the same time I was wondering how we could explain what the Feminist Movement was all about. I got interested in what had been done before I joined. The Movement started in 1971, and I had missed part of it. The idea grew in my head of writing a master's thesis about the history of the Movement. I thought the best way to gather an analysis was doing the research myself and writing about it.

Once the idea took shape, I needed an academic framework. To my surprise, it turned out to be easy. I once read in a new French feminist magazine – something like *Ms.* in its beginning – about a professor teaching a women's studies course at the University of Paris 7 – one of the faculties the Sorbonne split into after May 1968 – and I wrote to her. She agreed to be my advisor. For the next year I was busy writing the thesis, being in touch with her by mail, phone, and visits. I went to Paris for the defence, and upon completing it and an exam on feminist writings, I got the degree in 1981. I could then resume my feminist activities.

I joined the collective of Tsena U'rena, a women's centre here in Tel Aviv. As a collective, decisions were made on a consensus basis. We had bi-monthly marathon meetings that lasted through the night, usually on Friday. Friday night in Israel is a time for leisure and social life, and for us, this *was* our leisure and social life. We offered courses, CR groups, lectures. We also ran a coffee shop. The place was alive, and many women came and went on top of the core of close friends and fans.

We also had parties, and with all the lesbians around, we felt free. I am saying this because at the Feminist Movement's centre a few years before, visible lesbians felt strain around the straight women. Some very out and loud ones would say: 'Lesbianism is the only politically correct way,' or 'Feminism is the theory, lesbianism is the practice,' or 'Start sleeping with women even if you don't feel like it, then you'll see everything change.' Even if it did someone good to hear things like that, it felt safer to be outrageous on our own ground.

*

In 1982, I left my job, and I spent three weeks in the States. I was with lesbians all the time, and even had an affair with somebody, in a detached way. For once! [laughs] I think this did me good. Since then, I can say I've been *out*.

When I went into therapy one of the first things I said was: 'I want you to know women are *the* important thing in my life, so I don't want any negative comments.' My therapist said to me, 'Why women?' I said, 'You wouldn't ask, "Why men?"' so we never discussed it. Finally I unburied things that had accumulated for years.

Now the remaining problem was my mother, who is a protective, Jewish-mother type. You know, I ran away 5,000 kilometres from this symbiotic relationship, and one phone call from her would put me in a state for days. Last year I had this passionate affair with a woman from Quebec. We came to Paris and for the first time, I didn't stay at my parents' house. My mother asked a friend of mine, Renee, 'Who is this woman Emma's staying with?' I'd given Renee the green light to speak freely to my mother, so she answered, 'Her lover!' My mother's first question was, 'Is she Jewish!?' [laughs hard] And *then* she said, 'She's after her money.' Renee said, 'What money?' My mother said things like, 'I'll never accept it. This conversation between us never took place.' But Renee said, 'I'll do what *I* want. My loyalty goes to Emma.' She stood up for me, and it makes me feel good because now I know I'm accepted by my straight friends. I can share the hardships of life without feeling an outcast. And now I know I will live my life, even if my mother doesn't approve of it.

Since then I've had all kinds of crushes. How can I say: for me, they fell behind the main relationships I had before – the first ones, when I was young, and what I had a year and a half ago. I think this last was important because it was the best sexual experience I've ever had. I mean, if I must die now, I'll be happy! [laughing] I had never expected I could achieve this kind of – I don't know what to call it! – this level of excitement and satisfaction both.

*

In 1982 we closed the Women's Center. We had burnt out, and had no choice but to close the place with heavy hearts. I had this feeling of emptiness for a long time. There were other activities, though less intense. I ran CR groups and did workshops at feminist conferences, but I felt a big void in my life. Sometimes I felt like a snail without the shell.

Now I'm really interested in women's peace work. Things have changed since the 1982 Lebanon war: cracks in the consensus that all wars were wars of defence. I was taught to criticize what I don't like, but it took me *years* to be able to criticize anything about Israel.

Some of these changes in me came from my trip to Nairobi in July 1985, for the UN Conference on the Decade of Women. There were 13,000 women there from all over the world. I had more emotions there in two and a half weeks than during the whole rest of the year! Until then, it had been difficult for me to discuss the Israeli–Arab conflict with people who thought differently from me without reacting with my emotions and not my mind. In Nairobi, all this changed. The first workshop I attended was planned by the Israel Women's Network, and among the speakers were Israelis, American Jews, and a Black American activist. During the discussion an older Palestinian woman told how during the Six Day War in June 1967, she left her house in Jerusalem and moved to Kuwait. She cannot return to her home, and every night before going to bed she looks at the key to her house, hanging on her wall. This touched such a nerve: it made me think of my grandmother, who left a *shtetl** and never returned. I felt everything moving inside me and broke into tears and couldn't stop sobbing. Some of the Palestinian women talked to me, trying to comfort me. I went through such a turmoil it was cathartic.

Far away from my protected daily routine, I lost all my defences and let my emotions overwhelm me. Afterward, I finally could think with a clear mind and have discussions with people hearing things I didn't like and dealing with them on a rational level. This enabled me to be involved in women's peace groups after the intifada started and to work with women whose opinions I didn't necessarily agree with, but with whom I could find a common ground for a specific purpose. It also helped me see what we as Israelis had done and were doing wrong.

*

* Small Jewish village in Eastern Europe (pre-World War II).

There was a time when if somebody had said to me, 'You'll see, one day you'll be bored at feminist meetings,' I would have killed them! I would have said, 'How can you say that to me? [laughter] It's my *life*.' But you know what? I did get bored sometimes! Oy, I got *so* bored. I thought, 'If this bores me then what else do I have to live for? [laughter] What's going to be exciting? Nothing!'

Now I realize there are things I cannot do anymore. Other people should do them. And I don't feel I have to prove I'm perfect because I'm Jewish or Israeli. On the contrary, I can make mistakes and be unsure about all kinds of things – and I'm still Jewish, still Israeli, even still a feminist! I don't feel it's my duty to do things if I don't feel like it, or if I don't like people's attitude, or their behaviour, or their reaction. There are things I don't have to put up with anymore.

*

These past years, I don't make real friends with people if I cannot be out. You see – my life is not divided anymore, it's integrated. Finally! This summer is going to be twenty years since I came to Israel – about half my life. I have a perspective about the two parts: I feel at home in Israel *and* in France. I've managed a balance between living here because I want to, but knowing I *could* live there. I know part of me comes from France, even though the most important things in my life have taken place in Israel. I've grown roots here and I feel them very much. And though it's hard living as a lesbian here, I wouldn't want to live anywhere else.

רות
Ruth Kabri
Edited by Alexis Lieberman

• *Ruth Kabri, born 1949*

A hint of a British accent under the Hebrew heightens Ruth's understated phrasing. Her compact frame is muscled and tireless from a lifetime spent outdoors as an ecologist and avid hiker. Currently she is doing ecological consulting in the San Francisco Bay area waterways.

HOW many people in Israel in the 1950s could boast that their parents were *sabra*? Not many, but I could. Three of my grandparents came to Israel and one was born here. Dad's parents came from White Russia and from Georgia, in 1914 and 1921. Mum's father left Riga, Lithuania, in 1923 or so. Her mother, however, was fourth generation in Israel. Her great-grandfather was Rabbi Baruch from Baghdad.

I was born on a kibbutz when Dad was twenty-four and Mum was twenty. That was right after the War of Independence in 1948, a time when there was lots of enthusiasm and many wartime marriages. My father had helped found the kibbutz, and I lived there until I was ten.

The kibbutz was in the lower Galilee, which was mainly Arab before 1948. It was actually besieged; they used to shoot at the roads. I grew up on stories of heroism of kibbutz members who were killed on the hill patrolling, not far from the kibbutz. The fact that the kibbutz stood during the war was important because it helped maintain Israel's territory – it was a point on the map.

Growing up on a kibbutz wasn't just war-talk, though. It was fun being part of a group of kids, going places and doing things together. We lived together in the same house and saw our parents about two hours a day, and on Shabbatot in the morning. There were caretakers watching over us, who were officially responsible for everything about us, but there was still a lot of interest between the parents and children, and our parents always knew everything about us.

We left the kibbutz when I was ten. My mother had been unhappy there for a while because she wanted to study to be a teacher and the kibbutz wouldn't send her. My father, however, had been quite happy. The kibbutz had sent him to university to study biology but called him back in the middle of the course because there was a problem with the sheep business. They did everything they could to stop him from studying and he did everything he could to finish his degree. He managed to finish it and then got an experimental plot in the kibbutz. I believe he finally decided to leave when one of the other members took the tractor and ran over his experimental plot – ploughed it up completely and ruined his experiments. He'd been working on some of them for years, and it was a big blow.

*

I spent the seventh grade in Davis, California – 1961 and 1962. My father was working on his PhD in agriculture and he went there to get himself shaped up on statistics and population genetics. It was really funny because this girl who climbed trees and ran in the wadis and used slingshots suddenly found herself in a California junior high school with girls who were beginning to smear all sorts of paint over their faces, curl their hair and wear bras and narrow skirts. These were things which girls in Israel didn't do and I really never fit in. I did find my friends with whom I could climb trees and ride bikes. Naturally, I was a tomboy.

Back in Israel, a lot of boys began to fall in love with me, and I was interested in some of them too. There was also a relationship with a girl – a very deep love which started at the age of ten. There was no sexuality in it because I was not aware of my sexuality then. She and I were inseparable during our whole adolescence. She was a 'girlie' – a very girlish girl, and somehow we were an odd but also a very complementary couple. She taught me how to make dolls and I taught her how to shoot with a slingshot. She told me it's stupid to put rocks in my pocket because they might be dirty and what would happen if I wanted to put some biscuits in the same pocket afterwards? And I taught her how to climb a tree. She once climbed a tree and couldn't come down because she was afraid, and I had to rescue her. Anyway, we were very close and at times really inseparable.

In the Scouts, when I was sixteen, my most impressive relationship was with a woman, three years older than I was. We did a lot of talking and had a very special relationship. In one of the work-camps, I shared a room with her. I think that was the first time I had sexual feelings about a woman. I remember one moment when I watched her sleeping. In my diary I wrote the word 'lesbian' for the first time – I stated that my feelings for her were 'not lesbianism'. Years later, when I suspected my parents were reading this diary, I tore that page off.

*

I was drafted to the army in 1967, three months after the Six Day War. It was considered very pioneering to serve in the Sinai and I felt lucky that I spent a great deal of my service there. That area is, of course, no longer part of Israel, and to tell you the truth, I think it's better to cross over with a passport. At the time, though, between the Six Day War and the Yom Kippur War, there was a euphoric feeling about beginning new settlements and working in agriculture. We felt we were self-creating.

In the middle of my twenty months in the army, I served in the Nachal Settlement, an army camp in Sinai very involved in agriculture. That period was one of the most beautiful in my life. I was already being scientific, doing experiments in irrigation systems, growing cucumbers, tomatoes and peppers. It was actually conducted for someone else's master's thesis but I was in charge of the whole experimental plot.

In the settlement I had an affair with a boy, a sexual affair. I didn't go all the way, but I did act in expected, normal ways. And to tell you the truth, I quite enjoyed it. At the same time, I noticed I was taking too many photographs of one of the women in the group. Sitting and talking late at night, I would notice her deep blue eyes and feel something inside begin to grow. Yet I somehow couldn't believe it was me who was having sexual fantasies about her. I cannot be a lesbian! I was fighting it with my teeth.

After six months on the settlement, the boys went to advanced training and the girls went to a kibbutz where we were expected to stay and live. I left the group supposedly because that kibbutz didn't offer any school. But mostly, I knew it would be dangerous to live near that woman. From there I moved to the armoured forces and spent the next six months of my service with a group of the best fighters in the army. We were only three women in that group of about 150 men. It was a situation in which falling in love with another woman was nearly impossible and I think I put myself in that situation on purpose.

Israeli society produces a certain kind of average male who is chauvinist, and there's nothing to do about that. It's part of their training and the social selection pressures operating in Israeli society, including in the military. Masculinity is also measured by what kind of fighter a man is. Israeli society appreciates power. Today, I say power, in terms of *koach*, not strength, *hozek*. In the 1960s, the feeling was that these Israeli fighters are strong. They're *mentshes*. Now, I see it's not really strength – their strength is not internal. Rather, it comes from being able to exert power over someone else. This has become more straightforward since the war in 1967; the Israeli–Arab conflict is a very good source of doormats.

After I left the army, I spent the months before university doing a botanical survey of the Golan Heights. I lived in a rented room in a little town in the north of Israel. My boss offered me the hospitality of his own family in the evenings. His wife was very nice to me and I ended up spending most of my evenings in their house. She and I would talk and talk and I would see the way her eyes walked around my body, but for weeks, I didn't understand anything. One midnight as she was at the door saying good-bye, looking at me with a lot of fondness. I knew I wanted to touch her. Boom! It was very dramatic, this realization. I couldn't put the feelings I had been having for women aside anymore.

For the next few days, I fantasized about this woman and brought gifts to her. It was June and there were several beautiful dry plants in the Golan. One of them is a garlic which has large spikes that start in the centre and go all the way around. It's called the wheel garlic, because it's round and when it's ripe, it dislocates from the ground and the wind turns it around and takes it long distances, spreading the seeds. I brought her those and other things from the field. I was getting very, very gentle treatment at first. But several days later, after this euphoria, I saw that the boss was trying to prevent us meeting. I didn't feel this closeness with her ever again.

In spite of the clarity I felt about my boss's wife, my lesbian self remained hidden under many layers of oppression in my twenties. I went to bed with a boy for the first time when I was twenty-two, hoping he would save me from my lesbianism. I was disappointed to find out I was still attracted to some girls in my class. I went to see a shrink sometime after that and found out it was going to be a long treatment to get rid of my lesbianism and I couldn't afford it.

I learned it is not a good idea to tell anyone about my feelings towards women. Those were sad and lonely years. I was the only lesbian I knew in this world, and I thought other lesbians would be like those deranged personalities portrayed in the movies. I learned to separate the 'pure and noble' spiritual love which I felt for women from the forbidden desire, which I kept as a terrible secret.

*

I started allowing myself to indulge in art after I finished my MSc degree. I went to drawing classes and I also started playing with clay, and made my first sculpture. I found I had creative ideas that wanted out. Some of my work was to express the feelings I was having for women, but in a disguised way so nobody would know. One sculpture is of a woman, but there should have been another woman lying beside this figure in a way that shows a very close, caring relationship. But I was too scared to have two women look at each other in this way, so I made one of them a man. I never came around to doing the other one, with the two women. Instead I did another couple, a woman standing, man kneeling, like a Romeo and Juliet scene.

At twenty-seven I started therapy in a serious way. It took about three years until I reached the conclusion that I should meet those monsters called lesbian women and find out what was happening with me.

So I felt ready to look for women, but not before my father died when I was twenty-nine. I wouldn't have dared to do that when he was still alive. I was very attached to him and found myself doing things he used to do, travelling, visiting friends in England, buying avocado to take to Tivon. I trod in his path for several years. But I'm certain my ability to look at the newspaper, see an ad of a woman looking for another woman and answer it, is something I couldn't have done when he was alive.

Several months after he died, I answered this very ad. The woman was married, and her husband knew about everything – actually he suggested to her that she find a playmate. She was seven years older than I, had no children and was – well, something was very weird about her. She wouldn't tell me what she liked in bed for instance, but one time, her husband took me aside and told me what to do to please her. The relationship died several months after it began, but it got me started.

At thirty I had my own ad, and from one of the answers developed two intense relationships, first with the ex-lover of the woman who answered the ad, and several months later with the woman herself. It was a complicated triangle. I think this is where my adolescence begins actually. In most ways, I was very mature; I was quite good in my work, I was cultured, I had friends, I went on trips, I had a lot of interesting activities. Nobody knew I was still a baby inside – but I was. These two relationships and everything around them, including the short affairs, opened something. Those women reached my internal, hidden life.

During that time I became a feminist. My feminism woke up when a friend of mine, a young man, said women are less able with technical skill than men. I pounced on him and tried to show him this is not always true, and I had to articulate all sorts of ideas which were very vague in my head. In order to explain things to him I had to organize my thoughts. Later I went to a feminist conference in Jerusalem and met women who could help me phrase all these ideas and could let me check them. I believe the conference, in June 1980, was the third such gathering in Israel.

That same summer, a feminist centre opened in Jerusalem, Kol HaIsha. There I discovered some wise, competent lesbian women. They were not monsters after all! In fact, some of them were quite desirable. Pam, a member of the collective, and I were together for nearly a year – one of the happiest of my life. It was a year of unfolding, of opening, of learning. I was not a collective member, but I was a satellite putting in a lot of energy. It was really a euphoric year for the Jerusalem community.

I came out to my family that year. I decided it was the right time because I felt so good to be in the relationship with Pam. I prepared my mother slowly, speaking about homosexuals and lesbians in general, telling her more things gradually. Before I came out to her, I told Moishele, the friend Mum had after my father died, so he could help her. Mum took it hard, but did her best to understand. Of course she felt guilty like all parents do. Eventually, my family adopted Pam, whose family is in the States. On visits, Pam and I brought our families together like a married couple, and even after the relationship ended, the family connections went on.

During that year, my art work continued to be important to me. My grandfather gave me a small camera and I suddenly saw I could do all sorts of things with it. I learned to develop and print my films, and this opened a new field of creativity. Part of it was accidental – I had to finish a roll of film so I experimented. I realized I could express a lot by photographing my sculptures. My pictures were exhibited at Kol HaIsha in the spring of 1981. One sequence showed my hands holding a sculpture of a spirit woman, then letting her escape, and then seeing her up in the sky. I felt I was really telling stories there and other people told me so as well.

The next year, I met Yolanda. At first, it was really exciting. We were together for five years, underground, like moles because she was married. I think it was only a very strong love that would keep it going so long. The perpetual frustration and moral friction, and the fact that I had to hide, made it difficult. I was longing for her often because she could be with me only for very short periods of time.

The fact that I had come out to the family and to some degree at work, too, made me feel good about myself. So when I met Yolanda and had to go back to the underground, I felt I was regressing. I hadn't lived the liberated life long enough before I had to rebury myself. Yolanda and I separated when I realized it was too dangerous for me to continue. I noticed I was getting furious about things, becoming misanthropic. Afterward, I dived into work, and for a long time I did very little except work.

*

After I finished my PhD in 1984, I got a position as part of the University research staff in ecology. I had an ecological system to study and had to measure all sorts of things. I had to invent methodology for measuring things nobody measured before. And then I discovered a new realm of reservoirs, part of the beautiful Israel. I worked with farmers from kibbutzim who were using effluents from reservoirs to irrigate cotton and had problems with the algae growing in the reservoir. I devised an apparatus for untrained people to check the water to see what's in it, and nowadays it is in use by many people in Israel.

My work as an ecologist, with a feminist approach to nature, I think is important. This is what keeps me here. My children are the papers I produce and the ideas I try to inseminate in other people's minds.

מיכל

Michal Zohar

Edited by Yaffa Weisman

• Michal Zohar, born 1967

Lanky, dark and angular, wearing several different earrings of her own design, Michal is a twenty-two-year-old working on her Bachelor of Fine Arts in cinema at Tel Aviv University. Soft-spoken and articulate, her voice occasionally becomes stronger when she discusses issues she's passionate about, never losing sight of life's little ironies.

I COME from a Sepharadi family. My father is from Bulgaria and my mother's parents are from Greece. Both my parents lived in Tel Aviv most of their life, and so did I. My family is a bit traditional, not really religious. My mother and father are intelligent and young – not yet fifty. I have a younger brother, Ilan, who's in the army, and a sister, Shoshana, in junior high.

My father is more formally educated than my mother. He's a professor, while she doesn't even have a bachelor's degree. He's a scientist for the Ministry of Defence and the military. He lives in two separate worlds, but mostly in his career world, which ever since we were children we felt was more central in his life. Even when he's at home he reads and writes. His parents came from Bulgaria when he was a year old. They lived in the poorer part of Tel Aviv, and he didn't graduate from a good high school before he went into the army. He did everything on his own first, and later with the support of my mother.

My mother had to sacrifice her personal goals for him. She's a real estate assessor. She likes her work and she's good at it, but she was trained to be a technician for engineers, and she's very frustrated about this issue – but I'll just finish talking about my father first.

My father is a cultural person; he reads a lot, philosophy and such, but for years I thought he was narrow-minded, insensitive and somehow pragmatic. I knew that in his field he was very talented, but I didn't feel his wisdom. I'm talking in past tense because two months ago I found out he knew about my relationships with women. He just mentioned it naturally, and it really changed our relationship. It was much easier for him to accept than it was for my mother.

Anyway, now I even feel I love him, which is a thing I couldn't say before. But he's still not very involved in my life. I think he understands he missed something, but is trying to catch up now. With my sister, who is thirteen, he built a relationship – doing things with her, playing with her. He's more of a parent, which is nice to look at.

My mother, as I have said, didn't fulfil her professional ambitions. She likes to make a home; the house is always neat and clean and there's always home-cooked food. Sometimes she is rational, almost *too* rational, and sometime she is too emotional. I think she finds it hard to find the good middle road between the two. Her family has a different background than my father's. My maternal grandfather is an engineer, and that means a lot for Sepharadic Jews, because there are not many well-educated people of his generation of Sepharadim.

Both her parents were born in Greece, but she was born here, in Tel Aviv, and went to a very good high school. It's ironic because she came from a much more educated background than my father and she was very talented. For example, as a girl, she studied maths and physics – they had thirty-five boys in the class and four girls. She started to study in the Technion, majoring in engineering, but dropped out at twenty-one when they got married. One of them had to give up their studies and 'naturally' it was her – which was very hard for her, and still is, today. Her parents told her, 'You're a woman; you don't have to be educated – just get married.' Things have changed since, and her sister, who is only eight years younger, got all the support from them – everything.

The irony about my mother is she is very much a feminist. She resents that label, and when I got into all this business of feminism, she resented it. Considering how she educated us, she really is a feminist. When I look at my brother, I think his values and sense of feminism are *great*. If something like a feminist male exists – I think it does exist – well, he's a great example.

So, she has problems with my feminism, not to mention my lesbianism, and that's a sad paradox. Sometimes I get the feeling that my loving women – well, she has a part in it. A good part! I'm proud of her, I love her and she just can't see it that way. For her it was the 'Where did I go wrong?' reaction, and it's quite sad, because I can't share my lesbianism with her, although I want to.

She's afraid of us not going the conventional ways. I wish she could be freer – I think she's her own prisoner. I think many women are.

*

As I was growing up, I had the feeling of being loved and valued for what I did and who I was. I was easy to love because I was a good student, the kind of child you show off at family gatherings. I was mature and independent – only a little rebellious. Until I was seventeen I did things because everybody did them, but I didn't feel the kind of fulfilment and self-contentment I feel now. My relationships with boyfriends – though I didn't have many – were shallow. But then, I really started to change.

I think it began with several things simultaneously, but first of all it was film – discovering film was what I wanted to do, and starting to study it; first in high school, and later in the museum. I took a film course and started watching more films. I think it was a turning point in my life.

It was not one film that made me wake up one morning and say: 'That's what I'm going to do.' I was interested in art, like many other people, from quite an early age. I tried theatre, and I wasn't that good an actress. I tried creative writing and poetry, music and singing and playing, like everyone. But I wasn't really great at any of those. And then I discovered film, and things changed. I started to have more meaningful relationships, mostly with girlfriends. I don't mean sexual relations, but one of the most important things in my life, my relationships with girlfriends, started at that time. As time passed, and as I joined the army, I got more focused, more myself. And around that intensive time, I also understood I was bisexual or lesbian.

I had a sense of my bisexuality even before I had my first boyfriend, let alone my first girlfriend, which was *much* later – and it somehow was very natural. I remember myself from an earlier age interested in homosexuals in general, more from the ideological aspect. I told my parents, 'I'm going to be a heterosexual fighting for homosexual rights.' I was attracted to reading about it, but it was nothing personal. And then I had an intense and emotional relationship with a girlfriend and I just felt that, well! I'd like to kiss her, I'd like to touch her! These were very primitive feelings. It was a process – it took time. But the thought of it was never strange, as it is for some people. It was very, very natural.

The first person I told was my first boyfriend. He was supportive, and said he had guessed. I was glad to hear it and glad I said it. Later on I just started telling people about it.

And then I joined the army. I guess everyone remembers their *mackit*, the unit commander in basic training. She leads you through three intensive weeks for girls only, of shooting and running around and doing funny things girls have nothing to do with during their regular military service. Many girls suffer during that time, but I liked it. [laughs] Classically, anyone who loves women has a crush on her sergeant – it's not really that you fall in love. I myself had a crush on two of my commanders. That was the time I started noticing girls. I must have had crushes on maybe six girls, even though at the same time I had a boyfriend.

Then, in the middle of my army service, I fell in love. Even though nothing came of my crush, I told all the men I was dating about it, and they were all OK about it. None of these relationships with men were good, mostly on the communication level, rather than sexual. One 4 a.m. I told myself: that's the last man I'm going to be with and ... OK women – here I come!

When did *that* start? About a year or so ago. Several months after that realization I left home. I had my own apartment and I started going to women's parties, which for most of the time was quite frustrating ... that way of making acquaintances was not my cup of tea, but I had my first girlfriend a little less than a year after I'd had my last boyfriend!

I knew about my feelings towards women long before I had any experience. Many times friends asked me, 'Well, how do you know? I mean, you never tried!' And I just *knew* it. It really makes me laugh, because I say: 'Well, you knew you were attracted to men before you went to bed with them, so what's your point?'

At that time, when it was still very theoretical for me, I told my parents. With my mother it was terrible. She couldn't even say the word. She didn't sleep for two weeks for crying. What was hardest for her was that I said it was my choice and I was proud of it. I didn't say, 'That's the only way I could live' – because I was attracted to men too. She said, 'Well, if I knew that's the only way – then OK, I could cope with it. But when you said you have a choice and you're glad and proud about it?!'

She got in such a bad mental shape, she went to see a shrink. I was *glad* about that – and I told her so. She said, 'YOU have the problem,' I said, 'YOU have the problem,' and she wanted me to see him too. But I didn't want to – it was against everything I believed. It's such *shit* that most everybody coming out has a problem with themselves, and it takes them such a long time to accept themselves as gay people. Then, here comes me: a healthy person, who is glad about it, living with it in peace, in a very integrative way – and it can't be OK! But, at some point I understood that, diplomatically, it's the right thing to do. So, I went to see him – but we didn't get along too well. I didn't mind going to a male shrink – I even thought it was better because the interaction would be less complicated than with women. But we always argued – about methods, not about lesbianism.

Anyway, what is happening to me now – I don't know if it has something to do with him or not – is that I got to a point where I became very aggressive and resentful about men. Mostly I am indifferent to them, and more interested in women. But, as of a week and a half ago I'm involved with a man who – it's funny – used to be a lover of my ex-woman lover, and my being a lesbian is the first thing he knew about me. Before we got involved, we had lots of talks about it and it got us closer. We're not a couple exactly – I love him, but I can see it as a long-lasting relationship only in an alternative way. It's quite unique because I can tell him about meeting a girl who I was in love with last, and that we had a very important talk – I really wanted to share it with him. I think any relationship I'm going to have with a man from now on, this is the first or second thing I'm going to say. The involvement with women is so crucial to me – it must be part of a relationship with a man. And I think men will always know they're sort of secondary. I could see myself living in an alternative marriage, maybe not even living together – with a gay man, or a woman, or several women, or with men – I don't know.

I think being bisexual is sometimes harder than being a lesbian, because sometimes lesbians have problems with women who are bisexual and I can *really* understand it. I mean, I remember being with my ex-lover at the same time she was in love with a man. If she had been in love with another woman, it would not have been easy, definitely *not*. But I'm not going to have both a woman lover and a man lover at the same time, because I don't think that would be fair.

In the beginning, I didn't feel like sharing this with my mother because I had such bad feelings about her not accepting my experiences with women. I felt lousy about coming home and saying, 'Hi, Mum, I have a boyfriend now,' and her hugging me and kissing me. But I wanted to tell her I am more open-minded about men than I was before. I told her: 'Listen, I have problems telling you about it. I don't want any hypocritical support all of a sudden, and I really want to say I am *not* giving up women!'

And it was just great, because I discovered she understood much more than I thought she did. She said she appreciated my telling her about it, and understands she has to let me live my life. It was very important to me. I told her I think my relations with women improved my relations with men, and she said she can understand it *somehow* – it doesn't sound so absurd to her.

*

I just have to say I don't like closets. I live as out as I can. All my friends know about me. Even when it was kind of a risk, I didn't come out only to people I *really trust*, after examining them and having a long relationship with them. I just say it, in a tactful way and in the right context. I'm quite radical about that point. I have very hard feelings about women not coming out. I can understand it's complicated in Israel, but I am somehow angry about women who don't. For instance, there are two singers in Israel who are *very* successful. At this point they're so popular – what can they lose? I mean, maybe they can lose something, but damn it! I mean, you're not a teacher who has to hide it because you can be fired – you're *so* popular, you're so loved ... why don't you? All those love songs about men, all the lesbians coming to their shows and knowing they're really singing about women. It makes me angry, really.

My films, for example, are going to deal with it. It's not easy because it means everyone in your department knows, but then I say, what's the big deal? I feel when you live an open life you're not vulnerable. Everyone knows, so no one can threaten you about anything if you're strong about it. At the beginning of this year, I wrote a script for my ex-girlfriend that deals with two women and their relationship. My name is on it, and the minute I put out this film and everyone sees it – that's it. The film department is flooded with dykes – well, that's an exaggeration, but there are some women who are. And we all know about each other, but not all of them deal with it. Most of them *don't*. And it's hard! Our department demands teamwork, and everyone is very involved – everyone knows about everyone's social life. [laughing] I once had a quarrel with a girlfriend, and she screamed at me in the middle of the lawn in front of the department building where everyone passes during recess. People I know were going by, but I was into that fight, so I didn't really care. I figure if people treat it naturally, then maybe – it's kind of idealistic – but maybe it *will* become a 'so what' issue.

I do care about being out where my family is involved. I would have problems if my real name was published in this book, for example. But I think in the context of people I'm involved with now, or my good friends from the army or from school, or people involved with film, I want to be natural.

Being a lesbian in Israel is hard. Besides the social and religious reasons and the chauvinistic attitudes, socially it's a very limited 'market', I don't know how else to call it. I was in London last summer, and I was just amazed by how diverse it is. You open a paper, and you see parties and shows and films and support groups! Here you have very few places. Many women don't go to the Feminist Movement meetings in Tel Aviv or to CLAF events, and I don't know *how* they get to know each other. I assume there are lots of lesbians in Tel Aviv that just live their lives and never take part in activities. Sometimes I have the feeling Tel Aviv is just *full* of them! Just walking down the street I can exchange looks with three women on one street!

I don't want to sound too negative. I'm only beginning my

way as a lesbian or bisexual, but how can you survive twenty years in the same community which is *sooo* ... stagnant? I think one answer is just being with a lover and building a home or a family, an environment with your friends, where some are lesbian and gay, some are not. But I wouldn't want to be isolated in that way, because I feel I'm part of other things going on in Israel.

Another thing, you always have the feeling lesbian relationships won't survive that long. It's a terrible feeling. You see couples break up after two years, and that's a long time! This summer, when I was in Scotland, I went to the Edinburgh Theatre Festival and I met a couple who have been together for fourteen years, and I was so glad to find them.

The theatre festival was very fringey – lots of avant-garde productions, small theatre companies, women's productions and also lesbian and gay shows. I went to this reading night called 'Beware: Dykes Descending'. [laughs] I got to know some great women living there, and I got the feeling they really had a healthy community. They had a gay and lesbian bookshop that was the centre of everything, and some gay cafes. I made friends with a thirty-four-year-old theatre director. It was a very good experience, getting to know her, because although we became lovers it was more an emotional and spiritual thing. It was great! I discovered we have so much in common, despite our different backgrounds. She's Scottish, lives in London and Scotland, and the age gap between us is about thirteen years. We always knew what the other was talking about, even though we'd just met. Through her I got to know more of lesbian life, really from the inside. We went to London and lived for several romantic days at her friends' house. I saw established life, and couples' life, and cultural life – more lesbian life than I see in Israel.

I plan to go somewhere after I graduate and be involved with films, because filmmaking is also difficult in Israel. I am thinking about an English-speaking country, London probably, or Canada – places relatively advanced in the areas of women's and feminist film making. Eventually I will live here, possibly in Jerusalem, because it reminds me of things in England. But I don't really know – there is so much life between now and then.

היה

Chaya Shalom

Edited by Tracy Moore

● Chaya Shalom, born 1944

Born in Jerusalem, Chaya is fifth-generation Israeli Sepharadi. She works as an assistant to a woman Member of Knesset and as co-ordinator of projects at 'The Women's Network', a feminist activist and lobbying organization. Active in Women in Black, the weekly vigil against the Occupation, Chaya was a delegate to international feminist peace conferences in 1990–94. Chaya founded CLAF, the Community of Lesbian Feminists, and co-founded the Women and Peace Coalition. An interview with Chaya appeared in The Tribe of Dina: A Jewish Women's Anthology, *edited by Melanie Kaye/Kantrowitz and Irena Klepfisz (1986), and her poetry has been published in Hebrew and English.*

I WAS brought up in a lower-class Sepharadi neighbour-hood, where I still live. Living in a Sepharadi family, when I was a kid we were all together. Almost every evening we would sit and talk. The Ladino I know is because I had an uncle who used to tell fairy stories to our whole family, every evening of my childhood. How I loved it! Sure we had other problems, but this was the good part. But kissing his hand after the *kiddush** on Friday evenings was the worst!

I went to a girls' school, both elementary and high school. The environment was very *shamrani*, conservative, in the way they treated us and how we were to learn. It was a French school, so there was a great distance between the teacher and the students. And of course at home you had the same. My father was really a very patriarchal type. All in all, I grew up in very closed surroundings.

From this background I can talk about coming out. I think the first time most of us heard about lesbians was through the book *The Well of Loneliness*. It was in Hebrew, and I got it from the library. I think they must not have looked at it as *lesbian* stuff, just as a romance, just as fiction. But I don't really know because I never talked to anyone else about it! I couldn't allow myself. I was sixteen years old when I read it, and I was terrified because I so much identified myself with Stephen. *I* was feeling what *she* felt about some of the girls in school.

Although my school was for girls, we hung out with boys

* Blessing said over the wine.

from another school. But what was in my mind? I wasn't attracted at all to these boys, and all I was thinking was of my girlfriends. I was falling in love every other day with another girl. I tried to completely suppress the feelings, but I couldn't control my erotic dreams about making love to girls. So when I read *The Well of Loneliness*, I was really terrified, brrrr! Once one of the girls in class called out, 'You lesbian!' I had no idea why she said it, but of course I was terrified.

Two of my best friends in school were constantly together. Years later, one of them told me that in their last year in school and in the army they had a sexual relationship. They didn't see it then as lesbian. One denied it completely and got married, while the other one went on to be one of the leaders of the women's and lesbian movement here. But at the time, they didn't talk of it at all. It was a very innocent experience of love, and when they found out what it was, they stopped it. So lesbianism was around me, but nobody was open to talk about it!

In that time, always your best friend was a girl. But even though I had 'boyfriends', I never acted like 'I'm his girl.' One boyfriend asked me 'What's the matter with you? Why won't you be more intimate?' Because the *most* I would do was walk hand in hand, no more than that! So I replied, 'I have a defect.' And he said, 'Did you tell your sister or someone in the family?' I said, 'No, but it is a defect and I don't want to tell it to anybody.' This is how I looked at it.

In my twenties, yes, I had some affairs, and even can say I lost my virginity just to be like the others. I didn't want to be so old and still a virgin! But when I felt an attraction, it was to women. In my romantic, movie-star imagination *I* was the man – maybe a fairy-tale knight courting a lady. But in real life, who I could get was not women, but men.

In my late twenties, my best girlfriend, Ilana, was very hetero. She was fucking with boys all the time, and I didn't have even one boyfriend. Once I said, 'Let's go out to the movies Saturday night.' And she said, 'No, I don't want to. I only go out with boys on Saturday night.' I was jealous and offended. I was so in love with this girl!

All this time I suffered, because I so much wanted this intimacy, this love. I felt like I was losing time. Years passed by and nothing happened for me until I made friends with Hedva, when I was thirty-four.

Now, most of my family are politically from the centre to the right, so it was a complete change to hang out with someone on the left, like Hedva. It was the first time I heard about feminism from a personal level. I hadn't even been aware of the women's movement that started about five years before, in 'seventy-three.

Hedva opened my mind politically. She considers herself a heterosexual feminist, but it was from her I first heard you can be intimate friends with women and there is nothing wrong with it. She said, 'If you are close to a woman, why not be sexual with her?' She herself once had a woman lover. How she talked about it! It completely changed how I felt inside. More and more I understood who I am. Even though I didn't say 'I am lesbian' yet, I knew I was close to it.

In 1980 I travelled to the States, and by then it was firmly in my mind: I had to meet a lesbian. I was going to San Francisco, and I knew this is the place. But I didn't know how to meet anyone! Sure, I knew there are bars, but what do I do when I find one?

So I went to Castro Street. On the one hand it was really something for me because all the gays were out. On the other hand, I saw only a few lesbians at a book stand. They looked so masculine to me, the stereotype of lesbian just hit me. I was attracted and terrified! I didn't want to be like them, so much what they call masculine, what we call now the butch dykes. So even in San Francisco I didn't meet a lesbian.

So when I came back to Israel, I was really ready to meet a lesbian. And Hedva read me; she said she wanted me to meet a lesbian she knew called Zofi – the one who had been Hedva's woman lover.

When I met Zofi and felt her energy, I knew this was the right place for me. That first evening I went to bed with her! It was like trying on a glove that fits perfectly. I felt, 'This is it. The woman I am now and the woman I was all these years are one. I am not hiding it any more.'

This short relationship – no more than ten days – gave me the feeling I'm *there* and I'm *high*. And because I'm Sagittarius, I saw myself as a horse galloping in the sky, between the stars. Even though it ended awfully, I felt strong. I knew I'd never go back again.

Another thing I learned from Hedva was that a women's centre, Kol HaIsha, had opened only a half year before that. She mentioned the name of the member of the collective that started it, and she was one of the girls in the lesbian couple from high school! I found out there was a dancing party in a private house to raise money. I went there by myself. To this day, I don't know how I had the courage to go. I met all these beautiful, gorgeous women – and my friend from school too – and I danced and *danced*. Afterwards I went to the women's centre, asked a lot of questions, and suddenly everything matched together.

During this time, I had been working with a civil rights organization. So for me to come to Kol HaIsha was another step again. I knew the meaning of human rights, and further, of women's rights. So I felt open to hear everything and to observe, and to get what fits me, and to grow. In less than five months I was one of the collective. I started immediately to be active, doing even just shit work. After I joined the collective I did more, making decisions, making process. All this experience – being collective, consensus, everything – was so new to me. But when I came out and knew that I'm lesbian, it was like being reborn. Like a kid, you can really absorb everything that is new.

For three years I was a member of the Kol HaIsha collective. I grew many sides of myself: my personality, professional skills like PR and organizing. I learned to be a spokesperson – before that, I couldn't express myself at all.

At the same time, I was concerned because half the activists were either olot hadashot or Anglo-Saxon women who came to Israel for a short time. The point is, it was very American-oriented. I had to struggle with the language, and the only way I could know stuff was to read or talk in English with my Anglo-Saxon friends – mostly Americans. So on one hand I felt, 'This is my place,' and on the other hand I felt, 'This is too American for me.'

Sure, we Israelis had our own community. For instance, at least since the 1970s we've had a word-of-mouth network of lesbians throughout the country. If we had a picnic, all the lesbians we knew from the three cities and other places heard about it. In Jerusalem the lesbian community got involved with each other's needs. We helped women move from apartment to apartment or provided medical care for women who didn't want to go to hospitals. So it was really quite a lesbian community here, but we didn't have our own culture. This is still true today.

I have contradictory feelings about lesbian culture as I observe and experience it, because I know it came mostly from the American lesbian movement. It's what we've been most exposed to, whether from friends, music, reading, or visiting there. So on the one hand, when I'm in the States I feel comfortable: those lesbians are my sisters, and I'm glad I have built good friendships there over the years. On the other hand, when I am here – which is all my life! – I feel angry that we don't have the privilege of having a developed culture of our own.

The outcome is that most lesbians here are not feminists. If you go to the only lesbian disco bar – which is Tuesday nights in Tel Aviv – you won't see dykes. Most of them look very heterosexual, some of them are in butch-femme roles, and the environment is like any other bar: meat market. So lesbian feminists have our very close and small circle, and only slowly do a few more begin to be aware of what it means to live in Israel as women and lesbians.

So while I do have close Israeli friends, in wider circles sometimes I don't feel common with lesbians because they are not political. It is hard for me to feel it like that, because every Israeli lesbian, I want her to be aware of what it means to be a lesbian in a heterosexual society. I don't expect her to be radical feminist like I am, but at least to be conscious of what it means to be lesbian, what our culture is, that we are different, special, and it's great! That lesbianism is not a *bed* matter; it's cultural, with a unique community.

The only way I found to deal with that anger and frustration was to start CLAF, the Community of Lesbian Feminists, which I started in 1987. One of the purposes of CLAF is to build our own culture; to be involved with each other as community. This idea emerged for me at an international lesbian conference in Geneva, sponsored by ILIS. There I saw lesbians from Asia, from the Third World, fighting so hard to be lesbian in their own societies, and some of these societies are not very different from ours. We are a Middle East culture, and half of Israelis are Oriental, so we are as close to Asians as to Anglo-Saxons. When I saw these women, I said to myself, 'If they can organize lesbians in their countries, we can do it in Israel.'

One of the successes of CLAF is that it started with 50 on the mailing list, and now there are 250. The activities we have – discussions, cultural events, being out in nature – really influence women. More and more, some of them who had said when they first came, 'I am anti-feminist,' say now, 'I am feminist.' CLAF changes them a lot. But I have to say it is only a few. Of these 250 – and let's say maybe 150 are new to feminism – maybe only 15 or 20 per cent of them have been educated in this organization. It's a long process.

Talking about culture, there are more Israeli lesbians that sing or write than before, that are more out. But I want it to happen faster – that a woman will come one evening and the next morning say, 'Oh, I want to be an activist in the organization!' But it doesn't happen that way. And we struggle with the activists burning out and women coming less. I worry about the willingness of women to take on responsibilities. In truth, I doubt the future of the organization itself. It's not a matter of money, it's a matter of woman energy. A lot of women come to the discussion evenings and have a good time, and some even learn something, but they still don't see the connection that the next step is not to be passive, but to be *active*.

I don't want only to 'survive' – this is what I am doing always. I want us to grow, to really be a movement. Right now, we organizers have a problem. There are not many of us willing to be part of the lesbian movement, because we know we are a lot more than 250!

★

Fundamentalism, nationalism, and religion are against us. Also, with peace or national issues always taking priority, women become less concerned about our own situation. I hope women will realize we need to fight the growing fundamentalism and nationalism. But again I am not very optimistic, because in all these years of Israel's existence, we didn't get much progress in women's status.

Yes, feminism and peace activism have made me grow a lot. But – this may sound funny – but because I have only eight years of relationships with women, I feel like a very young lesbian. It seems everyone who is twenty-five years old already has five, seven years of intimate relationships! So I feel deeply all these years that I missed. For maybe twenty years, I didn't have the kind of relationship I would have had if we had another kind of society.

At forty-four I have yet to learn what it means to be in a couple. The longest relationship I ever had lasted almost three years, with an American woman who lived here at that time. And I don't even see all three years as being a 'good' relationship. Maybe because I was so desperate to have a relationship, it was like I got lost in it. I guess it's also her personality and my personality, which made us so dependent on each other. I learned a lot from this experience. Luckily, now we are very good friends as we both have changed, and accept each other.

I have to add that within our lesbian community, I can hardly see a model of a couple really being together. Either they are together for two or three years and break up, or they continue to be together because it's more safe, more stable, they can fight the outer world and survive. So it's not a matter of choice, but of survival. Maybe there are exceptions, but I hardly can remember more than two couples!

So since this three year relationship, I didn't have a long one. I had some romantic involvements, some with younger women, some with my age. We seasoned feminists don't see many women our age here, and the few that we know are friends, so there's no way we're going to be involved romantically. It's like being with someone in the family! It's easier for younger women to find partners. I meet wonderful women from outside of Israel. But here, only the young generation is growing. That's one of the reasons I find myself being involved with lesbians passing through, and this is not what I want. I want somebody here I can develop and grow with, a partner to be intimate with, that is not only my lover but also my friend. I really don't know how this issue will be solved, but it's making me, at times, quite distressed. I guess I just have to accept it.

Also I feel sometimes angry at women couples because I feel

singles are treated differently. As a single lesbian, I am having problems being friends with lesbians when they are in couples. I think they feel there is a threat around them, so mostly they hang out in couples. I guess this is true all over, but because we are so small a community in this country – the entire country is one community! – it is a problem.

For myself, I can't compromise and just have 'a lesbian'. She has to be political, she has to be part of our culture. I can't be with someone who is so much in the closet she is not aware what is going on. It's impossible! And I am not one to be with somebody just to have sex. I would love to have a sexual relationship with a woman if we could look at it as fun – like going out, having an evening together, not only to replace that I don't have a partner, but also that sex is *fun*. We used to call it 'sexual friends', do you remember? I think it's more American actually. That you're friends, but also you sleep together from time to time.

But this is hard. I would like to try it – but I don't dare. So many emotions are involved in such a step.

Bibliography

Israeli women

Azaryahu, Sarah, *The Union of Hebrew Women for Equal Rights in Eretz Ysrael: A Selected History of the Women's Movement in Israel (1900–1947)*, translated with an afterword by Marcia Freedman, Haifa: The Women's Aid Fund, 1980.

Benson, Miriam and Dorit Harverd, eds., *The Status of Women in Israel: The Implementation of the Recommendations of the Israel Government Commission of Investigation*, Israel Women's Network, Jerusalem, 1988.

Ben-Zvi, Rachel Yanait, *Before Golda: Manya Shochat*. Introduced by Marie Syrkin, translated from the Hebrew by Sandra Shurin, New York: Biblio, 1989.

Falbel, Rita, Irena Klepfisz and Donna Novel, eds., *Jewish Women's Call for Peace: A Handbook for Jewish Women in the Israeli/Palestinian Conflict*, Ithaca, NY: Firebrand, 1990.

Freedman, Marcia, *Exile in the Promised Land: A Memoir*, Ithaca, NY: Firebrand, 1990.

Fuchs, Esther, *Israeli Mythogynies: Women in Contemporary Hebrew Fiction*, Albany, NY: SUNY Press, 1987.

Glazer, Myra, ed., *Burning Air and a Clear Mind: Contemporary Israeli Women Poets*, Athens, OH: Ohio University Press, 1981.

Golan, Galia, 'An interview with Galia Golan', in *The Tribe of Dina*, pp. 247–57.

Hazelton, Lesley, *Israeli Women: The Reality Behind the Myths*, New York: Simon & Schuster, 1977.

Hazelton, Lesley, 'Israeli women: three myths', in *On Being a Jewish Feminist: A Reader*.

Heschel, Susannah, ed., *On Being a Jewish Feminist: A Reader*, New York: Schocken, 1983.

Hurwitz, Deena, ed., *Walking the Red Line: Israelis in Search of Justice for Palestine*, Philadelphia: New Society Publishers, 1992. Includes essays by Israeli women peace activists. See especially Yvonne Deutch, 'Israeli women: from protest to a culture of peace,' pp. 45–55.

Kaye/Kantrowitz, Melanie and Irena Klepfisz, eds., *The Tribe of Dina: A Jewish Women's Anthology*, Montpelier, VT: Sinister Wisdom Books, 1986. Updated and expanded edition published by Beacon, 1989.

Lipman, Beata, *Israel: The Embattled Land – Jewish and Palestinian Women Talk about Their Lives*, London: Pandora Press, 1988.

Moed, Lil, 'An interview', in *The Tribe of Dina*, pp. 256–63.

Rosenwasser, Penny, *Voices from a 'Promised Land' – Palestinian & Israeli Peace Activists Speak Their Hearts*, Willimantic, CT: Curbstone, 1992.

Shazar, Rachel Katznelson, ed., *The Plough Woman: Memoirs of the Pioneer Women of Palestine*, translated by Maurice Samuel, New York: Herzl Press, 1975.

Svirsky, Gila, ed., *Women in Black National Newsletter*, Jerusalem.

Swirski, Barbara and Marilyn P. Safir, eds., *Calling the Equality Bluff: Women in Israel*, New York: Pergamon Press, 1991.

Tiger, Lionel and Joespeh Shepher, *Women in the Kibbutz*, New York: Harcourt Brace Jovanovich, 1975.

Lesbians/Gay Rights

Beck, Evelyn Torton, ed., *Nice Jewish Girls: A Lesbian Anthology*, Watertown, MA: Persephone Press, 1982. Republished by Beacon, 1989.

Bloch, Alice, *The Law of Return*, Boston: Alyson, 1983.

Dyan, Ron, 'Gay Rights in Israel,' unpublished manuscript.

Freedman, Marcia, 'A lesbian in the Promised Land', in *Nice Jewish Girls*.

Israel Update, Bulletin of the Society for the Protection of Personal Rights for Gay Men, Lesbians, and Bisexuals in Israel, April 1993 and December 1993.

Katz, Sue, 'Melina: an echo on the line', in *Speaking for Ourselves: Short Stories by Jewish Lesbians*, ed. Irene Zahava, Freedom, CA: Crossing Press, 1990, pp. 102–8.

Maggid, Eliza, 'Lesbians in the international movement of gay/lesbian Jews', in *Nice Jewish Girls*, pp. 137–42.

Nachum, Nancy, 'Peaceniks,' *Sinister Wisdom*, 42, pp. 49–52.

Shalom, Chaya, 'An interview with Chaya Shalom', in *The Tribe of Dina*, pp. 214–26.

Shalom, Chaya, 'Conference for homosexuals and lesbians in Israel,' *Off Our Backs*, April 1993.

Svirsky, Gila, 'How I get started in a life of crime', *Sinister Wisdom*, 40, pp. 48–60.

Tall, S., 'Letter from a sabra to an American', in *The Tribe of Dina*, pp. 245–46.

Tilchen, Maida, with Helen D. Weinstock, 'Letters from my aunt', in *Nice Jewish Girls*, pp. 241–59.

World Congress Digest, Newsletter of the World Congress of Gay and Lesbian Jewish Organizations, Washington, DC, 1993 issues.

Oral history

Reimer, Derek, ed., *Voices: A Guide to Oral History*, Victoria, BC: Provincial Archives of British Columbia, 1984. A basic how-to with an extended bibliography for the careful oral historian on sound recordings.

Glossary

aliyah [ah-lee-YAH] immigration of Jews to Israel. The word literally means 'going up'. A Jew always 'goes up' when going to the Holy Land. The term is used for a wave of immigrants and for individuals.

aliyah or **aliyah l'Torah** the honour of being called up from the congregation to read from the Torah or to say the Torah blessings before and after the Torah is read.

Ashkenazi [*see also* Sepharadi] an adjective describing Jews and the characteristics of Jews who trace their ancestors to northern and eastern Europe. Ashkenazi Jews created the Yiddish language. Before World War II, 90 per cent of the world's Jewish population was Ashkenazi. In Israel in 1990 they represented just under half the population. The term also refers to a certain pronunciation of Hebrew, seldom used today.

Aza another name for Gaza (*see* Gaza Strip).

bagrut matriculation exams taken before leaving high school.

bar mitzva/bat mitzva (male/female versions) in traditional Judaism, the rite of passage from childhood to adulthood when a Jew becomes responsible for observing all 613 commandments. It occurs for boys at thirteen years, for girls at twelve. Secular Jews in Israel often have parties for their children at this age that do not contain religious elements.

challah a plaited bread specially baked for Shabbat and Rosh Hashanah.

Chanuka the Feast of Light or Festival of Freedom, usually celebrated in December and lasting eight days. Each evening, candles equal to the number of Chanuka days are lit. A minor Jewish holiday commemorating the victory of the Maccabees in 167 BC and repossession of the Temple in Jerusalem, it has become emphasized outside of Israel because of its juxtaposition to Christmas.

chupah the cloth canopy held over a bride and groom during a wedding.

chutzpadick presumptuous.

CLAF Community of Lesbian Feminists. Founded by Chaya Shalom in 1987 and organized by a collective of lesbians in Tel Aviv, it sponsors activities and keeps lesbians connected by a nationwide phone list and, since 1990, a newsletter.

co-counselling a therapeutic technique used by non-professionals working in pairs.

davka of all things! (but so idiomatic as to be almost untranslatable).

diaspora the lands of Jewish dispersion.

Esperanto artificial language devised in 1887 by the Polish linguist L. L. Zamenhoff in the hope that it would eventually become the universal language. Its spelling and grammar are completely consistent, while its vocabulary is based mainly on Western European languages.

galut exile, the condition of Jews in dispersion.

gan pre-school childcare (literally, garden).

ganenet (f.) childcare worker.

Gaza Strip a small strip of land on Israel's southern border with Egypt, densely populated by Palestinian towns and refugee camps. Under Egyptian control until the 1967 War, when Israel occupied it. It was not returned – or requested – as part of the 1979 Camp David Peace Accords, which returned the entire Sinai Peninsula to Egypt, but it passed to Palestinian control in 1994.

gehenom hell.

Golan Heights former Syrian territory occupied by Israel in the 1967 War and formally annexed in 1981.

Green Line name given to the *de facto* borders of pre-1967 Israel.

Gush Emunim 'The Bloc of the Faithful': religious–nationalist pressure group that believes in the divine right of Jews to sovereignty over Biblical lands. Settled widely in the West Bank during the 1970s and 1980s, and militantly opposed to concessions such as land for peace.

HaShomer HaTsair socialist Youth Movement.

Hasidism mystical Jewish movement; Hasidic men wear long sidelocks and black suits and hats fashionable in eighteenth-century Eastern Europe; women must dress modestly.

hevrah a social group.

Histadrut the largest trade union organization and largest employer in Israel after the government. With 85 per cent of workers as members, it greatly influences political, cultural, economic and social life in Israel.

hozek strength.

HUC Hebrew Union College – Jewish Institute of Religion, the Reform Movement's seminary, with campuses in Jerusalem, Cincinnati, New York and Los Angeles.

IDF Israeli Defense Forces.

ILIS International Lesbian Information Service.

intifada Palestinian popular uprising in the West Bank and Gaza begun in December 1987.

Jewish Agency executive body of the World Zionist Organization; works with Israel's government to encourage and organize Jewish immigration, and assists immigrants' social and economic integration.

the Joint The American Jewish Joint Distribution Committee; since 1914 it has made available funds, legal aid, foodstuffs and clothes to Jews in economic and political distress. It operated initially out of Austria and Hungary, currently out of Israel.

kabbalah [kah-bah-LAH or kah-BAH-lah] the most influential tradition of Jewish mysticism.

kaddish [KAH-dish] a prayer glorifying God that is used as a mourner's prayer.

kashrut kosher; following Biblical dietary laws.

kibbutz [ki-BUTZ] a collective farming settlement operated on ideals of social and economic equality.

kiddush [kid-OOSH or KID-ish] blessing said over the wine.

Knesset Israel's parliament.

koach power.

Kol HaIsha [coal ha-ee-SHAH] literally 'the voice of a woman', it was the name of the Jerusalem Women's Centre (approx. 1979–83). Feminists chose the name as a play on its use in a traditional Jewish context, where Jewish men are forbidden to hear a woman's voice during prayer, lest it lead them astray. It is also a pun because of its homonym meaning 'all women'.

kosher prepared according to Jewish dietary laws; also a term used to mean legal, appropriate, correct.

kvetch [Yiddish] as a noun, anyone who complains, whines, nags; as a verb, to complain, whine, nag.

Labor Party the major left-of-centre political party in Israel.

Ladino, also called **Judesmo** or Judeo-Spanish; the folk language of Sepharadi Jews; a combination of Spanish and Hebrew, with borrowed Arabic, Turkish and Greek words and phrases.

Law of Return the Israeli law permitting any Jew to immigrate to Israel.

Lesbit, Lesbiōt [lez-BEET, lez-be-OAT] lesbian, lesbians.

Likud Party the major right-of-centre political party in Israel, achieved national leadership for the first time in 1977 and was still in power in 1988–89; led by Prime Minister Yitzhak Shamir.

madrich, madricha Hebrew for 'guide'; thus, camp counsellors, tour guides, etc.

mahbarah a camp for new immigrants.

mentsh [Yiddish] literally a 'human being', a laudatory term for an honourable/good person valued by the community.

metapelet (f) babysitter, childcare worker.

mikveh women's ritual bath.

miluim [mil-oo-EEM] army reserve duty.

minyan ten Jews, traditionally only males; the required number for community prayer.

mishigas [Yiddish] craziness, nonsense, used in amused way.

mitzva, mitzvot commandment(s) from God given in Torah. In common English usage often means 'good deed'.

mizrachi/im [*see* **Sepharadi**] eastern or Oriental Jews.

MK Member of Knesset.

moshav, moshavim co-operative farm(s).

Na'amat organization providing services to women.

naches [NACH-iss] (Yiddish) pride, joy.

1967 War *see* Six Day War.

nu versatile Yiddish term; for example, 'Go on!' 'Well?', designating mild impatience, or 'So how are things with you?'

olah [oh-LAH] female immigrant.

olah hadashah [oh-LAH ha-da-SHAH] new immigrant (female). Male and plural forms are **ole hadash, olot hadashot, olim hadashim.**

oy va voy! same as **oy-vay**; Yiddish for 'Woe is me!' or 'Oh my!'

Passover English for Pesach.

Pesach the springtime festival of Passover, commemorating the Exodus from Egypt.

peyes/peyot sidelocks, worn by Orthodox males.

PLO Palestinian Liberation Organization, providing political, military, social and economic leadership of Palestinian people and its sub-organizations under Yassir Arafat.

'Purity of Arms' the concept of retaining one's human dignity and values, as well as the human rights of the 'enemy' while under fire in war; doing things properly, not losing one's humanness during war.

Rabbanut [rah-bah-NOOT] the rabbinate.

Reform Movement like Conservative and Reconstructionist, a movement within Judaism that is more progressive than Orthodox, the only state-recognized Judaism in Israel. The Reform Movement sponsors two kibbutzim in the Negev, Lotan and Yahel.

sabra nickname for native Israeli, referring metaphorically to the Middle-Eastern prickly pear cactus, with its prickly exterior and tender heart.

Sabra and Shatila Palestinian refugee camps near Beirut where, in September 1982 during the war in Lebanon, 700 to 800 civilians were massacred by Christian Phalangists with the tacit support of the IDF.

seder at Passover, the ritual evening meal recounting the liberation from Egypt, especially celebrated the first and second nights.

Sepharadi [*see also* **Ashkenazi**] adjective describing the descendants and characteristics of Jews living in Spain and Portugal at the time of the expulsion in 1492. In Israel, the term refers to Jews from Africa and the Middle East, most of whom immigrated after Israel was founded and who now comprise over half of Israel's population. The term also refers to the pronunciation of Hebrew used in Israel today. These people and characteristics are also known as **mizrachi**, from the word for 'east'.

Shabbat the Sabbath, religiously observed from Friday sunset to Saturday sunset. In Israel it results in many businesses and entertainments remaining closed, especially in Jerusalem.

shekel Israeli unit of currency, in 1988–89 valued at about US$1.70.

sh'lom bayit domestic harmony; peace in the house; a guiding principle for traditional Jewish households.

Shoah the Holocaust; Nazi genocide of Jews.

shtetl [Yiddish] one of the small Jewish villages in Eastern Europe where Yiddish culture flourished. Obliterated by the end of World War II.

Six Day War also 1967 War, in which Israel took control of East Jerusalem, the West Bank, Golan Heights, Gaza Strip and Sinai Peninsula.

slicha [slee-HA] 'Forgive me', 'Pardon me'.

sochnut immigration office.

social gap refers to the differences in economic, social and political standing between Ashkenazi and Sepharadi Jews. Especially pronounced in the 1950s and 1960s, the gap has narrowed with increased Sepharadi immigration.

Talmud the body of teaching (63 books) composed of commentary and discussion of the meaning of the Torah, assembled between the third and seventh centuries CE.

Tanach [tah-NAHKH] the Hebrew name for the Bible. It comes from an acronym of the Hebrew names for each major division of the Bible; Torah (the five books of Moses), Nevi'im (prophets), Ketuvim (writings).

tsuris [Yiddish] woe, troubles.

Tu B'shvat late winter Jewish holiday celebrating the renewal of trees and all of nature.

ulpan Hebrew language school.

wadi dry riverbed.

West Bank the area of Palestine west of the Jordan River seized from Jordan by Israel in the 1967 war. With Gaza, comprises the Occupied Territories.

WIZO Women's Independent Zionist Organization.

yeshiva Hebrew school in which religious and secular subjects are taught. It can also refer to an Orthodox rabbinical college or seminary.

Yiddish the folk language of Ashkenazi Jews, based on medieval German and containing elements of Hebrew, Russian and Polish.
Yiddishkeit is a term used to describe Ashkenazi Jewish customs and culture.
yishuv the Jewish community in Palestine before statehood; also refers to the period between 1900 and 1948.
Yom Ha'atzma'ut Israel Independence Day.
Zohar a lengthy collection of influential medieval mystical writings.